Commodity-linked Derivatives

IFR BOOKS

Commodity-linked Derivatives

Julian Roche

IFR Publishing

IFR Publishing Ltd, 11 New Fetter Lane, London EC4A 1JN

British Library Cataloguing in Publication data are available.

ISBN: 1 873446 66 7

Printed by CIP, Communications House, 14 Repton Close, Burnt Mills, Basildon, Essex SS13 1LJ

Contents

Introduction: The history and concepts of commodity derivatives

The concept of a commodity

The historical and conceptual analysis of commodity-linked derivatives starts with the trade of physical commodities. A commodity, in economic terms, is defined as a portion of wealth; something that is desired because it has the power to satisfy human wants or needs. It is limited in supply and therefore has value in exchange; it has 'utility'.

In trade terms, and when we speak of *commodity derivatives*, the sense of commodity is narrower. Commodities are natural substances, perhaps processed, which have economic value and can be perceived using human senses, can be quantified and measured for quality, and can — at least in theory — be owned. Very approximately they can be divided into the following categories:

- metals
- soft commodities
- energy
- others

Trading commodities

Almost all commodities in the trade sense are also economic commodities. Since relative scarcities differ, relative price structures also differ and trade occurs, initially in the form of barter. Trade allows both parties to specialise and thereby improve everyone's living standards. Economists justify international trade by providing the following definition: a country has a comparative advantage *vis-à-vis* another country in the production of an economic commodity in which it has a lower opportunity cost than the other country. So, if two countries are producing some of two commodities each, then the total output of both commodities can be increased if each country transfers resources into the production of the commodity in which it has a comparative advantage. The definition is of a comparative advantage, not necessarily an absolute one.

The US and Europe are both very efficient in agricultural production but, in a world where specialisation occurs, they are advised to import agricultural commodities of various kinds and to concentrate on the technological products for which they have developed specialist skills. International trade is, of course, not carried out by anthropomorphic individuals as Country A or Country B. In practice, international trade decisions are taken by thousands of interdependent decision makers: governments, firms and individuals, all making political and economic choices. International trade also depends *inter alia* on the mutual acceptance of separate currencies at fixed or varying exchange rates, as well as the determination of barter prices.

This price determination, whether in barter or through pricing of commodities, illustrates the next theoretical point about international trade; countries must exchange at a ratio of imported to exported goods. The quantity of a basket of exported goods that a country must give up to receive a basket of imported goods is called the 'terms of trade'. This is an important concept in international trade as commodity prices can move very suddenly in comparison to others. Some countries relying on certain commodities for their exports can suddenly find the terms of trade move radically against them. In the quest for a solution to this problem the origin of derivative products for commodities lies.

The origins

Trading started on a small scale with distances of a few miles, as villagers exchanged wool for fur or water for land. Several different types of primitive trade have been identified by historians; one is silent trade, or dumb barter. One party lays down goods and retires; the other party lays down goods that they consider to be of similar value and then also retire. The first party can then either accept or indicate the need for additions. No communication beyond the agreed general signals was necessary, hence the name. Leading on from this was barter itself — the direct transfer of goods for goods at a negotiated exchange rate. The possibility of haggling over quality and quantity exists but there must be a double coincidence of wants unless a multilateral barter arrangement is entered into. One step on from this is actual buying and selling of goods.

International trade is recorded throughout the ancient world, in monuments and writing. There was a continuous flow of exchange among the peoples of the Mediterranean basin and the Red Sea. Overland routes brought merchandise from the Yellow Sea to India, Arabia and the shores of the Black Sea. Certainly, the large cities of antiquity could not have existed without the continuous import of both food and building materials.

The eighteenth century brought new commodities such as cotton and tobacco from America. These assumed a greater volume and, eventually, value importance than the old precious commodities. From the end of the Napoleonic wars until World War I, Europe predominated in international trade. The UK was the mainspring and the clearing house of the worldwide flow of commodities. International trade was largely between Europe and the rest of the world. Between the UK and Continental Europe the volume of trade was considerable, given the population size. After World War II, trade became increasingly dominated, first by the industrial and agricultural might of the US, and then subsequently by the dramatic rise in importance of the Far East. The UN statistics on trade show the impact of the change.

Markets

Markets were created as soon as commodities were exchanged or traded. Primitive markets were varied and widely distributed across the world. Africa may have been the original home of the market, but they have also been described in Mexico, Hawaii and Peru. In rural European villages and towns there are still weekly markets, each often concentrating on different commodities. In times of recession, markets become more important relative to conventional retail outlets, as people seek to obtain value for money in preference to convenience; markets often involve low relative overheads compared with conventional retail outlets.

Markets existed in Britain even before the Romans arrived in AD43. These markets were usually directly between producers and consumers. This method cut the number of individual profits that had to be made to make trading effective. The Romans, partly through their introduction of coinage, were responsible for the evolution of these individual markets into a system, which was crucial in replacing barter. Product specialisation in regions, and commercial specialisation in towns, led to markets in particular commodities developing in particular towns. Officials established reserve stocks, ran market administration, including weights and measures, and collected taxes and other dues. The main characteristics of a market are:

- the set time;
- the regular occurrence;
- the definite limited place of assembly;
- the existence of regulations governing the exchange of commodities;
- the maintenance of order.

The complex commodity markets of the today are descended from of these rural markets.

Subsequent developments

It is believed that forward trading in soft commodities began as early as Saxon times in England, when fish was traded on such a basis at Billingsgate. This site was close to Tower Hill where London's soft commodity markets are still situated. By the Norman invasion of 1066, commodity markets of a form were trading in Mark and Mincing Lanes. Market charters were granted by Church and State Institutions. All merchants are involved to some extent in speculation as they are risk-takers. It was through the development of forward markets however that prompted the evolution of voluntary risk-takers: they have since become known as *speculators*. Speculators used forward contracts and kept stocks of commodities. The forward contracts themselves were originally viewed a little suspiciously by the authorities of the time — as are the complex derivatives contracts of the late twentieth century. They were difficult to tax and account, and thought to contribute to price volatility and speculative trading profits.

In the Middle Ages more sea traffic and a better road system throughout Europe increased trade. In England, towns such as London, which were close to both sea and inland river systems, were well placed to develop their trading role. Royal authority in England asserted its right to control and profit from both domestic and international trade. Trade expansion brought more markets. The main characteristic of the markets of the Middle Ages was their local nature; almost all commodities would be sold at every major market. International and national trade fairs also started and these became an important part of the marketing system. Such fairs permitted market areas to trade between themselves, and they helped to level prices that had diverged widely between areas. It was at these fairs that the idea of *open outcry* for commodities was first introduced. Open outcry is still used today in the international commodity markets. Fairs developed specialisation in a single commodity and sophisticated clearing and credit systems evolved.

Traders also gradually began to specialise; dividing first into international and national merchants and then by commodity. Markets became progressively more vulnerable to attempts to monopolise supplies and almost as a by-product of this commodities acquired characteristics that approached quantitative and qualitative standardisation.

The Royal Exchange has been in London, on the same site, since Sir Thomas Gresham's original building was opened by Queen Elizabeth I on 23 January 1571. By that time, Lombard Street was the main gathering place for merchants. The original Royal Exchange, designed to compete with the trading centres of Amsterdam and Antwerp, was burned in the Great Fire of 1666, but was speedily replaced.

Despite the fall in the proportion of goods that arrived in England specifically by the Port of London, the huge increase in trade volume during the eighteenth century rendered the Royal Exchange inadequate. Business centres grew up therefore at the new coffee houses, which had become popular with the arrival of new goods from the colonies. Governments have traditionally seen price stabilisation as a policy objective. At the coffee houses and the Royal Exchange, merchants and brokers met to exchange information on trade, cargoes, and ship movements. Each commodity's merchants tended to concentrate in a particular coffee house. These eighteenth century coffee houses were the origins of many of the trade associations that subsequently developed into the financial institutions of the City of London.

In the eighteenth century local authorities succeeded the Crown in the administration of markets and this resulted in increased forward trading. Forward trading was not, during this period, conducted to raise capital in advance of physical sales, nor was the objective simple forward selling. The aim was, in fact, to reduce the inherent risks in long-term trade with short-term price movement, and certainly to ensure continuous commodity supply. Economists now recognise that although not every market actually follows this process, forward trading is an almost inevitable corollary of spot market cash transactions. Even now, however, economists are far from agreed on why some spot markets fail to develop derivative markets — or why the types of derivative markets that develop vary so widely between apparently similar commodities. The best example is probably that of coffee and tea — the former with a fully fledged futures market, the latter completely without one.

In 1746 the Mark Lane Corn Exchange was founded. Exchanges became popular throughout Britain during the nineteenth century and forward trading became immediately popular at these exchanges. The process has been described (Courtney) as one of 'negotiation, registration, formalisation and execution'. Most contracts at this stage however were forward deals done as price protection. Storage costs, risk premium, and good faith deposits, almost invariably created contango markets (when the nearby month is trading at a premium to the deferred months). Speculation began to enter trading on a regular basis.

The Mark Lane Exchange was the first recognisable forerunner of the London Commodity Exchange — now the London Commodity Futures and Options Exchange (formerly London Fox) — the centre of London trading for coffee, cocoa, and sugar. Although the Mark Lane market was not an official and regulated market, it was similar to a commercial sale room in that samples of merchandise were available. The London Commercial Sale Rooms were opened in Mincing Lane, in 1811; they were a concentration of auction centres. The futures markets proper, or terminal markets, which developed in the later nineteenth century, were accommodated on the floor of the Subscription Room of the London Commercial Sale rooms.

The invention of the electric telegraph in 1847 was vital for organised international futures trading. The first telephone was installed in 1880 at a time when contracts were still unofficial and loosely defined. Cotton was the outstanding traded commodity and it spurred futures trading in the UK by substantial amounts. Cotton traders were frequently at risk for months between their US purchases and sales in the home market. The Cotton Brokers' Association was formed in 1841 and it included the 'arrivals' trade. The first hedge trades were thus of cotton with the Chicago Board of Trade (CBOT) being established in the US at approximately the same time. The first futures contract was traded on the CBOT on 13 October 1865 and was based on the Liverpool Cotton Exchange physical contracts. Many commodities subsequently adopted the futures trading methods rather than exclusively using auctions and forward sales.

Metal markets had developed in parallel. In the mid-nineteenth century Britain was the world's largest producer of tin and copper, but in the latter half of the century the country increasingly had to import metals from new mines in South America, Africa and the Far East. Sea transport for all commodities, at this time, was hazardous, so a market in the 'future arrivals' of metals developed. Merchants established forward prices based on their analysis of the likely future supply and demand balance. Dealing was through open outcry, as for other commodities, and the market traded principal to principal. The London Metal Exchange (LME) was formally opened in 1876. Premises were acquired in Lombard Court and telegraph links established. The three month metals contract, which became standard, was based on the approximate sailing time between mines in Santiago and Singapore to the ports in the UK. The LME quickly acquired a reputation for flexibility and satisfying its users' needs. By 1920 all metals were traded in the main ring. The authorities' attempts to prevent trading outside hours led to dealings taking place outside in the street, hence the expression 'kerb dealing'. Trading has continually increased, except when suspended during both World Wars, and is now recognised as the world's leading centre for the establishment of metals prices.

The traditional soft commodity (including rubber) markets meanwhile continued to dominate futures trading until the formation of The London International Financial Futures and Options Exchange (LIFFE) in 1982. The London Traded Options market was created in 1978, and the European Options Exchange in Amsterdam was created at the same time. But it was LIFFE that really turned the tables on the commodity markets in London, turning them by 1990 (with the exception of the energy markets) into poor relations of the financial futures industry.

Since the early 1980s financial futures have grown in importance. Today they represent over 60% of exchange futures and options trading and the figure continues to rise. Innovations in technology, new products and new contracts are tending to be driven by the financial futures side — and this applies not just to the US but to elsewhere in the world. It really needs to be said that financial futures are no friends of the commodity derivatives industry. They make *using* commodity futures easier and more attractive, as they can be used to take away associated currency and interest rate risk. Speculators became increasingly attracted to financial futures because of their liquidity, and although in many markets commodity futures volumes have increased, their rate of expansion was undoubtedly slowed by the growth of financial futures. New exchanges were formed throughout the world in the 1980s, and many countries still intend to introduce them. Competition has increased between exchanges and between different contracts. But it must be conceded that commodity futures are now the Cinderellas of the piece, and the trend is continuing that existing commodity futures exchanges (Marché à Terme d'Instruments Financiers (MATIF), for example, or the Kuala Lumpur Commodity Exchange (KLCE)), are seeking a piece of the action in financial futures where volumes are usually ten times greater, rather than concentrating either on developing new soft commodity contracts or expanding the volumes in their existing contracts.

The US

Commodities trade has always been important in the country's development. The two most important commodities were originally tobacco and cotton. The futures markets developed in a similar way to those in the UK: the Tontaine Coffee House was opened in 1792 in central New York. The Coffee Exchange of the City of New York established uniform guidelines on trading procedures, fixed standards for coffee grades, and set up arbitration courts that were generally recognised. The CBOT was established in the mid-nineteenth century to provide a central market-place in response to Chicago merchants' problems of standardisation. The CBOT became responsible for grading, quality and inspection rules for agricultural commodities, especially grains. World War I gave a major boost to the US, as the sugar exchanges in Hamburg and London were closed. In December 1914 the US launched a sugar futures contract, creating the New York Coffee and Sugar Exchange which opened in 1916. In 1925 the New York Cocoa Exchange was created, a world first.

The next major period of expansion for the futures markets in New York and Chicago was after World War II, and the demise of price controls. Exchange members saw a critical need to develop new contracts, to expand their markets, and to identify industries that could make use of futures in their economic planning. This drive to develop new products has become the hallmark of the US futures industry.

Before the 1960s, commodities contracts had been written only on storable, non-perishable goods that could be traded in the future, regardless of harvest time. In September 1961, however, the Chicago Mercantile Exchange (CME) began trading a new futures contract based on pork bellies that became one of the world's most successful futures contracts. The strong performance of pork bellies convinced the Exchange to develop other contracts based on meats. In 1964 the Exchange introduced futures trading on live cattle. Live hog futures were started in 1966 and feeder cattle futures in 1971. By the 1970s, the CME was the world's largest trading centre for meat and livestock commodity futures.

In the US in 1977 the Coffee and Cocoa Exchange relocated to the World Trade Centre, where the Commodity Exchange Centre was constructed, housing all the New York commodities. Combined trading volume grew dramatically after 1977, from 8.7 million contracts in that year to 71.5 million in 1991.

Futures accelerated in importance and use in every part of the world economy. In the early 1970s, approximately 13 million futures contracts were traded in the US annually. A little over a decade later, that number exploded to over 23 million. By the 1980s there were futures contracts for grains and oil-seeds, interest rates, stock indexes, manufactured and processed products, non-storable commodities, precious metals, foreign currencies

In May 1972, the Exchange inaugurated trading in contracts based on seven foreign currencies — the first futures contracts on financial instruments. The rapid success of foreign currency futures stimulated the development of other financial contracts, namely, interest rate futures and stock index futures. At the same time, options were first traded on the Chicago Board Options Exchange (CBOE), and these equally rapidly became an important part of derivatives trading. In April 1982 the CME established a division for the trading of indices and options. The first contract was based on the Standard & Poor's (S&P) 500 Stock Price Index; futures trading had at last become accessible to participants in the equity market. In the first three years, more than 27 million S&P 500 stock index futures contracts were traded.

Most of the world's futures trading takes place in the pits of the 11 US futures exchanges. Users represented a broad range of worldwide interests — from individual investors to governments; from trading houses to foreign banks. Some 70% of all futures trading in the US takes place in the pits of Chicago. Of the nearly 313 million contracts traded on domestic futures exchanges in 1989, more than 24 million changed hands on the floors of two of Chicago's futures exchanges — CBOT and the CME. Together, they traded 10 of the industry's 12 most active futures contracts. The Exchange's efforts to develop new markets rapidly extended beyond the US. For example, in 1980 the CME became the first US exchange to open an overseas office (in London) which it now shares with the CBOT, and which is highly successful in promoting the work of the US Exchanges in London. The London office sustains marketing and educational support throughout Europe, the Middle

East and Africa. There are 150 CME member branch offices in those areas. In 1987, a CME Tokyo office was opened. Major exchanges are moving towards worldwide representation.

In 1984, recognising that the financial world was at the threshold of yet another revolution — a technological revolution — CME became the first futures exchange to establish an international trading link. This mutual offset arrangement with the Singapore International Monetary Exchange (SIMEX) gave the Exchange an edge in the race toward the inevitable full day-and-night trading cycle. The two exchanges — the CME and SIMEX — are independently owned and operated. They maintain separate clearing houses and audits, compliance and surveillance departments. The key to the success of the trading link is the ability to offer interchangeable futures and options contracts that can be offset on the other exchange.

If the picture of futures trading in the 1980s was still of agricultural futures such as pork bellies being traded on the US pits, by the early 1990s, and especially in Europe after the virtual collapse of the EMS under the impact of financial (currency) futures trading in September 1992, the clear new agenda was financial futures. And in Japan, electronic trading as well.

Japan

The Japanese also have a long and distinguished record of commodity derivative trading, almost contemporaneous with the West. Futures trading has always been accepted in Japan as a very natural corollary of physical commodity trading. In 1730 the Osaka Dojima Rice Trading Board was officially allowed to trade rice futures (*choaimai torihiki*) for the first time. It is believed that futures trading was based on the commercial custom of *Choninkuramoto*; the merchant warehouse keeper, who had been entrusted *Kuamai* (stored rice) to sell on behalf of the feudal clans.

The Rice Exchange, which was established under the Rice Exchange Law and the Exchange Law of 1893, was followed by the foundation of a series of commodity exchanges where the key commodities traded were rice, raw cotton, raw silk and sugar. The Tokyo Commodity Exchange was established in 1894, combining with the Tokyo Rice Exchange in 1908. Silk and rice were the principal commodities in which Japanese traders had a particular interest. Once World War II broke out commodity prices fell under government control and there was no opportunity for the Exchanges to fix prices so they ceased trading. In 1950, another Commodity Exchange Law was enacted in Japan, and further commodity exchanges were established throughout the country. The Tokyo Grain Exchange (TGE), for example, was established as an agricultural commodity exchange in September 1952, encouraged by the lifting of control over grain in 1951 (the Tokyo Rubber Exchange was set up the same year), and trading began in October 1952 in the old building of the Tokyo Rice Commodity Exchange. The TGE started with just three futures contracts: domestic soyabeans, red beans and potato starch, and later added three more commodities: white beans, Chinese soyabeans and US soyabeans. Apples, poultry and frozen egg futures were traded at a later date and, in 1954, futures on iron and scrap steel were also added.

The Tokyo Sugar Exchange was established on 7 May 1952 listing and commencing trade in refined white soft sugar and raw sugar. Subsequently, in 1959 and 1960 brown sugar and beet sugar were traded on the Exchange.

On the Tokyo Textile Commodity Exchange, raw cotton was listed from 1961, adding to the existing staple fibre commodities of rayon yarn, cotton yarn and woollen yarn that commenced trading in 1951. Turnover on the Exchange became the highest in Japan. In 1982, the Tokyo Gold Exchange was established and platinum and silver were listed from 1984. The three existing commodity futures exchanges, the Tokyo Textile Commodities Exchange, the Tokyo Rubber Exchange, and the Tokyo Gold Exchange merged to form the Tokyo Commodity Exchange (TOCOM) in order to maximise trading liquidity. In 1988, TOCOM began gold spot trading, and also trading of warrants. In 1990, the Japanese amended their Commodities Exchange Law, to encourage more trading and to permit index contracts.

The concept of derivative markets

The first distinction is between the *physical* (actuals, or spot) market, and the *derivative* market. The physical market and the physical or underlying commodity need not necessarily be a tangible commodity; it could be a government bond, an insurance contract, or a given quantity of a certain currency. In Chapter 3, the different types of commodities and derivative markets are analysed. What the derivative markets have in common is that they are all based on physical commodities. The market to buy and sell the physical commodity, whether it is rice, government bonds or property, is called the spot market. When a house is bought for £50,000, in derivative market terminology the underlying product has been traded at £50,000 on the property spot market.

'Forward' markets are a form of derivative markets. All agreements to buy and sell in the future are called *forward* agreements. So futures markets are types of forward markets. Like spot contracts forward markets are subject to national laws. In many cases international obligations are involved and there may be counterparty risks of non-payment: these risks helped futures markets to develop.

In the derivative market, all market users are called players. Brokers buy and sell on behalf of market players. When players buy or sell in derivative markets, they *take*, and *hold* a 'position' in the market. They are consequently 'exposed' to a risk of price movement in the market; the extent to which they are exposed to risk is known as their *exposure*. Exposure is either being long of any market and short. If you buy a house, in derivative market terminology, you are long houses; if you rent you are short houses. If you can buy the physical commodity and sell in the futures market you can be neither long nor short. If you do both to the same financial amount, you can be neutral —neither long nor short. A price change in the market will leave you unaffected. Derivative markets have the distinctive characteristic that players can sell before they buy — thereby benefiting when the price falls.

Notes:

David Courtney, *From Futures to Futures*, Credit Lyonnais Rouse, 1991.

Chapter 1: How futures and options work

All commodities are subject, in varying measure, to price volatility, and this price risk has been a constant source of concern to traders over the centuries. As the twentieth century has progressed, the price volatility of most commodities has increased. Only very recently (1990–92) has this trend been reversed for some commodities. Increased price volatility inevitably means increased business risk for all those involved in manufacturing, producing, processing, distribution and selling commodities. All the elements in the chain have increasingly looked to derivatives markets, whether over-the-counter (OTC) arrangements such as forward purchasing agreements, or futures markets, as an alternative to international agreements as a way of protecting themselves against the often massive effects of adverse price movements on profitability. Such effects can easily outweigh any effort to control costs or increase profitability internal to the firm.

Commodity 'producers' face risk regarding uncertain weather, which affects feed costs, the availability of feed and forage, storage and growth rates for crops, conception rates, survivability of young animals and shipment costs. Another risk is the constant threat of disease and livestock producers know that animal health management requires effort and expenditure.

Producers manage such production risk by adopting good husbandry practices. Husbandry alone however cannot eliminate market risk — the uncertainty of prices at market time owing to shifting supply and demand factors. The derivatives markets have evolved to satisfy the need of businesses for a form of 'price insurance'. Price risk exists for the merchant, the producer, the distributor, the retailer, the consumer and anyone holding a stock of a commodity. Any exposure to price volatility by producing, holding, selling, or needing to buy a commodity, creates a need for a means of controlling it.

Derivatives markets provide precise price information and make it possible to transfer risk from those who want to reduce it (hedgers) to those who want to take it on (speculators). These important benefits — price discovery and risk transfer — extend to all the sectors that have created such markets and economic risk. So, in the simplest terms, derivative markets are where hedgers and speculators come together to agree the future price of a commodity and protect against (hedge) price risk, which is taken up by a large pool of risk capital.

Physical commodity markets vary enormously at present. The international market for crude oil, for example, is both liquid and complex. There are many different sub-markets, each individual in terms of participants, structure, pricing and geography. For example, the Rotterdam spot market has dozens of participants, most of them in major oil and trading companies; the European naphtha market consists of the commodity in transit to Europe with fewer than a dozen traders in key oil and trading companies; the Bangkok rice market is dispersed across several different locations in and around Bangkok; and the market for some commodities, for example gold, is completely international but handled by very few companies and governments such as De Beers. As a corollary of this, the different contracts that exist between and within each physical or forward market for a commodity vary enormously.

Most international commodity spot markets indicate a general price level for each type and location, published either electronically or in local or international media. Some commodities are far better price reported than others. Rice is especially bad in comparison with cotton, for example, which has an immensely prestigious daily index published in Liverpool. Whichever commodity market it is, however, the trading community reacts to changes with tremendous speed. There are few commodities where the price does not change daily and where traders worldwide know of all important deals the day after they have happened. Companies such as Tom Slayton Associates, experts in rice analysis, or Cotton Outlook, provide such information daily to their clients if necessary.

Forward contracts

Forward contracts — everything from real-estate leases and fixed-rate loans to credit-card agreements and magazine subscriptions — are commitments between two parties to exchange a specific product or service at a specific price on a specific date. For example, it could be an agreement between two individuals to sell a particular property at an agreed price in six months' time.

Forward markets, like other OTC markets, are more impenetrable as far as price is concerned but crucially, physical and forward commodity markets usually involve principal-to-principal contracts. Brokers get involved, but counterparty risk and information costs are always present, and in some markets such as rice, traders understand the risk of default. Despite the apparent simplicity of forward markets in comparison with futures or options, there are usually fewer physical than derivative traders. Derivative markets involve 'closing out', avoiding any direct involvement with the physical commodity, and this encourages high levels of participation. Physical markets, by comparison, are tightly organised and exclusive; outsiders are not welcome. An excellent example of this is the international rice market where virtually all the leading rice traders of the world know one another, and many are related by blood or marriage. The European naphtha market is even more exclusive with one annual dinner uniting virtually all the participants. Physical traders of commodities tend towards a jealous partisanship in favour of their 'own' commodity. Participants in physical markets are often therefore obliged to use experienced traders and brokers to escape the difficulties summarised by Battley:

'1 The problem in ascertaining accurate market prices
2 The administrative burden in finding potential counterparties
3 The need to establish the standing of a counterparty
4 The possibility of default
5 The price risk.'

These problems are often exacerbated in the forward markets, where the opportunity exists to sell on forward cargoes, hopefully at a profit, rather than take delivery. A producer, for example, may sell to a trader — who never intends to take delivery — a cargo of 10,000 tonnes of rice that is to leave Kohsichang in three months' time. One month later, the trader accepts a higher bid for the rice and sells it on. Similarly, some oil cargoes may be sold 10 or more times before they actually arrive at their destination. A default by one of the intermediate buyers — all of whom have legally binding contracts with their seller and their purchaser — often causes the whole chain to collapse. Expensive and lengthy arbitration and litigation frequently follow such a collapse. Unlike exchange-traded futures and options contracts, forward contracts are negotiated privately and are not actively traded in any central market-place and they do not necessarily need to be standardised. In fact, in most cases, they are as varied as spot market contracts. Forward contracts do carry risk; there is always the possibility that one or the other side is negotiating in bad faith or without sufficient creditworthiness, or that subsequent events might prevent one of the parties from being able to fulfil the forward contract.

Futures contracts

A forward contract is an agreement to buy or sell a standard quantity and quality of a commodity at an agreed time in the future, in a market-place, with terms agreed in advance. *Futures* contracts, by contrast, are standardised;

quantity, type, grade and approved delivery points are all known before active trading begins. The identity of the buyer and seller are the only unknown factors before the actual contract is made.

Standardisation opens futures markets to any commercial interest that wants to manage business risk by hedging. Hedgers, whether pension funds, corporations, insurance companies, commodity producers, farmers, packers or processors, all have the same objective: to gain financial protection in the conduct of prospective business and to maintain, and if possible, increase their profitability.

The first principle therefore behind the development of futures markets is hedging. Hedgers aim to establish an equal and opposite position to that taken in the physical commodity, to ensure protection against adverse price changes. In derivatives market terminology, they aim to offset their long physical position by being short the derivative, or vice versa. Any price movement in the physical commodity will be reflected in an equal and opposite move in the price of the derivative contract. The least volatile markets of all are those which are regulated by the government, for example regulated rents. These markets have, however, been circumvented in the past by market forces to create black markets very much dependent on supply and demand and often very volatile in price. Clearly, the more volatile the price, the greater the risk associated with an exposure to the commodity. It must be remembered that the risk is equally applicable to a long or short position. A company that needs pearls tomorrow is as much at risk to price change as a company that sells them tomorrow — it is just that the risk goes in the opposite direction — they are short the physical commodity instead of long it.

Moreover, companies compete in an international market-place, so they usually find it impossible to maintain artificial prices for long periods. A problem with forward contracts is that with fixed future prices individual companies may find themselves forced to buy or sell at prices that are not the current market price, which has changed, perhaps substantially, since the contract was negotiated. Consequently some of these contracts have to be renegotiated. Forward contracts are not always available because of the difficulty in matching buyer and seller and then in agreeing mutually acceptable terms within a useful and cost-effective time frame. Spot markets such as in Memphis for cotton or tea auctions avoid this problem, but they provide no certainty for future supply and delivery ('spot' is used both for the nearest month in a futures contract and the cash markets themselves). This largely accounts for the development of futures markets.

The simplest forms of hedging are the purchaser's hedge and the seller's hedge, which are designed for those short and long the physical commodity respectively.

A purchaser's hedge

Example

On 1 January an investor, or pearl retailer, analyses the likely price developments for the pearl market for the year. He has been offered a certain quantity, say 100kg, of pearls of a known quality, to be delivered on 30 September, at whatever price prevails then. The risk to the purchaser is that the price will exceed the current futures price that is, say, $1000/kg. The investor therefore buys 100kg worth of pearls through the futures market. If the futures contract is specified as 10kg of pearls this entails buying 10 contracts. If, by September the price of pearls has risen, for example, to $1500/kg, the investor will have to pay $500/kg more on the spot market. The value of the futures contract however would have risen to an equivalent amount, and can be sold for a profit of $500/kg. The effect of having taken an equal and opposite position in the futures market to that in the physical market is to lock in the price to be paid.

If, however, in January the purchaser negotiates a deal for September at a price of $1000/kg and he believes that pearls will be more expensive than $1000/kg by 30 September, he will probably buy, and if he expects pearls to be cheaper than $1000/kg, he will not. If the investor accepts the contract however and is then proved wrong, he will own 100kg of pearls on 1 October, for which he has paid $100,000, and for which he may only be able to obtain $80,000 on the spot market. If the purchaser were to sell futures contracts on 1 January however, when the market generally agreed with him that the likely price on 30 September would be $100/kg, then on 30 September he will be able to recoup losses in the physical market, as the futures will have fallen to $80/kg as well, and he will be able to buy back the contract at a reduced price, thereby making a profit. Again, the equal and opposite position in the futures market balances the physical market position.

A seller's hedge

This hedge is the exact opposite to a purchaser's hedge. The seller intends to establish a selling price for a cash commodity before the delivery date. The correct strategy for the hedger is to sell the futures contract month. On 1 January a pearl fisher analyses the likely price developments for the pearl market between then and the end of the year. He will have 100kg of pearls to sell on 30 September, at whatever price prevails then. The risk to the seller is that the price will be less than the current futures price, which is, say, $1000/kg. The pearl fisher therefore sells 100kg worth of pearls through the futures market. If the futures contract is specified as 10kg of pearls, that entails 10 contracts. Should the price of pearls have fallen by September to $800/kg, the fisher will receive $200/kg less on the spot market: but the value of the futures contract would have fallen to an equivalent amount, and could be bought back for a profit of $200/kg. Again the effect of having taken an equal and opposite position in the futures market to that in the physical market is to lock in the price, in this case the sales revenue.

Suppose, however, that in January the pearl fisher negotiates a deal for September at a price of $1000/kg. If the fisher believes that pearls will be cheaper than $1000/kg by 30 September, he will probably accept the offer, and if he expects pearls to be more expensive than $1000/kg, he will not. But if the seller accepts the contract and is proved wrong, then on 1 October he will have a cheque for $100,000 instead of the $120,000 that would be possible were the pearls available to be sold on the spot market. If the fisher however were to buy futures contracts on 1 January, when the market foresaw the likely price on 30 September to be $100/kg, then on 30 September he will be able to make the profit missed through the original contract, as the futures will have risen to $120/kg as well, and he will be able to sell the contract at an increased price, thereby making a profit of $20/kg *and* having the assured sales market.

Clearly in a market composed of both retailers and pearl fishers, some with agreed forward contract prices and some not, and all with varying expectations about the future, there is ample scope for trading, and this process is the essence of all derivatives trading. Risk is exchanged for certainty. When the investor, trader and producer must either hold or sell a quantity of a physical commodity, they sell the futures to obtain a balanced position — which is called shorting the futures market. Futures can be sold without buying them first, as can most physical commodities. Traders often make commitments to sell quantities of rice, for example, before actually possessing the stock to enable them to do so. The risk to the trader in this case is that the price will rise before his sale date. The hedging position on a futures market is therefore the reverse of the previous example: the trader buys futures and protects against a price rise. Should the market price rise, in the worst case actually above the price at which he has agreed to deliver the pearls, then the futures contract price will also have risen by a similar amount and the trader will have been protected.

In practice the 'perfect hedge', in which the present or anticipated cash position exactly matches the futures position, is extremely difficult — if not impossible — to achieve. This is because a futures or an options market concentrates buyers and sellers in order to permit the transfer of risk. One immediate problem is that some traders may be exposed to the price changes of oval pearls, and others to round pearl prices. The supply and demand characteristics and the price implications of those pearls may be very different. If oval pearls are mainly produced in Hawaii and there is a hurricane there which destroys stocks and disrupts production, the relationship between oval and round pearl prices will change, often for long periods of time.

Futures contract designers must produce contracts that combine as many potential participants' exposure as possible. This encourages the maximum number of participants into the market and hence creates liquidity. Futures and options contracts are usually based, for commodities, on a frequently traded grade of the commodity, deliverable in one or more commonly used locations. The futures contract specification frequently reverses, to become a benchmark for physical spot contracts and for comparison with other qualities and locations. It is usually more difficult to achieve with commodity futures than with financials, because of the enormous variety within each commodity of types, growths, locations and associated production and freight costs as well as important differences in market prices. The cotton trade is an excellent example of this phenomenon. The figure below shows different cotton growth prices

NY Nearby *vs* 'A' Index *vs* Memphis

CIF Northern Europe, 7 January 1988 – 23 July 1992

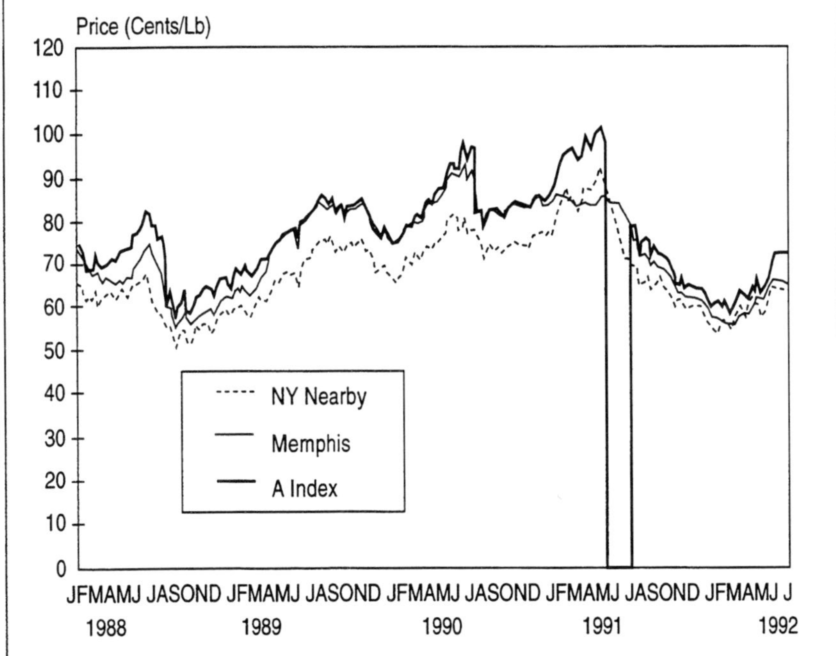

Weekly prices ended Thursday
Source: New York Cottn Exchange

from the Liverpool Cotton Outlook, and illustrates the difficulties associated with using even the new contract at the New York Cotton Exchange (NYCE) based on the 'A' Index to hedge any one growth. The more specialised the product, the more idiosyncratic the supply and demand considerations. Futures contracts, are however, designed to maximise liquidity and are therefore the most 'average' type of the commodity. The tendency therefore is for the future to be a less effective hedge, the more specialised the commodity or sub-type.

Physical and futures prices certainly do not always move exactly in parallel. There is ongoing debate about the degree to which futures prices reflect spot prices for commodities, and it is generally believed that they do although there are frequent occasions when there are discrepancies. These discrepancies could, for example, be due to major speculative interest in the futures that is unlikely to be reproduced in the physical commodity. It is interesting that far more academic attention has been paid to option pricing, which in the case of exchange-traded options relies on future prices, than on the determination of futures prices themselves.

There may be a mismatch between the time of the physical transaction and the futures month available. A trader might be expecting a consignment of pearls in November, but the only available contract expires are October and December. The solution, in this case, is to spread the contracts, producing what is called a 'strip hedge'.

Basis risk

The gap between the price of the specific physical commodity to be hedged and the futures price is called the *basis risk.* The relationship of the local cash market price and the futures price at marketing time is called the *basis.* Knowing the likely basis enables the hedger to translate an available futures price for deferred delivery into an expected cash price that will result from a hedge. The basis is calculated by subtracting the price of the appropriate futures contract from the local cash market price.

Basis = cash price – futures price

If, for example, the cash price for pearls is $50.00 per pearl and the futures price is $52.00 per pearl then the basis is 50.00 – 52.00 = $2.00, or $2.00 under. With a cash price of $49.50 and a futures price of $48.50, the basis is 49.50 – 48.50 = $1.00, or $1.00 over.

The figure opposite shows the relationship between cash and futures prices.

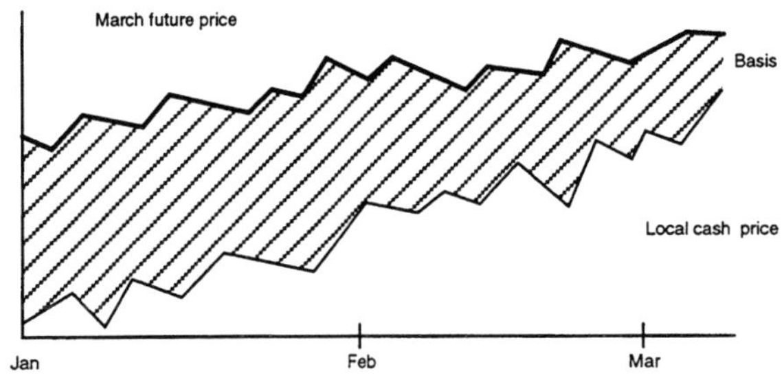

Futures and cash prices

Futures prices are determined by the cost of delivering a defined commodity of a particular quality to specific locations and according to procedures prescribed by the contract specifications. Cash prices are determined by the cost of delivering the commodity to the same or different places under procedures specified by particular contracts. The delivery costs for livestock, for example, include transportation and marketing costs such as commissions, yardage and weight shrinkage. The possibility of delivery on the futures contract generally causes the futures price during the delivery month to become identical to the cash prices at the futures delivery locations. If there are wide differences among these cash prices, the futures will also tend to become identical to the lowest one.

Basis differs from one location to another. Depending on how the local market is placed — its distance and direction from the futures delivery points, — the basis may be consistently positive (over) or negative (under). It may reflect a seasonal pattern; stronger at one time of year, for instance, when local cash prices are high relative to cash prices at futures delivery points because of seasonally strong local demand. Each local market has its own seasonal supply and demand pattern and relationship to the nearby futures price.

The aim of a hedger is to lock in a favourable forward price. Knowledge of the expected basis is used to translate a given futures price (for a deferred delivery period corresponding to the expected market period) into a likely cash price at that time. The decision is then taken as to whether that is favourable. If it is favourable, a futures position is established as a hedge. If the hedge is kept on until the livestock actually move to market, the total price risk is reduced to the amount by which the actual basis differs from the expected basis. For the short hedger, the more positive (stronger) the basis when the hedge is offset, the greater the actual price received. For the long hedger, the more negative (weaker) the basis when the hedge is offset, the lower the actual price paid.

Basis and the hedger

	short hedger	long hedger
stronger basis	higher price received	higher price paid
weaker basis	lower price received	lower price paid

Hedgers will seek to minimise their basis risk. Having decided that they wish to use a futures contract, they must then choose the right contract. They aim to use the contract with the closest price correlation in the past to the commodity class and type being hedged. It is when a large segment of the commodity class being traded lacks an effective hedging mechanism, because its price behaviour is radically different from that of other segments in the class, that the exchanges start to see the possibility of introducing new contracts.

Secondly, hedgers choose whether to buy or sell and their decision is determined by whether the physical commodity to be hedged is to be purchased (buy) or be held or sold (sell). Since spot and futures prices are usually correlated well, the futures price will rise when the spot does and vice versa.

The third factor is the number of contracts to be traded relative to the spot transaction. All futures contracts are denominated in volume terms (if for physical delivery or of any commodity), or as a multiple of an index point (if an index contract for cash settlement). If a trader has bought 100 pearls and the futures contract is for 50, he will clearly need two contracts to hedge his position. It is often not possible to find an exact exchange-traded futures hedge. In the example above, if the trader had bought 125 pearls, he would probably be advised to take out either two or three contracts, either leaving 25 pearls ($2,500) unhedged or being 'short' a net equivalent of 25 pearls on the futures market.

The timing of the hedge is important as well. Two questions must be answered: when to trade and in which expiry months to trade? Futures contracts expire in different months. For example, the Goldman Sachs Commodity Index (GSCI) contract on the CME expires in February, April, June, August and December. In futures market terminology, each month has a specific letter attached to it (see p.28). The contracts stop trading on the fourth day of every month. The fundamental aim is to 'put on' the hedge, ie, to buy or sell the futures contract, as soon as the risk is perceived, and to buy or sell the expiry month closest to when the risk is actually to be faced. So, a trader in April planning to sell shares in a commodity firm in October would probably elect to sell a combination of August and December GSCI futures to the value of the shares in order to protect himself against a fall in the price of commodities that would affect his shares' price. In practice, most hedging is carried out 'dynamically'; the level of the hedge and the expiry months are constantly held under review and changed. In the above example, if the GSCI started a rapid climb in May, the trader may decide to buy back half the GSCI futures at that point; if the climb continues through June, he may sell the rest, and only buy them back when and if the GSCI falls back to the level at which he originally bought. Dynamic hedges can compensate for changes in the direction and volatility of prices in the underlying commodity, or for fresh information. However, since buying and selling futures involves a cost each time, there is a transactions price to be paid for a dynamic hedge strategy.

Spread trading

Spread trading is an example of a more complicated strategy involving the simultaneous buying and selling of futures. It is usually carried out by a trader seeking to take advantage of a view about relative prices between months or contracts. In the same market, the trader could, for example, believe that the December GSCI contract is overpriced relative to August. If the trader were to sell December, and buy August, he would be exposed only to the relative change between the months and not to the absolute value of the index. If both rise by 50 points in the largest bull market for commodities ever seen, the trader will neither lose nor gain, and the same is true for a massive fall. Should the gap between August and December narrow however, due to a fall by 50 in the December contract and a fall of only 45 in August, then he will profit by 5. The best examples of trading between commodity markets can be found in the energy futures markets. The 'crack spread' between crude oil futures prices and those of petroleum products is an example. Such trading allows a refiner, for instance, to lock his margin in over a future period. The crack spread between crude oil and refined products can vary substantially over time, but the refiner has locked in the existing projected rate of return as depicted by the futures prices by selling the product futures and buying the crude oil futures. A decline in the refining margin due to increased crude oil prices will be offset by the profits from the crude oil futures. And, if refined product prices fall, which would also narrow the crack spread, the refiner profits from the short product position. The effect is that the refiner has traded away possible gains from either level or falling crude prices and rising product prices and rising or level product prices and falling crude prices — in return for a guaranteed future return, set by the two futures prices at the time of taking out the crack spread hedge. As with all stable price environments, this increases the refiner's ability to make plausible plans, increase efficiency, use cash effectively, and obtain favourable borrowing rates.

Initial margin

Whether selling or buying futures contracts, an *initial margin* (initial deposit) must be deposited with the broker. This deposit is a small percentage of the value of each contract traded. Interest is paid on the initial margin whilst it is held by the broker. This payment system is controlled by the exchange clearing house (see Chapter 2), in transactions with all clearing members/brokers who in turn 'settle up' with each of their own customers.

Derivative exponents claim this process reduces the amount of money required for trading to a prudent minimum, while ensuring financial integrity in the market-place. This in turn facilitates trading and encourages liquidity, so that users can enter into and exit from futures market positions easily.

Variation margin

Whilst a position in the market is held, the broker calculates the value day-by-day. This is called marking-to-market. If the value of the position falls and thus the account balance falls below a certain amount (called the maintenance margin level), the broker will issue a margin call, asking for more money for the account. Responding to a margin call serves to top up the margin deposit — and the same arrangement by all traders serves to ensure the financial integrity of the entire market-place. Failure to respond to margin call involves the automatic closing out of the position. Examples of margin calls are given below:

Short hedge with pearls

One December 10kg of pearl futures is sold at $1000/kg, the total value of the contract being $10,000. A gain will be made if the contract is bought back for less than $10,000. As the futures price falls below the selling price, the position improves, but if the futures price rises above the selling price, the position worsens.

The initial margin is approximately 10% of the contract value, in this case a deposit of $1000. Suppose that by the end of the second day, the contract has decreased in value by $320 — that is a gain would be made if it were bought back for $320 less than the selling price. The $320 is credited to the account obtained from a market user who is long the same contract at $10,000. Not until the fifth day does the futures price begin to rise again. This time the contract value has increased by $340, which is subtracted from the account balance.

If the account falls below the maintenance level agreed in advance the broker will ask for a margin call for another $320 to bring the balance back up to the original level. If the contract value then falls considerably, and a gain would be made by buying back at this lower price, the user may decide to buy back the contract. The gain will be the reduction in price, which will already have been credited on a daily basis to the account, plus the return of the initial margin. Commission would then be deducted from the account.

Long hedge with feeder cattle

Suppose a farmer plans to purchase 120 head of feeder steers in March. The initial margin requirement is $600 per contract, and the maintenance margin agreed with his broker is $400 per contract. The farmer deposits $1,200 in the hedging account for two contracts and buys two March feeder cattle futures contracts at $66.00/cwt.

The total value of the two contracts is $58,080 (880 cwt). As the futures price rises above the buying price, the position improves and as the futures price falls below the buying price, the position deteriorates.

The farmer started with a margin deposit of $1,200. By the end of the second day, the contracts increase in value by $308 — that is, he would realise a gain if he sold them back for $308 more than he bought them. The $308 is credited to his account. On the fourth day, the price returns to his buying price. The farmer's account balance returns to its original balance. If his account falls below the maintenance balance of $800, he will receive a margin call to bring the balance back up to $1,200.

If the farmer sells back the two feeder cattle contracts at $68.90/cwt he will receive back his margin deposits less a commission fee of, say, $150, and have realised a gain of $2,552 on the transaction.

Cash settlement

Traditionally, futures contracts were always either closed out or the underlying commodity was delivered (to the longs by the shorts). Rather than purchasing an offsetting contract, a trader with a short position would want to deliver the commodity if futures were high relative to cash. Conversely, if the futures were too low, a trader with a long position would prefer to take delivery and then sell into the cash market. These situations were rare because of the accuracy of futures pricing. With 'cash-settled' contracts, the exchange reports the closing price of the futures contract as a sum equal to the prevailing cash price. By definition, futures prices converge to cash prices at contract expiry. The CME initiated cash settlement in Eurodollar futures trading and the idea was later applied to all stock index futures ideas and to some agricultural commodities. The trend continues to spread, although some traders accustomed to this type of contract find index contracts more difficult to understand, but in fact they are just as straightforward. If a trader has bought 100 pearls, at $100 each ($10,000 of exposure), he needs to replicate that $10,000 of exposure. Suppose the Pearl

Index used by the exchange is currently at 200, trading at $25 per index point. The trader will need to sell (200 x $25) x 2 = $10,000 contracts to hedge his position.

The idea of cash settlement in energy futures, pioneered by the International Petroleum Exchange's (IPE) Brent contract, is now widely accepted throughout the energy industry as preventing the complexities of administration and quality associated with physical delivery. More than 2% of Brent contracts are cash-settled, compared with fewer than 1% of physical delivery contracts actually going to delivery. Cash settlement for textile contracts is now widespread in the world cotton contract, and even in soft commodity markets the idea can be expected to gain ground.

In the cash settlement procedure, all long contracts that remain outstanding after the last day of trading are automatically offset by the clearing house or exchange against all remaining short contracts. Consider the example of the CME feeder cattle contract, which is cash-settled. The price settlement is set equal to the US Feeder Steer Price (USFSP). All the contracts are cancelled and, using the normal margin system (see below), money moves from losing accounts to profiting accounts, based on the final one-day price change — hence the term cash settlement. The best way of describing the procedure is that it is as if all the remaining contracts were simply offset by open outcry on the last day of trading, and all at the value of the USFSP.

The USFSP is a national average feeder steer index calculated by Cattle-Fax, a non-profit cattle-marketing service in Denver, Colorado. The USFSP, approved by the CME and the Commodity Futures Trading Commission (CFTC) for use in the feeder cattle contract, includes auction and direct sales of 600–800lb feeder steers in 27 states over the previous seven calendar days. Although a price is calculated and released daily it is used for cash settlement only eight times a year — on the last day of trading of each contract month.

So, an option for the futures contract designer is to use an index of familiar grades or locations. An example of such an index contract is the Baltic Freight contract on London Fox. Index contracts for commodity contracts are always cash-settled rather than deliverable. A good example of the index contract is the Brent Crude Oil contract on the IPE. The IPE states, 'The Exchange will prepare daily an index called the Brent Index which will be the average of cash market prices for Brent Blend traded on the previous business day taken from Tokyo opening through Houston close. These cash market prices (or 'deals done') are quoted and published by the independent reporting services, the media, used by the oil industry. Where there is an insufficient number of contracts in the cash market to calculate a satisfactory Brent Index, the Exchange, at its absolute discretion, shall determine the Brent Index by using the average of assessment prices as quoted and published by the media'.

The absence of physical delivery helps to avoid a 'squeeze' on prices where certain market participants obtain a large percentage of the physical commodity in order to complicate the delivery process and drive futures prices up or down close to the delivery date. It must, however, be said that some traders are suspicious of the process of calculating an index: if traders are supplying the information to the exchange for the calculation of prices, there is a risk that they may be biased depending on their position in the market. Exchanges can employ a variety of methods to reduce this problem. The most obvious is to eliminate the top and bottom price quotes before averaging the price. The other check, which exchanges are not entitled to do, is to covertly discover traders' positions before analysing their price input. Although this practice is very fair to the market in general it does rather negate the principle of anonymous trading in the market.

Terms of contracts

A futures contract will contain the following terms all of which must be decided upon before the contract is launched. Although it is possible to change all of them, alterations must not be allowed to affect already open positions.

Size of the contract

For a physical delivery or cash-settled specific commodity contract, this will be expressed in tonnes and for an index contract it will be $ per point. If the contract were for 10kg of pearls, for instance, and the average price of pearls was approximately $1000/kg, then the 'face value' of the contract — the price changes that affect the participant directly — would be $10,000. A 10% change in the price of pearls would change the value of the user's account by $1000. With a pearl index, it could be at 100 when the contract was launched, with each index point counting for $100 — producing a contract of approximately $10,000. The contract size for each contract (or 'lot') is usually determined by the trade in question. They consult with the exchange before a contract is launched. Consequently, the face value of contracts varies enormously depending on the practice of the trade. At London Fox, for instance, the lot size for coffee is 5 tonnes; for cocoa, 10 tonnes; and for sugar, 50 tonnes. As a rule of thumb the larger the market, the larger the face value. It is difficult for the exchange to choose the face value of a commodity contract: too large, and too few contracts will trade to create sufficient liquidity, and the exchange will receive no revenue (given that an exchange receives a small 'turn', usually between $1–5, for every contract traded on it); too small, and there will be complaints that the exchange and its brokers are exploiting their clients by exacting too many transaction fees for any given physical volume of transactions.

Months traded

How far ahead, and in which months, do traders in a particular commodity want the contract to be traded? Typically, futures contracts for soft commodities 'go out' between 15 months and two years. On futures exchanges worldwide, each month is given a standard letter coding shown below.

Jan F	Apr J	July N	Oct V
Feb G	May K	Aug Q	Nov X
Mar H	June M	Sept U	Dec Z

Quotation price

This will be expressed in a specific currency. Most commodity contracts are expressed in US dollars, but there are notable exceptions such as the London Commodity Exchange's cocoa contract which is expressed in sterling. It is, however, relatively easy to lock in exchange rates, in order to convert contracts to dollars.

Managing delivery procedure

This applies only to those contracts that are not settled in cash. The delivery mechanism must specify:

- where the commodity is to be delivered, whether premiums or discounts are associated with any particular delivery points, and if so what they are;
- over what time the delivery period extends;
- what premiums or discounts are associated with particular deliverable grades, or condition in which the commodity is delivered — for example the age of the commodity, density or moisture limits, requisite packaging;
- the method of delivery, whether Free On Board (FOB), Free Along Side (FAS), Cost and Freight (C&F), or in warehouse;
- documentation required by the contract specification;
- arbitration procedure.

Futures contracts are often said in their contract rules to 'turn into' a physical contract governed by, for example, the rules and regulations of the US Rice Millers' Association or the Malaysian Rubber Exchange. This helps the clear pricing of the futures contract: buyers and sellers know what they are trading and what they may receive or must deliver if they do not close out the contract in advance of the delivery dates. It is important to note that very few futures contracts, fewer than 5% on all markets, actually result in physical delivery where the contract specification includes such deliveries. In the remaining cases the contracts are bought or sold back (closed out) before delivery is made or received.

Delivery dates vary between markets. For some markets delivery dates matter in relation to the underlying physical market contracts that often call for delivery of the commodity by a particular day of the month. Every delivery date is followed by a roll-over date, at that date the next futures month to be traded starts trading, and price displays are shifted up one month. So for example, when the near June stops trading (on say the last business day of May), a new far month starts trading. Where expiry occurs at the close of the last business day of the month, the roll-over date is the first business day of the following month. In such markets there is never fewer than the full number of delivery months available for trading.

The more complex the delivery procedure, the fewer contracts are actually delivered. The administration of deliveries is a major expense for exchanges and consequently they do not usually favour them on their markets. The delivery process is usually complicated and unappealing in comparison with spot markets or straightforward forward contracts as a means of obtaining stocks of the physical commodity. When contracts are held through to expiry, delivery occurs through a process known as tendering. Short positions holders in the market, on expiry of the contract, contact the clearing house (or the exchange as appropriate — see Chapter 2) with the details of their delivery intentions. With soft commodity contracts, a sample is delivered to the exchange's grading panel for assessment. The grading panel must approve the particular sample for quality and decide on any premiums or discounts that need to be applied. Some commodities such as rice, coffee or cocoa are highly sensitive to quality differentiation. By contrast, oils and metals although difficult to categorise are relatively straightforward to assess for quality. There are several different quality assessment procedures depending on the contract specifications. For example, inspection before or on delivery, or the requirement for warrants declaring the quality to be satisfactory. Finally there may be provisions within the contract specifications discouraging the delivery of small amounts of the commodity, for example on the IPE gasoil contract, or the London Fox rice contract.

Deliverable grades and locations under exchange contracts will not satisfy all trades. Some traders will want to exchange a different quality or use a different port. In the short term they must either arrange a specific contract with another counterparty, and avoid the futures market altogether, or establish an agreed discount or premium to the market and trade with a side contract to their futures position. In the longer term, they must become involved in exchange politics and seek to alter the contract specification.

Trading hours

Considerable variation exists in attitudes to trading hours and how they are arranged. Some exchanges, such as the LME, arrange their trading hours in short 'rings' so that each metal is traded for no more than 20 minutes; this is also the common practice in Japan. Other markets such as the US and LCE allow trading during a full working day with a break for lunch. Trading hours depend on the normal trading hours of the physical commodity, and crucially, on the time zone of the exchange. They may be adjusted in Europe, for instance, to encompass the end of trading in the Far East or the beginning of trading in the US. Electronic trading is continually extending trading hours although commodity markets have been slower to react than financial markets.

Price fluctuations

The minimum price fluctuation, known as the tick size and the maximum price fluctuation, if any, are set by the exchange. A tick size which is too large will cause the market to lack liquidity as it will take too long for the market to adjust to spot market changes. Too small a 'tick size', will cause the market to fail to trade large quantities at one price because the price will have fractionally moved before all the trade can be executed. Maximum price fluctuations, limits on trading, are usually such that prevent movements of more than $x within one trading session. Movement of x% will result in exchange officials closing the market for 15 minutes, and reopening it at the previous limit with another similar $x being imposed as the new limit. These limitations, which only exist on some markets, are designed to prevent price changes over-reaching market participants, causing severe fluctuations before they become self-perpetuating; for example, fund sales 'stops' (eg, sell everything if the price falls below £Z), and producing accelerating changes. Maximum price limitations are accused of forestalling price changes thereby reducing the effectiveness of the market in reflecting prices, but they are allowed by exchanges even when they are quite complicated, for example when trading is only permitted within a certain band. Sometimes there are also speculative or hedging position limits, set by the exchange or the clearing house, limiting the number of contracts that any one market participant can hold at any one time. Most market players employ more than one broker, however, so these are virtually impossible to enforce. Major US corporations sometimes hold more than 50% of the open interest in smaller US futures contracts.

Exchange levy and clearing house fees and margins

These are usually the same for all contracts on an exchange and for all contracts cleared by a clearing house. Occasionally both or either can reduce or waive their fee, most usually in the introductory phase of a new contract. The clearing house — or the relevant department of the exchange responsible for clearing as is common in Japan — also sets the initial margin for the contract. Usually this is set to equal the average daily fluctuation in the price of the commodity. Clearing house experts calculate this from the historical volatility of the price of the commodity in question: initial margins can therefore be changed after the contract has been launched, depending on whether the commodity increases or decreases its volatility, in the months after launch.

Liquidity

Futures market designers and players all strive towards a truly liquid market: how to get it, how to increase it, how to preserve it. The most liquid commodity futures markets are basically those with the highest volume turnover, and are therefore the most successful. But what is liquidity? A market is liquid if you can get what you want done in it without moving the price. A market would therefore be perfectly liquid if an infinite amount of volume could be transacted there without moving the price at all. Markets clearly differ enormously from one another in their degree of liquidity, and equally importantly, in the degree of liquidity that they need. For example, the physical property market is notoriously illiquid. To sell a physical property takes both time and money. The faster you want to sell, the lower price you will receive. Large amounts of money entering the market always change the price, and information is at a premium. All deals are conducted in secret although all this is changing very gradually with the development of reliable property indices that one day may form the basis for sophisticated property derivatives. However, other markets are clearly already adequately liquid for their participants. Most cocoa traders believe that the LCE cocoa futures market, for instance, enables them to transact whatever business they require without moving market prices. As a general rule the larger the market volume, the more liquid the market. Liquidity also depends on the structure of the market. Forward and physical markets always tend towards illiquidity because all bargains must be matched with one another. When the market is falling buyers become scarce and vice versa. Periods of sharply rising or falling prices will often reduce the numbers of participants. This is true also in futures markets but many futures market participants are 'jobbing' — trying to make short-term profits or minimise losses quickly. This helps to explain why futures markets frequently have participants willing to trade at almost any prevailing price. Complex trading strategies such as differential and basis trading make this even more likely. The other general point is that the more varied the participants in the market, the more liquid it is likely to be. Liquidity exists when there are potential buyers for every seller and potential sellers for every buyer.

Conversely, without liquidity, futures markets fail to achieve their risk-transfer function. The greater the liquidity, the more attractive the market is to the broadest possible range of potential users. Liquidity, then, along with standardisation of contracts, allows futures contracts to be bought and sold in the open market quickly and at fair prices. For a farmer or producer, this means that he can sell an agricultural commodity futures contract at what he feels is a fair price, thereby at least guaranteeing the cost of production. When the contract expires several months later, he receives the agreed selling price, whatever has happened in the cash market. Corporate or institutional investors benefit significantly by hedging with futures, provided the market is sufficiently liquid.

With many traders wanting both to sell and buy, the gap between sell and buy prices will be very narrow, only one or two ticks. Indeed, this 'bid-offer spread' is a good measure of liquidity. Illiquid markets and less liquid months have much wider bid-offer spreads. Another measure is the number of outstanding —'open' — contracts, and how many participants are holding them. Almost all open contracts will be closed before delivery. The clearing houses and exchanges keep records of the open interest figures from the returns submitted by their clearing members — the market positions of their members' clients will complicate the market and make it more liquid than the net long and short positions of the clearing members themselves.

Liquidity is of particular significance when an exchange launches a new market. On launch there will be no open interest and no prices. If action does not appear quickly, participants will shy away from the contract and it will fail, however sophisticated the contract specification or effective it is in meeting the trade's needs. Potential users will be advised against joining the market because they might be unable to close out their contracts before delivery, thereby receiving unwanted physical deliveries or squeezes. Consequently, exchanges need to establish, in advance of a launch who will make a market in the new contract, and how wide bid-offer spreads can be expected to be. This leads inevitably into delicate territory with the regulators who are suspicious of what they see as attempts to create false markets.

Speculators

On the opposite side to a hedger are two types of market participant. It could be another hedger with an exactly opposite problem or it could be a *speculator* — a market participant without an equal and opposite position in the physical market. In a futures market, speculators are extremely important; they add to the efficiency of the market by enabling trades to take place because there are always willing buyers and sellers. Speculators do not create risk; on the contrary, they assume the risk that already exists for the producer or the user of a commodity. Not only does the speculator assume risk, he also contributes much of the capital that ensures a large pool of liquidity. It is however wrong to argue that speculators never cause price changes, and that they use the market in order to profit from price fluctuations. The price of grain, for example, is usually low at harvest time when the supply is normally plentiful. Bad weather, or a disease blight during the growing season can send prices back up, hence the fluctuations. It would be pointless to deny though, especially in the wake of the UK's currency crisis, that concerted action by speculators cannot affect prices even in the largest of markets.

Speculators look at changes in actual price levels. Their desire for profit motivates them to gather information on supply and demand and they use this data, to choose their positions in the market. They thereby provide information to the market about the impact of current events on expected future demand. So the price of a contract combines all the information that speculators and other market users have at any given time. This improves the price efficiency of the market. Exchanges gain speculative interest from two major sources; managed futures under institutional investors, and local members. 'Locals' importance derives from not only buying and selling a variety of contracts, but in improving price efficiency. Their involvement creates tighter bid-offer spreads (the gap between prices at which sellers are willing to sell, and prices at which buyers wish to buy), and their action in taking on risk gives the opportunity for those with physical market exposure to off load it. The prime function for a futures market, and indeed for any derivative product is to transfer risk from those who wish to divest themselves of it to those who want to assume it. In the less liquid futures contracts it is often locals who enable a two-way trade through their willingness to provide a two-way price. This improves the market's price accuracy. The frequent pricing gives investors a guide to the current market price of any listed futures or options contract, even if in practice the locals would not be able to sell or buy many contracts at those prices. Much criticism, directed at smaller exchanges throughout the world, is based on their failure to encourage or sustain a locals system similar to that which operates at the CBOT or CME. In London, locals on LIFFE are very effective and those on the IPE are gaining in stature, but there are virtually no locals making markets at LCE.

Types of options

An option contract is the right, but not the obligation, to buy or sell a specific quantity and quality of a commodity, share, index or futures contract at a specific price on or before a specific date in the future. One simple example of an option is a theatre ticket: there is no compulsion to attend the performance once the ticket has been bought. There are two major types of options that are important; the first is an option on a physical commodity and the second is a traded option. The former is, in essence, of the type 'A makes B a payment of value X to buy (or sell) a quantity Y of commodity Z specified according to criteria I at or by time T at a price of S'. The latter can, of course, be very complicated in structure and scope: it may provide difficult risk management problems that need to be confronted through derivative products of one type or another. Options terminology is as follows: all options on commodity Z are said to be of class Z; all options having the same expiry date and price are said to be of the same series.

Those who buy options are called buyers, holders or takers, whilst the sellers are also called writer and granters. One can either purchase a right to buy or to sell — this illustrates the first difference between the two primary types of options. Commodity call options are defined as the right, but not the obligation, to buy an underlying commodity at a certain price (known as the 'strike' or 'exercise' price in consideration of a payment (known as a 'premium')) and at or by a certain date (the 'expiry' date). Commodity put options are the opposite — the right, but not the obligation, to sell an agreed quantity of the underlying commodity at a given strike price. In the physical market for commodities traders, therefore, have four strategies, not two — they can buy or sell calls and they can buy or sell puts.

A second distinction between the two main types of option is 'at' and 'by' a certain date. Clearly one possibility is that the option may be exercised by the holder at any time between the agreement and the expiry date. This is known as an 'American' style option. The second type is exercisable only at expiry, and is known as a 'European' style option. The third distinction is that conventional options, whether European or American, expire at a certain date. The strike price is determined at the outset. The alternative is an average rate option, known colloquially as an 'Asian' option.

This allows a hedger to tie protection more closely to actual risk; he can choose the points over which the contract measures the commodity's price; on the settlement date an average is calculated which provides the final exercise price for the option, which combines a range of potential price movements. One option can therefore be used to hedge a series of cash flows. One metals broker in London, Brandeis, reports that between 55–60% of its brokered tonnage is average rate optioned, achieved mainly in the larger tonnage deals. These options are currently traded off-exchange, but they will probably be introduced on exchanges themselves as the exchanges fight to regain volume lost to OTC contracts.

Options contracts on physical commodities are written either to be completely specific to the two companies involved or they can be tradeable. Options are called 'traded' because there is a market, usually an exchange authorised by national legislation, in which they are bought and sold before expiry. An example was the London Traded Options Exchange, now merged with LIFFE. The traded option is bought and sold freely at an appropriate price until expiry. The strike price and the expiry (prompt) date are fixed and the premium varies over time. Options premiums quoted by market makers reflect three factors:

- current spot and futures prices of the underlying commodity;
- length of time to expiry of the option;
- supply and demand for that particular option.

A company can trade an option by signing an opposite contract with a third company — in which case it would have traded out of its physical position entirely. Suppose company A pays an option premium to company B to buy 100 pearls in six months' time at a price of \$100 each. The current price is \$90 and the market generally believes that the price of pearls will increase by \$10 over the six months. A consignment of pearls is then discovered to be fake, and counterfeiting rumours sweep the market. Prices rise to \$110 immediately. Clearly, A's option is now more valuable than it was, and can be profitably sold, if A can find a buyer easily and cheaply enough. The opposite is that if the spot price falls, the value of the option will tend to fall too.

An option is said to be 'in-the money' when, in the case of a call, the underlying commodity is trading at above the strike price, and for a put option when it is trading below. An in-the-money option will make money if exercised, and an 'out-of-the-money' will not. An 'at-the-money' option is one where the underlying commodity is trading at the same price as the option itself. An option is out-of-the-money when, for a call, the underlying commodity is trading below and for a put above the strike price. There is no point in exercising an out-of-the-money option and they expire valueless and unexpired. In derivatives market terminology the intrinsic value of an option is the amount of money that can be made by exercising the option. The other part of an option's value is the extrinsic value that is determined by how long the option has left to become in-the-money or more in-the-money, the volatility of the price of the underlying commodity (the more volatile the greater the chance of an out-of-the-money option acquiring some or more worth, and vice versa), and interest rates. Together these produce an overall expectation of whether an option is expected to become profitable before expiry: as the option approaches its expiry date, the likelihood of it becoming more (or less) valuable reduces accordingly, ie, the time value of the option diminishes.

Options also exist on futures contracts and are traded on commodities exchanges. Options on futures contracts are traded between different holders. With physical options contracts there are almost always problems in finding a buyer who wishes to acquire precisely the type of option that the company wants to sell. Although on an exchange full of interested parties, the chance is greatly increased even if in practice it is often quite slim. Exchange-traded options can often have a surprising lack of liquidity with, depressingly, very few contracts being traded for futures contracts, especially for some less traded months. Very wide spreads between buy and sell quotes tempered by realism and personal judgement are often the result. Most brokers to varying degrees are usually able to provide strike price quotes for all expiry months if asked.

Exchange-traded options do assist holders to close out their positions. There are several ways of closing out from an exchange-traded options contract. The holder can offset the position by buying an opposite position in the market at the same strike price. Company A, for example, having bought a call option for 100 pearls at $100 each in six months' time, buys a put option so that it can sell the 100 pearls for $100 each in six months' time. Its net exposure is now zero — it is square against the market. This is clearly one strategy. It has involved two option premiums for no eventual net gain, but it does have the advantage that either option can be exercised at any time until expiry.

In order to offset an option position, one must buy or sell the option with an identical strike price and contract month. Furthermore, a call option cannot and does not offset any put option position and vice versa.

Example

If a March $3.50 pearl put option is bought on 10 January, to offset the position a March $3.50 pearl put option must be sold. If a March $3.50 pearl call option or a March $3.40 pearl put option or a May $3.50 pearl put option is sold, the original position of buying the March $3.50 pearl put option will not be offset either completely, or in some cases, at all. The company could exercise the option, changing the company's exposure into a futures position at the buyer's instigation. The seller must conclude the physical transaction or futures transaction at the strike price.

'Option exercise' is the term used to describe the action taken by the option buyer who acquires a position in the underlying futures market at the option strike price. Since a put option gives the holder the right to sell at the strike price upon exercise, the put buyer will end up selling a futures contract at the strike price to the put seller. Therefore, if a March $3.50 pearl put option is exercised, the holder will receive a short March pearl futures contract at $3.50 and the put seller will assume a long March pearl futures contract at $3.50 per pearl. Once futures positions are established through the option exercise, both the option buyer and seller are margined (marked) to the market according to their respective futures positions. That is, the difference between the $3.50 strike price and the settlement price on the day after the option is exercised would be credited or debited to the respective futures positions.

The option expiry date is the last day an option can be exercised. With the CBOT Wheat Options contract, it is the Saturday immediately following the last trading day — the last Friday preceding the first notice day of the corresponding futures contract by at least five business days. Because the first notice day of a futures contract is the last business day of the month preceding the delivery month, the last trading day and expiry date of an option are always in the month preceding the delivery month. The option can expire worthless if not exercised. This will happen automatically if the option expires out-of-the-money. On the last day of trading the clearing house or exchange will cause all in-the-money options to be exercised.

Wheat option premiums

These are quoted in multiples of one eighth of one cent per bushel, representing $6.25 per contract (ie, 1/8 cent per bushel $00.125 x 5000 bushels). The Table below shows an example of how the prices appear in a newspaper. The premiums are computed, assuming the underlying futures prices are at $2.60, $2.50 and $2.40 for March, May and July options respectively:

	Calls			Puts		
Strike price	Mar-C	May-C	Jul-C	Mar-P	May-P	Jul-P
220	40	30	22	1/8	1/2	2 5/8
230	30	21 1/4	15 1/8	1/4	1 5/8	5 1/2
240	20 3/8	13 7/8	9 3/4	5/8	4 1/8	9 3/4
250	12 1/4	8 1/4	5 7/8	2 3/8	8 1/4	15 1/2
260	6 1/4	4 3/8	3 1/4	6 1/4	14 1/8	22 5/8
270	2 5/8	2 1/8	1 3/4	12 1/2	21 5/8	30 5/8
280	7/8	7/8	7/8	20 5/8	30 1/4	40

Each option month is usually followed by the letter C or P, designating call or put options respectively. The strike prices and the option premiums are quoted in cents per bushel. Therefore, the premium of a March $2.20 call option is quoted as 40 cents per bushel (ie, $2,000 per contract).

Since the March futures price is assumed to be $2.60 per bushel, the March $2.20 call option is in-the-money by 40 cents per bushel. The March $2.60 call option is, on the other hand, at-the-money and commands a premium of 6 1/4 cents per bushel (ie, $312.50 per contract) which represents solely the time value of the option. The March $2.80 call option has a premium of only seven eighths of one cent per bushel (ie, $43.75 per contract) because it is out-of-the-money by 20 cents.

Given that the May futures price is at $2.50 per bushel, the at-the-money May $2.50 call option has a premium of 8 1/4 cents per bushel (ie, $412.50 per contract). The reason the at-the-money March and May call options have different premiums is due to the difference in their times to maturity. The March option expires about two months earlier than the May option. The strike price of the May call option that is greater than $2.50 is considered to be out-of-the-money and commands a smaller premium than the at-the-money call option. On the other hand, the strike price of the May call option that is lower than $2.50 is considered to be in-the-money and commands a larger premium than the at-the-money call option.

Given a March futures price of $2.60 per bushel, for example, the at-the-money put option has a strike price of $2.60 and commands a premium of 6 1/4 cents per bushel (ie, $312.50 per contract). An in-the-money put option would be any put option with a strike price greater than the at-the-money strike price of $2.60. The March $2.80 put option, for instance, commands a premium of 20 5/8 cents per bushel (ie, $1,031.25 per contract), which is higher than the at-the-money option's premium. The March $2.20 put option would be out-of-the-money and commands a premium of only one eighth of a cent per bushel (ie, $6.25 per contract).

Intrinsic and extrinsic option values

As with the futures contracts, exchange-traded options trade in different contract months. Trading in options is not allowed for those months in which the corresponding futures do not trade.

The *intrinsic value* of an option is the amount that would be realised if the option was to be exercised. An option will not trade at a level less than its intrinsic value; if it did, arbitrage opportunities would be created — arbitrageurs would quickly buy options, bidding their premiums up to at least the intrinsic amount. For example, suppose a call option is struck at $3.00 per pearl when pearl futures are trading at $3.20. This option is 20 cents in-the-money. However, suppose the option may be purchased for 15 cents per pearl.

Arbitrageurs can be expected to buy the call option at 15 cents per pearl, and immediately exercise it by purchasing pearl futures for $3.00 when they are trading at $3.20. Thus, the arbitrageur will realise a 20 cent gross profit upon exercise of the call, less the 15 cent premium, for a net profit of five cents per pearl. Although an option will not trade at less than its intrinsic value, an option will often trade at levels greater than its intrinsic value. This is referred to as the option's *extrinsic value*. In common usage, extrinsic value also is called 'time value'. However time value is only one element of extrinsic value. Several factors influence the extrinsic value associated with an option, including:

- the time remaining until the option expires;
- the volatility of the underlying futures market;
- the relationship between the futures price and the option strike price.

Example
Assume it is March, the July pearl futures price is $3.40 per pearl and a July call option struck at $3.00 is held. The intrinsic value of the call is 40 cents, but perhaps the premium for the call is now 50 cents per pearl. If the holder exercises the call, he will assume a long position in the pearl futures market at $3.00 when pearl futures are actually trading at $3.40 realising the 40 cent intrinsic value. On the other hand, if he sells the call for the 50 cent per pearl premium it now commands, he realises the 40 cent intrinsic value, plus an additional 10 cents per pearl in time value.

Notes:

Nick Battley, *An Introduction to Commodity Futures and Options*, McGraw Hill, 1989.

Chapter 2: Exchanges and clearing houses

Exchanges

A futures exchange is an organised, central market-place for the trade of futures and options contracts. There are now over 50 futures exchanges trading commodities throughout the world that provide internationally recognised locations where traders can meet to trade 'their' commodity or instrument, quote swap prices and other information. To trade at a futures exchange traders must become members. The exchange provides support and encouragement for trading. National regulations however, normally preclude the exchange itself from trading, establishing prices or otherwise actively promoting trades.

The exchange is also responsible for the establishment, usually in conjunction with main market users, of trading rules and, in conjunction with national and international regulators, for their enforcement. The establishment of an exchange must be in accordance with national rules, for example those of Securities and Investments Board (SIB) in the UK for a Recognised Investment Exchange (RIE). In some cases, notably in Japan, the exchanges also provide the clearing mechanisms described below.

The exchange provides the physical location for the trade of the contracts. This can be a specialised trading floor, such as the US pits, the LME rings, or the floor of LCE. *Rings*, are specially tailored for the trading community of particular commodities. *Pits* enable traders to trade several commodities, thereby encouraging liquidity and highlighting those commodities which are most actively traded in any one trading session.

Around any trading floor in separate firms' booths, or ring desks, are the telephones that connect the floor traders with their back offices at the brokers they represent or are acting for. Floor traders try to execute their orders — to 'get them filled' — as best the market rules allow: they cry out their orders and signal by hand to other traders in the pit or around the ring. There are no telephones in the actual pit itself so runners are required to carry orders to the traders themselves.

Distribution of prices

The prices themselves are recorded by exchange staff (in pits and rings) or run off feeds from the electronic trading systems directly, to systems which sell the data to quote vendors — companies such as Reuters and Telerate — which provide the information on screens to their clients worldwide. A number of exchanges in the UK use the Manifest system which displays information for each delivery month of each contract as follows:

Sell	– the lowest price in real time being offered ('asked' in US terminology)
Buy	– the highest price bid in real time

The gap between these two, which will be a certain number of ticks, is the 'bid-offer spread' for that contract month.

Trade	– the price at which the last recorded exchange took place
High	– the highest traded price that trading day
Low	– the lowest traded price that trading day
Volume	– the number of contracts traded that trading day
Time	– the time of the last trade

The screen also shows the total daily volume of the contract and the current time. Some US price reporting systems are not as detailed; they show only the 'trade' and quotations. In January 1992 the IPE introduced its own price reporting system, increasing the data and quality of reporting available on Brent and gasoil options contracts. Options premiums and volatilities are updated in real time, and the at-the-money options are permanently highlighted. The IPE believes that the introduction of this system has been instrumental in increasing option volume. Since the summer of 1989, subscribing TOCOM members have been able to obtain data on the trading results of commodities listed on the Exchange *via* video monitors linked to the TOCOM Market Information System.

Information provision on derivative and physical business has an $8bn annual turnover. The market is dominated by such companies as Reuters, Telerate, and Knight-Ridder, and they provide everything from news services and simple prices to personalised pages, and spreadsheet integration. As some exchanges sell their data directly, smaller firms have been breaking into the market. This worldwide distribution of information on a real-time or near real-time basis ensures that international futures markets do not often get out of line with one another. When they do, arbitrageurs step in at once, often alerted by their own electronic systems monitoring of relative prices, to ensure that they make a riskless profit and return the relativities between, for example, New York and London coffee to their correct level.

The New York Coffee, Sugar and Cocoa Exchange's (CSCE) experiment using hand-held terminals for price reporting is designed to improve accuracy and significantly increase the speed of price dissemination. With this system, Exchange members around the trading rings enter data about their trades into a hand-held computer terminal, which passes the information *via* radio to the CSCE central computers and the Commodities Exchange Center system, disseminating prices on the floor and around the world. The CBOT and CME are working together to develop a hand-held electronic trading card that will surpass all US government trade-reporting standards, providing an audit trail that will record every transaction on the Exchange floor or other system at the time it is made. Mock trading in the first of two chosen contracts, on the CBOT's wheat pit and the CME's Deutsche mark pit, is currently designed for the introduction of the system for locals in 1993 and for all traders by 1994.

Exchange funding

Each exchange is funded through a levy placed on members for every futures and options transaction handled — normally about $2/£1 per 'round turn' (buy and sell) and as a result each exchange can only grow by expanding volume. This in turn demands marketing and business development staff (who are costly), in addition to staff required for compliance, audit, accounts and running both physical and electronic markets. Some people have suggested that exchanges will contract out business development work in the future. Major exchanges can have over 2,500 members and hundreds of permanent staff.

In a number of markets or exchanges, price movement is restrained by a limit that is defined in the exchange contract rules. Limits are usually based on settlement prices. Trades may take place at the limit price but cannot be exceeded. So if there are unfilled bids or offers at the level, the limit comes into operation. In those London markets that have limits, this usually entails the closure of the market for a period of time, after which the session is reopened according to conventional opening practices. Spot delivery months are often limit free, and trading can continue in them even though the others are closed. Limits are designed as braking mechanisms in volatile markets, and are arguably anti-competitive and an unwarranted interference in the market. They have no real technical purpose and basically exist to force players to stop and assess the situation. Hence after the 1987 stock market collapse, it was suggested that limits (which were not in force in either the stock market or the stock futures market) would have slowed or mitigated the crash, but it has equally been argued that limits generate pent-up demand which in turn creates price volatility that would otherwise be dissipated through the normal market mechanism.

In the US, markets that reach limit usually operate a pool system. The market closes and buyers and sellers put their orders to buy and sell at limit into a pool. The market can only reopen if the price reverses, either by the buying (at limit-up) being met with sufficient selling, or by the selling (at limit-down) being satisfied by buying. If not the market remains closed for the rest of the day with a new limit in operation the following day.

US exchanges

There are several exchanges, for example, all trades at the CBOT are settled by the Board of Trade Clearing Corporation (BOTCC), an independent entity that handles the Exchange's clearing functions and ensures the integrity of the market-place. In this capacity, the BOTCC acts as a guarantor for all trades cleared by it, reconciles all clearing member firm accounts each day to ensure that all gains have been credited and all losses have been collected, and sets and adjusts clearing member firm performance bond margins for changing market conditions. The BOTCC has been a model of financial integrity for more than 60 years. In fact, since its inception, no clearing member firm has ever defaulted on its contractual obligation to the Clearing Corporation.

The Clearing Corporation of New York (CFCCNY) will clear for the CSCE and the COMEX from 1994 onwards if agreement is reached. CFCCNY will be jointly owned, financed and operated by the CSCE and COMEX, and may be joined as principals in the Corporation by the NYCE. CFCCNY will clear all trades executed on CSCE and COMEX, and will have sufficient capacity to clear trades for other future exchanges. Presently, trades on COMEX are processed by the COMEX Clearing Association, while CSCE's trades are cleared through the CSC Clearing Corporation, both of which are owned by their respective clearing members.

Asia

In Asian exchanges the role of the clearing house is usually performed by the exchange itself, or by a specialised corporation particular to one exchange. In some countries, such as Malaysia, there is only one exchange. Malaysia's Futures Clearing Corporation (MFCC) replaced the International Commodities Clearing House's (ICCH) computer software with its own, and has carried out further development work since. In 1991, for example, the Corporation developed a client accounting and risk management system for brokers (called KRIS — Klein Risisko Informasi System), which the Exchange is encouraging them to use as it provides for standard accounting procedures and can be run on a personal computer. At present the system handles only futures contracts but will be modified to accommodate options later.

All trades in Malaysia on the KLCE are cleared by the MFCC clearing house which has an authorised capital of M$50m and issued capital of M$25m. The Exchange and clearing members together own 70% of the shares of the Clearing Corporation and the balance is owned by banks.

A corporate member of KLCE may be admitted to clearing membership if it satisfies the following requirements:

- its paid-up share capital of not less than M$1m and Net Tangible Assets of at least M$2m;

- it owns two exchange memberships.

On admission, a clearing member will be required to purchase up to 3% shares in the Clearing Corporation, and to provide a security deposit amounting to M$500,000 to MFCC either in cash or in bank guarantee.

Electronic trading worldwide

On the whole 80% of international futures trading in commodities is carried out through open outcry on exchange floors. Although the percentage is bound to increase over time, the existing floors of exchanges are set to continue into the twenty-first century. Some contracts are, however, not traded on trading floors; the requirement for the traders to meet in one physical location is therefore removed if the contracts are traded electronically. If this is the case the futures exchange is a more abstract concept, with a physical location combining the central computer, audit, compliance, administrative and business development functions.

Japan

The Japanese lead the world in the use of electronic trading for all markets, but especially with regards to commodities. The change to electronic trading also resulted in the demise of the traditional price determination method: the *Itayose* auction method, still used in the rings of the LME, has been replaced by the *Zaraba* or continuous method of trading. The Zaraba method is standard for Japanese securities and commodities futures markets in the US and Europe.

The TOCOM diagram over explains the difference between electronic and open outcry trading systems. The key differences lie in the areas of trading and daily schedules; the trading method and the determination of price, including price fixing; the placing of orders and order and transaction types, and price level indication.

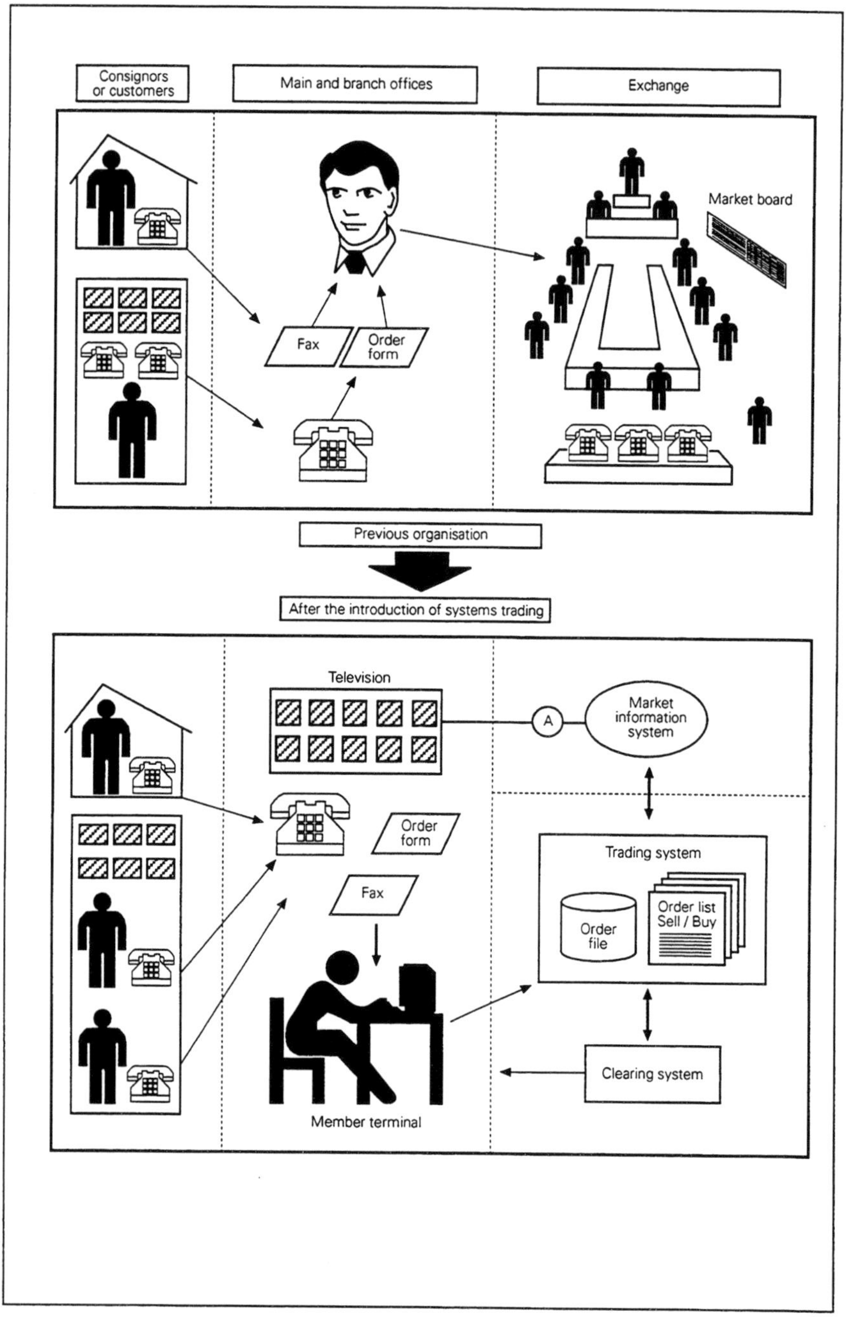

Adapted from TOCOM literature

TOCOM's initial step towards electronic trading was the establishment in April 1990 of the Commodity Systems Trading Corporation (CSS) — a joint venture between TOCOM and NTT Data Communications Systems Corporation — for the operation and maintenance of the TOCOM systems. TOCOM expects CSS to become an important information and support organisation for the commodity industry within Japan. On 1 April 1991 TOCOM introduced electronic systems trading for precious metals (gold, silver and platinum). Plans exist to put other TOCOM commodities such as cotton yarn, rubber and woollen yarn onto the electronic trading system as part of TOCOM's drive to become a genuinely global market-place. This would mean 24 hour trading and computer links to other exchanges worldwide that would allow electronic trading for stock market members hedging positions in securities markets. This development is expected during the 1990s depending on demand for the commodities markets in question.

Members enter market orders from computer terminals, in their own firms, connected directly to TOCOM. The TOCOM computer centre houses the central system which matches and clears contracts, including credit control and market information dissemination. To protect trading data from manipulation or sudden changes, the Open System Interconnection (OSI) communications format has been adopted.

The system goes on line at 08.00; orders are accepted for the morning session from 08.20; and from 09.00 authorised terminal operators hit bids and offers to determine the opening price. The market then moves into continuous trading on an order matching basis until 11.00. Similarly in the afternoon, orders are accepted from 12.30, and trading takes place from 13.00 to 15.30. (These arrangements are frequently changed and each exchange should be consulted for its current trading times for each contract).

The Tokyo Sugar Exchange also uses electronic trading. Electronic trading for raw sugar futures began on 5 November 1991, and on 6 May 1992, the Exchange commenced options on raw sugar futures using the CTS/2 system. Since 22 June 1992 the Osaka Grain Exchange has switched to electronic trading.

Australia

The Sydney Computerised Overnight Market (SYCOM) began on 30 November 1989 in response to demands, from both domestic and overseas participants, for longer trading hours. SYCOM now accounts for 3–5% of the total Sydney Futures Exchange (SFE) volume. The system can accommodate up to 100 terminals and up to 1000 delivery months and option strike prices can be quoted. SYCOM takes over trading for financial contracts at 16.40, 10 minutes after the close of local trading, and finishes at 14.00 the following morning. The Exchange has not as yet placed its commodity contracts onto the system and current volumes certainly would not justify the move. Since its inception in November 1989 volumes have grown steadily. Nightly turnover in 1990 was 727 and by the following year it had increased to 1474. An upgraded version of SYCOM was introduced in May 1991 that provided more screen and contract capacity and, more importantly, permitted SFE to list options on SYCOM. An example of the growing use of SYCOM, particularly from overseas, was emphasised by the extension of trading hours in March 1991 to 02.00. The numbers of operators by the end of 1991 had grown from the original 45 to 135. Versions of the SYCOM system were adopted by the New York Mercantile Exchange (NYMEX) and London Fox.

The UK

London Fox's experience with electronic trading has been mixed. Starting with the ATS/1 and then ATS/2 systems of the ICCH, the original project was for the white sugar contract only. Sugar traders liked being able to watch and trade whites from their offices whilst being in telephone communication with the raw sugar floor. Fox then tried to launch new contracts on its replacement system, Fast Automated Screen Trading (FAST), which was also an order matching system but a cheaper and simpler version. These contracts failed partly because it is difficult to build liquidity on an exclusively computer-traded system. Existing members were allowed to buy licences for £400 to trade a new contract, which enabled them to hit a key to change screens. Existing members preferred to keep their screens fixed to white sugar, understandably, and so attention was diverted from the new screen-based contracts. In fairness, lamb futures, launched on the floor of the Exchange, did little better. Fox eventually decided to scale down both its contracts and its electronic trading, and the system has reverted to trading just white sugar only.

USA

The CME, realising that technology has created an increasingly sophisticated but indisputably smaller world — in which political or economic developments in one country immediately influence markets in each of the world's financial centres — decided that this new global market would insist on a liquid trading system which was available around the clock. So, together with Reuters Holdings plc and the CBOT, the Exchange developed and introduced Globex on 25 June 1992.

Globex is an electronic trading system for futures and options that provides investors with a single, continuous, worldwide trading system available virtually 24 hours a day. Globex's interactive network will be capable of linking thousands of terminals, in every corner of the world, into one deep and liquid market-place.

Reuters, an international communications organisation with few competitors, specialises in financial news and information; it has an integrated global network — 165,000 terminals in 118 countries. Reuters has been a trading service industry pacesetter with transaction networks enabling dealers in stocks, bonds, currencies and bullion to execute confidential transactions *via* computer terminals. The Reuters Monitor Dealing Service in particular, links nearly every currency-trading organisation of significance. The CME and CBOT will be joined in Globex by a number of other exchanges in the US and around the world, all of which will have access to terminals and equal trading rights. These partner exchanges will retain control, ownership, clearing and financial responsibility for their own products. They will also choose the hours during which their products are to be traded on Globex. Other information vendors will also be invited to join the Globex network. These other vendors can, through their own systems, provide their customers, who are members of partner exchanges, with the ability to submit orders for Globex products.

Globex's dedicated interactive network links Reuters Digital Equipment Corporation mainframe computers to smart trading terminals built around 386+ microprocessor technology. The network, which relies on dedicated, fully redundant subordinate computers or concentrators, is exclusive to Globex, remaining entirely separate from the Reuters Monitor Network.

A Globex transaction proceeds in the following way:

1 Orders are entered through Globex terminals.

2 A credit-control module verifies creditworthiness based on clearing-member determined parameters.

3 Orders are matched based on time and price priority.

4 Matched orders are confirmed the instant a match is made at each originating terminal. Meantime, all unmatched orders remain in the system until matched or withdrawn.

5 The instant a trade is executed, all participating quote vendors receive last sale price and quantity data, as well as updated information on best bid and offer and size of each.

6 As each trade is confirmed, it is routed to the CME clearing system for settlement.

7 Clearing member firms adjust buyers' and sellers' accounts for position and margin.

If Globex succeeds, it will be a matter of time before a new generation of traders starts to doubt the importance and loose the skills of the trading floor. The decline, once it starts in earnest, could be rapid and will almost certainly be cumulative. Traders will however want to see a few years of successful Globex trading first, before they push for the scrapping of expensive trading floors and floor traders.

In addition to Globex in the US there is CBOT's Project A, which is designed to assist the Exchange in competing for OTC business.

Globex was designed originally as a method of exporting Chicago's financial futures contracts to protect the US Exchanges' revenues. The system was developed by the CME and Reuters, with the CBOT joining in later. The close focus at all stages on using it for financial futures probably owes more to questions of priorities, and unwillingness to risk losing liquidity in the commodity pits, than any great belief that Globex is intrinsically unsuitable for commodity contracts. Indeed, it is very likely that the biggest losers from the success of Globex could be the small commodity exchanges worldwide; especially if the liquidity and costs prove to be greater and less substantial respectively. The MATIF has already joined Globex which is a far-sighted move. Offset deals between exchanges, and global combinations of contracts must be imminent. Even the LIFFE is talking to Globex and there is likely to be fierce competition over Globex entry between LIFFE and the Deutsche TerminBörse (DTB). However, large exchanges like these have the ability to extract good deals for listing their contracts, and may be able to construct parallel trading or out-of-hours arrangements. The same is not so for the smaller commodity exchanges so Optionsmäklarna (OM), for example, or the KLCE, should talk to Globex now.

In London two conflicting approaches have brought radically different results. LIFFE's incremental approach for financial futures concentrating on after-hours trading has brought acceptability for the Automated Pit Trading (APT) system, but London commodity traders have become suspicious of electronic trading after the Fox debacle. Any revival of electronic trading in London for commodities is likely to come from other sources, for example, the direct installation of Globex terminals, or the expansion of OM London (or even LIFFE) into some form of commodity trading, perhaps property futures — for which neither exchange has immediate plans. As for the IPE, its most recent official publication states that after extensive study of the issue, nothing is to be done at present. The IPE is closely watching Globex and will no doubt wish to participate in the system if it proves successful and is adaptable for after-hours energy futures trading; the same is true for the New York exchanges.

The SFE has plans to trade options all day on SYCOM, and to modify the system to incorporate a price discovery mechanism which takes into account such variables as implied volatility and strike price delta. The SFE is also talking about becoming part of Globex, as are Japanese exchanges.

There is opposition to all forms of electronic trading from floor traders and all of those — both traders and analysts — who believe that open outcry trading has irrefutable advantages. They argue that the logic of floor trading, through the subtle perceptions of traders on the floors, creates liquidity itself. Expert floor traders — especially locals — claim that their awareness of market 'feel' is precisely what enables them to trade successfully; bluntly, that they can sense, from the behaviour of other traders around them, whether prices are about to rise or fall. These traders believe that liquidity is lost in electronic markets. They are almost certainly right or at least until a new generation of trader emerges, traders who have never known a floor market and who actively seek to create liquidity on screen. This view is reflected by clients who demand that certain floor traders act on their behalf, a form of exclusivity, which some brokers believe electronic trading will destroy. This is particularly important when regulators worldwide are placing an increased emphasis on the necessary legitimacy of methods used to create initial liquidity in contracts. Client companies may themselves, in the future, obtain electronic systems. In practice however this is a distant and receding fear as client companies do not wish, (a) to identify themselves every time they trade; (b) to incur the fixed costs associated with the installation of electronic systems, back offices, trading experts etc and (c) to change the nature of their own business, offsetting these costs by competing with brokers for other business. Client companies have chosen not to install electronic trading systems yet, and it is actually highly improbable that they will. Many commodity exchanges have made substantial investments in their trading floors; SFE and London Fox are good examples . Where the exchanges are tenants, a decision to abandon the trading floor at the end of a lease effectively means a complete commitment to electronic trading something exchanges are not planning to do in the next decade. Instead they prefer to wait to see how effective Globex proves to be, and whether it proves possible to unite different trading systems. In London, the issue is bound up with the lease held on the specialised trading floor at Commodity Quay on the one hand, and the major investment placed in Cannonbridge by LIFFE/LTOM on the other.

However, the success of Österreichische Termin und Optionbörse (OTOB), DTB and OM London and the widespread availability of effective clearing demonstrates conclusively that given the right contracts, adequate capital backing and a good computer system, exchanges can be established and succeed even amidst already strong competition. It is likely that such exchanges will continue to grow at the continued expense — at least the relative expense — of the traditional floor markets, especially in the US. The fate of London Fox, confused by its scandal and premature speculation in electronic trading and new contracts, has and will really be determined by the decline in its traditional markets, especially sugar and coffee.

Globex is not designed to clash with pit trading and exchanges are unlikely to upset their existing pit liquidity by casually discarding them in favour of electronic trading. Traders, who make up a large power on the governing boards of exchanges, on the whole oppose electronic trading. Regulators, by contrast, generally prefer it as the audit trail is so visible.

In the long term however all the advantages of electronic trading will continue whilst all the disadvantages will gradually decrease. Electronic trading is already cheaper, and the reduction in the price of suitable electronic terminals will without doubt continue. Exchanges exclusively using electronic trading will be able to drastically cut their overheads. Electronic trading will increasingly allow the stationing of terminals internationally, a major reason Japanese exchanges cite for their interest. At present it is regulatory difficulties that prevents this, and there is unfortunately insufficient political will from the international trading community to overcome it. Globex screens trading numerous commodities, and with slave systems displaying a variety of contracts, including inevitably commodity contracts, such as crude oil, will begin to appear once the system has really proved itself. The CBOT is currently investigating the possibility of clearing OTC contracts as part of the campaign to win back business from the burgeoning OTC markets. It is certainly possible that banks, for example, having devised OTC products with at least some standardisation of terms so that a number of clients might be interested, would want to list such products on Globex. As with initial listings, this is most likely to begin in the financial and energy areas and spread later to the soft and other commodity derivatives areas.

Electronic trading is as yet not a satisfactory medium for the promulgation of new contracts as it is impossible to co-ordinate the development of liquidity. This will change as Globex develops and becomes more sophisticated.

There is no doubt about the shape of the future but how quickly will it come? It seems possible that electronic trading will remain peripheral to commodity derivatives trading for at least the rest of the century.

The clearing house

In various countries, particularly the US and Europe, commodity exchanges are allied to clearing houses that act as the principal for each exchange trade registered with it.

Risk management is both the purpose and the key ability of the clearing house. The extent of risk for each clearing member is proxied by the size of their net open position across all the different markets. Each trade is recorded by both seller and buyer; a net neutral position is reached by 18.00 each day in London (trades made after 17.00 are cleared the following day). The business day is divided into a series of periods to ensure the quick resolution of mismatches to 'square' the market.

When exchange clearing members enter into contracts with one another the contracts are registered with the clearing house. The clearing house is substituted into the contract by novation, and thus becomes the principal in the trade. As a result of novation the clearing house accepts legal responsibilities including the orchestration of transactions and their finance. The clearing house also carries counterplay risk; it deals only with its clearing members, and settles all transactions at the end of each day's trading. By interposing itself between the two transacting parties, it guarantees the contractual obligations of the transaction. It allows each party to offset the transaction without having to reach a new agreement with the same party. However it takes no legal responsibility for the agreements between parties and their clients. The clearing house must through its facilities, procedures and regulators be able both to:

- register and monitor transaction registrations to the satisfaction of its clearing members (even if dealing by proxy with a non-member), and ensure an equable trading outcome in the various trades dealt with worldwide. It must also ensure that data on, or provision of, relevant political, climatic, and product characteristics can be deployed in efficient decision-making during the period of transaction activity.

- monitor the performance of the trade (be it a commodity or a financial instrument) to ensure that, for example, quality, delivery, post-delivery and legal aspects are to the satisfaction of the members, and that full payments have been made at the correct times.

London Clearing House

The London Produce Clearing House was established in 1888 to clear sugar and coffee trading in London. It became the ICCH in 1973, and its role is now crucial to the development of commodity and derivatives in London and abroad. In 1988 the ICCH set up the London Clearing House (LCH) as a division to reflect a specific commitment to the London markets. LCH is the independent counterparty and guarantor to all contracts traded on specified RIEs in the UK, and hence all trades registered with LCH in the names of its clearing members. This creates economies of scale; for example, clearing members benefit from more standardised back-office trade processing, and centralised payment and receipt procedures. London RIEs are:

- LIFFE;
- IPE;
- London Fox;
- LME.

which means that inter-office trading is brought within the clearing system.

As these organisations are all independent clearing house members the key advantage is that they are insulated from the effect of a default by another member. They do not need to provide a bond or guarantee themselves.

Membership requirements

Applicants are vetted for membership of clearing houses; this is an integral part of counterparty risk management. Membership is available for companies or partnerships who meet certain criteria concerning financial integrity and probity, net worth, management reputation, parentage, type of business and administrative efficiency. These criteria are the same as those for seeking authorisation in the relevant category by the Exchange and Regulatory Authorities. Not every exchange member is a clearing member.

Every exchange has its own membership requirements and application procedures. For example, to be considered for membership of LCH an applicant must provide the following background information and documentation:

- Latest audited accounts;
- Memorandum and Articles of Association, Certificates of Incorporation;
- Details of group structure, including the audited accounts of the parent company (if any);
- Identity of any major shareholders;
- Names of directors and relevant senior executives;
- Business and senior personnel profiles.

Clearing members must sign a standard clearing member agreement establishing the legal nature of the relationship between the two parties.

Clearing, settlement and deliveries

The LCH clearing, settlement and delivery systems ensure that members' net worth is normally not required to pay market losses, as in most cases the monies are already held as initial margin within the clearing system.

Clearing houses worldwide are either independents or owned and operated by exchange members as is the case in the US. Counterparty risks are minimised by the structure and financial resources behind a clearing house. The ICCH in London, a profit-marking concern, clears for a number of exchanges worldwide and is owned by six of London's largest clearing banks (Barclays, Lloyds, Midland, NatWest, Standard Chartered and the Royal Bank of Scotland). The LCH has, what is universally described as, discrete backing of £200m provided by the banks and the insurance market. Worldwide coverage enables ICCH to see the exposure of its members in other exchanges, but does not show their commitments in the OTC market. Clearing houses also provide registration, clearing and settlement, central banking and treasury services, and the administration of the physical delivery of futures contracts. To facilitate improved trade registration as volumes mounted during the late 1980s, the LCH, in conjunction with the UK exchanges, developed and has now introduced Trade Registration Systems (TRS).

Shorts in the contract submit tender documents between determined hours on the expiry day, and the clearing house/exchange allocates them to those who are long in the contract. Although the total number of shorts and longs will be equal, the numbers of market participants may differ, and the clearing house's responsibility will be to allocate them amongst market participants most efficiently. Some longs ask the clearing house for a revision of clearing allocations and a process of negotiation may ensue, but the political power lies with the clearing house. A long cannot refuse a delivery which is in accordance with the delivery regulations of the contract. Longs can only reject tenders for reasons of quality failures and cannot exploit any gap between tender and expiry dates to run their position on the market and either close out or take delivery later, in the hope of a better delivery in terms of location or quality.

The clearing house manages the delivery process itself, although in practice the matched market participants may communicate with one another. Once delivery has physically been made, the product risk — and therefore the need to have insurance — passes to the buyer. Property rights over the commodity pass when the correct paperwork, detailing the quantity and quality of the commodity delivered is exchanged. Arbitration procedures are agreed in advance in the contract specification and are administered between the clearing house and the exchange. In the event of default the clearing house will try to ensure a satisfactory agreement between the parties, and will also carry out 'invoicing back' between participants in the event that force majeure prevents the efficient execution of the contract.

The clearing house guarantee continues until after delivery has been made and as a result it has an interest in the efficiency of the delivery mechanism for every contract. The clearing house may increase its deposits and sometimes demands proof of the deliverable commodity. The objective is to avoid a squeeze. For example, for the IPE gasoil contract, deposits are doubled five days before tender, and doubled again three days before delivery. Similarly, the last settlement price on the day before the expiry day is sometimes used for the calculation of invoice value, in order to avoid a squeeze price on delivery.

All open positions are revalued on a daily basis and any profits or losses are paid or received by the clearing house in terms of variation margin, (except for the LME — see below).

Managing the risk

Initial margins

The LCH is the ultimate counterparty to every trade and the guarantor of the markets — LCH is at risk to the default of a clearing member. It therefore requires collateral or deposits called *margins* to be met on all open positions held by clearing members to cover its risk exposure. This requirement is referred to as *initial margins*. These are calculated principally as a weighted average number of trades with respect to price of the trades done on the trading floor in a closing sequence of the trading day. Initial margins are set by the LCH in conjunction with the exchanges, and are set 'broadly to cover one day's price risk with reference to the volatility of each contract; they therefore may vary from time to time. Contracts traded out will have no outstanding payments to make or receive, as the market-to-market process will have already collected or paid them, except for what is done as a result of the day's trading'.

The initial margin charged depends on the volatility of the underlying commodity and hence of the futures contract. It is usually between 5–10% of the face value of the contract. In general, clearing house members maintain enough capital in their clearing house accounts to meet their needs. If a squeeze or corner is threatened in a particular market, the clearing house raises deposits with the aim of encouraging members to close out their contracts. Initial margins should give the LCH sufficient liquid funds to make good any losses following the default of a clearing member.

Variation margins

Few elements are as important or as difficult to understand for new participants as *variation margins* and their applications. These were devised to protect clients in the event of the collapse of a clearing member. This 'no-debt' system, in which losses cannot accumulate over time, protects the Exchange against default by its clearing members, since its debt exposure is limited to only one day's price movement. Each account must be settled on a daily basis, affording clearing members protection against default by their own customers; clearing members are also required by exchange rules to collect settlement variation from their customers on a daily basis.

All clearing members must provide full variation margins daily; during periods of extreme volatility the LCH may call additional variation margins to be paid during the day, to supplement the initial margin and any variation on margin already held. These must be paid within an hour of such a call being issued. LCH may also require additional margins in other special circumstances determined by the clearing houses. Clearing houses have the whip hand in determining margins, and exchanges often believe that they are set high to minimise clearing house risk rather than low to encourage trading. Sometimes exchanges rebel and establish their own clearing houses as is common practice in Japan.

Some exchanges, for example, the CME, maintain a daily 'intra-day' settlement cycle. Routinely, this cycle is run at 13.30. Variation payments are determined by applying current market prices to the previous day's final positions by firm and origin. If, for some reason, market conditions warrant it, another intra-day cycle will be run at any time during the trading day.

Margin liabilities for both futures and options, whether cash-settled or physical delivery, are assessed at the end of each day, and all open contracts are revalued at the day's closing price. Settlement prices are determined by the relevant exchange, but the clearing house reserves the right to determine its own official quotation prices.

Settlements

The margins are paid to the LCH through, for example, the Protected Payment System (PPS) which is an internal transfer system operating between accounts at the same bank branch. All clearing members must hold an account at a bank branch operating the PPS. They sign a mandate allowing the LCH to make direct debits from their account for the amount of liabilities called. The bank then credits this amount to the LCH account held at the same branch for the other clearing member. Repayment of surplus cover to members and also the collection of exchange and clearing house fees from clearing members also uses this system.

Daily settlement prices are calculated principally as a weighted average (number of trades with respect to price) of the trades done on the trading floor in a closing sequence of the trading day. Contracts traded out have no outstanding payments to make or receive, as the marking-to-market process will have already collected or paid them, except for what is due as a result of the day's trading. Once established, the settlement price is used for all new and open (unliquidated) positions to compute the settlement variation for futures and the premium pass-through and increase or decrease in margin for options. LME contracts, however, cannot be settled before the prompt day. Each open contract is however, compared with the day's closing price and a 'contingent variation margin is calculated'. If this is in credit it may be used to offset contingent debts. Net debits must be covered in the same way as initial margins. If a member does not have sufficient cover lodged with LCH, a PPS call (margin call) is issued to his bank by 08.30 (06.40 in US).

A common misconception is that all margins must be met in cash. In fact, they must be covered in one of the forms of approved collateral which currently are: cash, certain Government securities, and Bank guarantees from LCH approved banks. Members are paid a reasonable rate of interest on most of their margin deposits. An important difference between the UK clearing house and brokers and those in the US is that UK brokers may extend credit. To reduce costs and capital outlay the LCH allows for all margin requirements to be covered by these bank guarantees as well as cash and other forms of collateral. In contrast to the ability of brokers to extend credit, clearing houses do not do so. If a position has lost value since the previous day, that loss is treated as a debt to the clearing house — a debt which must be made good in cash by 06.40 the next business day. If a position has gained in value, the clearing member's account is adjusted. The gain and loss adjustment is called *settlement variation*. In turn, the clearing member must collect or otherwise adjust its customers' accounts. This marked-to-market system does not apply to options on futures contracts. For options, the full value of the premium is debited from the buyer's account and credited to the seller's account by the next trading day. Hence, for the duration of the option, irrespective of any change in the option's settlement price, no cash flows between buyer and seller. Nevertheless, the possibility that the seller of an option may have to deposit additional margins to secure his position still remains.

The level of margins

Margining is on a 'net' basis across all positions held by the clearing member. Net margining ensures that the margin held is directly proportional to the risk inherent in a member's position in a specific contract. However, overall risk is clearly more complicated than the risk inherent in one contract's price movement. Consider the example of two commodities, pearls and swine. Over the past 10 years it has been observed that pearl prices always rise when swine prices fall. There is, to use economists' terminology, a perfect inverse correlation between the two. If a clearing member is long 100 pearl contracts and short 100 swine contracts, then if the contract sizes are identical, the net exposure of the clearing member is zero.

In practice, the method of calculating initial margins for LIFFE, Fox and IPE is Standard Portfolio Analysis of Risk (SPAN). This was first introduced by the CME in June 1989 and has become a widely used method for exchanges in the US. Initial margin is calculated by evaluating the risk of an entire portfolio and matching margin to risk. To do this, it simulates how the portfolio would react to changing market conditions. The margin requirement is the largest overnight loss that might reasonably arise as a result of these changing market conditions. Where appropriate, inter-month spread charges and spot month charges are added to this, and intercommodity spread credits are deducted to produce the final initial margin figure. SPAN has needed changes from previous delta-based hedging methods; it has involved many substantial programming alterations for many back office accounting systems, although it has demanded few changes to clearing reports and procedures.

SPAN is currently being studied by the Sydney Futures Exchange Clearing House (SFECH), which has used delta-based initial margin calculation methods since its inception in December 1991. SPAN provides a more accurate assessment of risk, especially in respect of offsetting trades within a portfolio; in general, it has tended therefore to reduce total initial margin liabilities. It is also fast becoming an international standard and as such eliminates the necessity for any one exchange or clearing house to study, for example, improvements to the delta hedging system.

LME contracts, however, cannot be settled before the prompt day. But each open contract is however compared with the day's closing price and a 'contingent variation margin is calculated'. If this is a credit it may be used to offset contingent debts. Net debits must be covered in the same way as initial margins.

Clearing members must segregate customer funds from their own, except where certain permitted investors contract out of the requirement. LCH, for example, provides facilities for each clearing member to use two separate clearing accounts; one for trades and positions of the member's business for customers requesting segregation, and another account for all in-house and other non-segregated business. Both accounts are margined separately on a net basis with separate margin calls, payments and receipts. Neither LCH nor the clearing member is allowed to net or offset between these two accounts.

At clearing house level, funds and collateral passed to the clearing house by its clearing members are dealt with according to house regulations. The clearing house itself is not usually subject to national client money regulations and the rules relating to the safe keeping of investments.

In some cases, LCH has established further sub-divisions of clearing members' non-segregated business, for example, between house and non-segregated client trading for position maintenance and to satisfy regulatory requirements.

Administrative functions

Clearing houses provide their clearing members with centralised delivery and banking facilities.

The clearing house has an essential role in the final settlement of futures and options contracts at maturity. The clearing house effectively guarantees the financial performance of the contract by both clearing members. The wide range of products cleared by the LCH includes physical delivery and cash settlement contracts. The LCH administers the allocation of sellers to buyers of physical contracts. In most instances neither party will know the other's identity.

To ensure the integrity of the market, the seller must deliver to the LCH prior to receiving payment and the buyer must pay the clearing house before receiving delivery. If the underlying cash or physical market allows, same-day delivery against payment is undertaken. The clearing house ensures:

- timely delivery by the seller of the exact quality and quantity of the commodity or financial instrument;
- full and timely payment by the buyer.

Whilst most futures contracts are liquidated before expiration, the remainder must be delivered or settled in cash according to detailed specifications.

Managing the markets

The LCH's central role in the London markets involves monitoring liabilities to reduce counterparty risk for those dealing on London's derivative markets.

The LCH is responsible for the prompt payment of any profits arising out of dealings on the exchanges. Payment of members' profits is not dependent on receipt of losses, as LCH is committed to meet its obligations to members, even if it suffers a default for non-payment by loss making counterparties. That is now the guarantee of the exchange-traded derivative markets, setting them apart from the OTC markets practice. Each LCH department operates risk management procedures, designed to minimise the chance of such a default.

These procedures — covering accurate margining practices, efficient treasury systems, thorough credit analysis and comprehensive risk assessment and monitoring systems — account for the majority of the administrative costs of the clearing house. Clearing house staff in performing these functions do assess the risk management procedures they apply to each of their clearing members at regular intervals. They study the member's level of initial margin in relation to the firm's financial resources, the size of the firm's absolute and relative positions in particular commodities, the pattern of margin payments, large option writing positions, and in general, the financial performance and risk liability of individual members.

Under the General Regulations of LCH, a wide range of circumstances may cause a clearing member to be deemed to be in default, for example, a breach of relevant LCH, exchange or regulatory body rules or procedures, a failure to make any payment due or failure to perform any tender or delivery obligation, or a bankruptcy or winding up order on a clearing member, or where an administrator or receiver is appointed for a member.

The clearing house under such circumstances may close out and settle open accounts, transfer open contracts to another member with the recipient's agreement, call in any relevant bank guarantees, and realise any relevant securities being held as collateral.

Clearing members of exchanges do go bankrupt and cease trading either because of their own trading problems, or because they are commodity subsidiaries of other companies. Financial difficulties of clearing members affect the market when there is a default.

The default procedures embrace account segregation: collateral held for a member's segregated business account may only be realised in respect of a default involving a member's segregated business account. In addition there is no offset between a member's house and segregated business accounts. These are precisely the sort of steps that occurred in both the cases cited above.

Clearing for tomorrow's markets

The LCH is wholly dedicated to the support and promotion of London's derivatives markets, both in the UK and internationally. Its independent status enables maximum attention to be paid to the paramount objective of market security.

In providing clearing services to all the London Futures and Options Exchanges, the clearing house is able to offer a centralised service to its members. This allows for significant economies of scale; for example, clearing members trading on London's exchanges benefit directly from more standardised back-office trade processing procedures and centralised payment and receipt routines. In addition, the absence of a mutual guarantee reduces the costs and liabilities of all clearing members in the event of a default by another clearing member.

Faced with increasing competition from other international exchanges and with the advent of the single European market, the London exchanges are meeting the challenge by developing new contracts and improving established ones in order to ensure the UK's continued competitiveness. The clearing house actively contributes to the planning and development of contracts and systems designed to facilitate more efficient and cost effective trading.

Against this background of dynamic change and fast moving development, the LCH is well placed in providing security, promoting confidence and supporting the growth of the London exchanges for the benefit of all market participants.

Chapter 3: Commodity-linked exchanges and contracts

Hedging, developed by the cotton trade, was crucial in the trade of commodities. Many commodities traded by other methods, such as forward contracts or at auction, made the transition to futures. Today, commodities traded on the world's futures and options markets include metals; agricultural products such as wheat, barley and potatoes; energy products based on oil; and 'soft' commodities such as cocoa, coffee and sugar.

The current and historical selection of commodities in which there are active futures markets appears at first sight to be practically random. Coffee is one of the most actively traded futures markets in New York but tea has no active futures market anywhere in the world. Cotton is a dominant soft commodity market. Rice however, the world's most important food, has always struggled as a futures market, and indeed the last attempt to establish an international rice futures contract, at London Fox in 1991, was a failure. What is the explanation for these differences?

Savaiko suggested in 1985 that the traditional soft commodities of the futures markets — coffee, cocoa and sugar — differed very importantly from the more 'basic necessities' such as the grains. Cocoa and coffee, he argued, are luxuries, and therefore the demand and production of them is a small fraction of what can be expected for grains such as wheat and maize. Savaiko's argument was that precisely because these commodities are not necessities, demand fluctuates more substantially during periods of recession. In addition, medical knowledge has suggested that reducing consumption of sucrose and caffeine may benefit one's health and cultural practices in the West have changed towards soft drinks, in particular fruit juices — the fastest growing commodity markets in the world at present. Sugar, also has had to compete with substitutes such as isomerose or high fructose corn syrups. Looking in more depth at such commodities — Savaiko includes rubber which was still traded in London in the mid-1980s — he says that understanding the supply side of the equation is very complex; small geographical areas concentrate production and both climate and politics can have dramatic effects on their prices.

Savaiko's explanation accounts in large measure for the growth of futures trading in these commodities, but since 1985 in particular a very different judgement must be made about commodity futures. The markets that are the most successful are clearly the oil markets, closely followed by the metals markets. Volumes for 1991–93 suggest that this trend is continuing. Following on from the oil and metal markets are the grains markets and finally the traditional softs markets.

Development of contract specifications

Extensive research must be carried out before a futures contract is introduced — or an existing one is modified — to ensure that it will coincide with current industry practices and norms. Industry experts and contract users are consulted, in some cases forming a committee to decide on specifications, along with academic experts, graders and futures brokers.

Since the terms and conditions of a futures contract are established to encompass the mainstream of the commodity in the marketplace, convergence between futures prices and major cash market values can readily occur. This is because sellers of futures can easily find products to deliver when futures prices are high relative to cash prices, and buyers of futures can easily find an outlet for the product they might receive on delivery, making them comfortable to 'stand for delivery' when futures prices are low relative to cash prices. A stable and predictable basis (cash – futures difference) results for most hedgers, so they find it conducive to use the contract. Few deliveries are therefore needed to achieve convergence — the possibility of delivery is usually enough.

Cash market practices and norms change over time and the futures contract terms need to keep pace accordingly. The process of altering futures contract specifications however is lengthy; separate studies and approvals by the exchange, and later by the regulatory authorities, are required. The process may last for several years. Once a change that has an effect on prices has obtained final approval by the regulatory authorities, it can only be implemented on contract months not yet listed or traded in order to avoid changing the rules affecting contracts already being traded.

Most commodity contracts are expressed in dollars. For those that are not, investors wishing to obtain a return in dollars, or any other currency, must use currency futures or other hedging instruments to ensure that their calculations are not completely offset by adverse currency moves.

In addition, there is always the danger with new contracts that exchanges see what they want to see and introduce — or seek to introduce — new contracts when it appears to suit them rather than when the cash market participants actually want it. That is part of the reason why new contracts often fail.

Which exchange?

The question of where the contract is traded is important. Put a frogs legs contract on the floor of the CME and, if the price is reasonably volatile and there are some interesting things to say about frog-spawn, it will probably trade thousands of contracts a day. Put the same contract on FAST at London Fox and it will probably not trade at all. These are unpalatable facts for all the European exchanges, but they must be faced. The traditional soft commodities are rapidly moving down the list of important traded commodities: sugar volumes are falling dramatically in New York, Tokyo and London as it simply no longer commands the trade interest that it once did. Coffee, divided between robusta in London and arabica in New York, has probably reached its sensible levels of trading judging from the statistics and consumption evidence. As Fox's failed arabica contract demonstrated, there appears to be little scope for another coffee contract. Cocoa may still be over-exchanged and traders have often suggested that there is really only room for one international cocoa contract in the world. From Savaiko's model the biggest change is undoubtedly in rubber. It is no longer traded in London, despite several attempted relaunches, and trades in small quantities only in the Far East.

Success or failure

The trend, undoubtedly, is away from the traditional soft commodities in the short term, and towards those commodities where there is a sophisticated demand for products that need to be hedged on futures markets.

New 'commodities', whether abstract or traditional can, of course, be introduced at any time; the principles of futures can be applied to an unlimited variety of trades. Most exchanges however, do not believe in introducing new contracts on a 'random' basis. They research very carefully, in advance of the launch, whether their planned new market is likely to succeed. Despite extensive research, however, commodity traders do not always tell exchanges either the truth about their intentions or, more usually, what eager exchange officials want to hear, ie, that their proposed contract will succeed. Consequently, many new contracts do not actually succeed in the accepted sense of:

- providing adequate liquidity for their most likely users;

- trading at least the exchange average number of lots. For example, the IPE's naphtha futures contract. After just over one year of trading, the IPE Board of Directors decided to suspend trading in the naphtha contract from 21 May 1992. Although the contract had started out on an optimistic note interest in the contract declined until trade became sporadic at best.

Futures traders are quirky. Contracts usually have to succeed quickly, especially if they are launched on an electronic system, or else traders will soon ignore the new contract. This produces a vicious spiral of little interest, few trades, wide bid-offer spreads, and progressively less interest. Really important changes are developing from new technology. Through communications and collaboration, futures markets, along with other markets, are becoming global rather than international. Twenty-four hour trading is approaching, with international participation. Computer exchanges need not follow market hours. Terminals in members' offices networked to central exchange computers match bids and offers. Global markets result in lower costs and tougher competition.

Not all commodities (according to the definition in the Introduction) have futures markets. Numerous commodities do not yet have, or have ceased to have, active derivative markets. A good example of a commodity that used to have a derivative market in Europe but no longer does, is rubber. Rubber prices are still quite volatile, but due to the particular way that rubber is traded internationally, it appears impossible to construct a straightforward futures contract that works. It looks likely that sugar, in particular, may go the same way. Agricultural commodity futures markets in Europe are clinging on with some difficulty.

Although the SFE, for example, is enthusiastically pressing forward with plans for further automation, including elaborate ideas of voice-to-computer software for price reporting, there are no plans for more commodity contracts.

Some financial derivative innovations, such as some exchange-traded futures and options on certain commodities, have not survived. They have either lacked a commercial or economic reason to be traded or they were too expensive to trade. Many financial innovations, however, such as stripped bonds, have indeed survived and provided incremental and valuable hedging and investment additions to the financial markets. Commodity futures and other derivatives now follow the principal that whatever is introduced first in the financial derivatives market can eventually be expected to surface in the commodity markets. In the worldwide recession of the 1990s, however, the length of time between introductions of new products and between their multiple applications across different markets is increasing. The slow development of soft commodity swaps is an example of this and the rate of introduction of new contracts by exchanges throughout the world is another.

Opinion differs widely on whether commodity index contracts such as the GSCI and the CBOT agricultural index are likely to succeed. The consensus view is that they will achieve modest but respectable levels of liquidity, but that they are far from being the third wave much sought by futures industry members. Not every index contract succeeds. London Fox's Metallgesellschaft Metal Index (MGMI) and Elgin Oil's jet fuel index are good examples of failures. The major lesson to be learned from these two examples

— and it will almost certainly apply throughout the 1990s to all new contract development — is, to be successful in contract Y you need to be already successful in X and Z. Had the LME launched the MGMI or IPE the jet fuel index, the chance of success would have been very much higher.

Despite pioneering work by Gordon Gemmill at the London Business School and by others, it is still not certain as to which derivative products are likely to succeed and which are not. Theoretical analysis is relatively straightforward: a new type of product is a socially useful innovation and enhances investor welfare if:

- it allows investors/hedgers to create a return/risk configuration not previously available, thus helping to complete markets;

- it allows investors/hedgers to obtain their goals in a more efficient and/or less costly manner.

It has been argued that derivatives fill needs not presented by other securities, particularly because of costs, taxes and other frictions. As has been pointed out, however, innovation is not a static process; the goalposts keep moving, so it is difficult even to establish a coherent theory of success for derivative products.

The absence of liquid energy derivative markets in the Asian time zone strongly suggests the likelihood that the Japanese exchanges will, eventually, introduce energy derivatives. Steady deregulation of the cash market is the probable prerequisite.

Observing recent new products suggests that there is no limit to what can be produced if the need is there. An example of a product that was specifically designed to fill a need are 'U Choose' oil warrants issued during the Persian Gulf War. These warrants were exercisable into a specified number of barrels of oil but could be converted from a call to a put at the holder's option. The motivation for a new financial product issue may not always be derived from the demand side. It could be that the product is launched on the inspiration of exchange officials because it is new, looks interesting and is difficult to value.

Exchanges could be forgiven for believing that there is no possible innovation left in the exchange-traded energy derivatives area. NYMEX, however, has recently launched both a Gulf Coast unleaded gasoline contract and a natural gas options contract, with the hope that it may eventually trade more than the futures contract. The Exchange is also considering introducing strip trading (contracts in a series of months), subject to concerns about diluting liquidity on the existing contracts. In terms of entirely new contracts

NYMEX, like the IPE, is examining the possibility of creating an exchange-traded electricity futures market by the end of the decade. COMEX is deciding when to launch the Dubai contract and is also planning a jet fuel contract, possibly in conjunction with the CSCE.

A successful innovation is characterised primarily by being useful, and ultimately beneficial to social welfare. It should also fulfil the following essential conditions:

- Hedging. A new commodity derivative should provide some opportunity for users to alter their risk profiles.
- Arbitrage. Those selling the derivative must be able to reduce their risk by using other products.
- Speculation. If the product can also attract speculators, liquidity and trading activity will probably be greater — often the difference between success and failure.

Other factors include similar but non-identical products, experienced traders and analysts who understand the product and its likely market and, finally, the existence of an underlying spot market which is a requisite for the efficient pricing of the derivative product.

An example of the types of problems that new innovations can face is that of piggyback deals. A piggyback deal allows the holder, *via* an option, to acquire a futures position at a given strike price. If exercised before, after, or between certain dates, the holder receives an additional piggyback futures position at another strike price. The initial warrant is a compound option because it contains an option on an option. But is this a valuable instrument? The piggyback feature adds to the difficulty of valuing the option, and there are other problems. If the holders exercise at any time other than the optimum, the underlying issuer's dividend, capital structure and investment policies will be affected, quite possibly adversely. The piggyback option was not a response to market need; indeed it confused rather than clarified. A similar, possibly even more severe, problem exists with options exercisable into two different types of futures contract. This particular type of option is difficult to value and is of varying utility.

Some of these more complicated types of financial futures products, however, which already have limited uses in the financial futures industry, can be expected to make a slow entry into the commodity derivatives industry. For example, OTC options on differentials between different contracts. Indeed, some futures contracts themselves such as the CSCE arabica contract are already based on differentials and this can be expected to increase as a factor in the market-place.

The CBOT has received CFTC approval to trade innovative new futures and options contracts based on the Environmental Protection Agency's (EPA) planned market for sulphur dioxide emission allowances. The underlying instruments for the futures contract are the sulphur dioxide emission allowances being issued by the EPA under the 1990 amendments to the Clean Air Act. Clean Air futures trade in units of 25 one-ton sulphur dioxide emission allowances. Minimum price fluctuations are in multiples of one dollar per allowance. Created in response to a strong industry demand, the CBOT plans to add catastrophe insurance futures and options contracts to its soon-to-be-launched insurance complex. Catastrophic losses will be based on a large sample of reported incurred losses for a quarter caused by wind, hail, earthquake, riot, or flood, as appropriate for each applicable property line. This data will be calculated by the Insurance Services Office (ISO) which has been in business for 21 years, and is responsible for collecting claims-loss data for companies representing approximately 85% of the insurance industry. The CBOT has claimed that these insurance contracts are a breakthrough in futures markets on microeconomic indices, providing the basis for a third wave of innovations after agricultural and financial futures. The price of a contract at any time will reflect the market's expectation of a quarter's catastrophic loss in relation to that same quarter's estimated property premium. The final value of the contract at expiry will equal $50,000 times the ratio of quarterly losses to estimated property premium. The futures markets are in need of their third wave now as 1991 showed — a year of declining volumes for many exchanges.

The CBOT has also received CFTC approval to trade futures and options on health insurance. These contracts will have a proposed trading unit of the gross profitability on one hundred thousand dollars of premiums earned. The price of health insurance futures will be quoted in points, with each point equalling $1,000. The final settlement amount will equal $100,000 times the ratio of total claims paid to total premiums earned on all policies in the underlying insurance pool during the calculation period.

Finally, for insurance futures, the CBOT received CFTC approval to trade futures and options on homeowners insurance which are included in the new CBOT insurance complex which was launched in 1992. The unit of trading will be the profit on one hundred thousand dollars of premiums earned. Prices will be quoted in points equalling $1,000. The final settlement amount will equal $100,000 times the ratio of total claims to total premiums earned on all policies in the underlying insurance pool during the calculation period. However, the development period for insurance futures has already been very long, and there is still no certainty that they will succeed.

The CBOT is already the leading successful innovator amongst world commodity exchanges. Permits are already being traded on the CBOT, and interested parties are proposing that similar permits be traded in Europe and Japan. It seems likely that this idea will eventually catch on, although it may take well over a decade.

The CSCE is understood to be researching a dairy contract and is reported to have more exotic ideas in mind. CSCE officials are well aware of the central dilemma faced by all exchanges; they needs to diversify to survive. Futures contract designers and consultants, from Sandor in the US to Miller in the UK, are convinced there is a third wave. Finding it, however, costs money at the very time when cash is short and exchange members are looking unsympathetically on expensive business development programmes. They will compare the unhappy experience of London Fox in 1990–91 with the NYCE, which has placed its hopes on the further development of the world cotton contract launched on 1 October 1992. In the short to medium term the NYCE is unlikely to be very successful but the contract is conventional, relatively straightforward and likely to create good volumes in the end. But what will happen to the NYCE when its competitors have diversified? There is no obvious third cotton contract waiting to be launched, and sooner or later the NYCE will face competition from OTC business.

Eventually, this will be the basis for a new generation of derivative products designed to allow risk transference for hitherto unhedgeable risks. In the climate of the 1990s, however, it has proved exceptionally difficult to introduce these new contracts, and the launch dates for many of them have been continually put back. LIFFE in London, which at least understands the difficulties associated with the re-introduction of property futures in London, is not intending to relaunch them in the foreseeable future after their failure on London Fox. But the CBOT has won regulatory approval for barge freight futures, for an agricultural index (which will provide fascinating arbitrage opportunities with the GSCI) and clean air futures. These are planned to be launched on Project A, the CBOT's own screen trading system, but they may eventually find their way onto Globex. Three other commodities of major international importance without an active exchange-traded futures market are:

- water, for which there are currently no contracts in existence or planned;
- electricity, mooted by the IPE and London Fox, but this eventually became a moderately successful contract traded by Gerrard & National Inter Commodities (GNI) in London. The difficulty with electricity futures has been in designing a contract which caters for both average and 'spike' demand, in providing a contract useful to both electricity generating companies, and the distribution companies. This difficulty

explained the exchanges reluctance to launch contracts when the industry was privatised. GNI has now launched an OTC electricity market (see Case Study, Chapter 4);

- air, which is already sold in limited quantities in a spot market in Japan.

There are two types of innovation in the derivatives industry. Firstly, there are innovative mechanisms, such as those discussed above. Secondly, there is the application of financial product technology based on derivative contracts to new areas, new commodities. Numerous examples of commodities do not have active derivative markets but for which there are occasional OTC contracts. Probably the best known commodity is land and property. London Fox attempted to establish a property futures market in 1991, but this initial attempt was a failure. The property industry, even in the UK where it is at its most sophisticated, was not ready for a fully-fledged exchange-traded futures contract. A much more careful OTC approach that did eventually bear fruit, and which will certainly be repeated, was the OTC contract entered into by the Burton Group in 1992, arranged by Citycorp.

Basic commodities with existing futures markets in other countries, or in very similar products do not stand as much of a chance of success as they did in the 1980s. The evidence of the London Fox rice, lamb and arabica contracts, naphtha on the IPE and the New Zealand Futures and Options Exchange's (NZFOE) wool options, are good proof of this. Launching contracts where there is:

- an active forward market currently in operation;
- another liquid futures contract elsewhere in the world;
- opposition to any form of futures market from traders;

is not likely to enjoy any success in the 1990s. Exchanges have largely taken this on board.

The KLCE is studying the possibility of introducing a palm oil kernel contract in consultation with the Malaysian Edible Oil Manufacturers' Association. The Exchange says that, 'The general view of the industry is that there is a need for the contract and with increased production of palm kernel oil and a structural change in the utilisation of the palm kernel oil in the country, the contract would be viable.' Correctly, as part of the product development process the Exchange has identified certain statistical facts about this commodity, for example that world production has increased from 1,294,000 tonnes in 1989 to 1,421,000 tonnes in 1991, with Malaysia accounting for 55% of the total world supply.

One crucial problem in the launch of new commodity futures contracts in the 1990s is the gathering of initial liquidity. There are two ways to make a new contract work. One — used very effectively for the white sugar contract in London when it was relaunched — is that a number of brokers agree to promote the contract by buying and selling amongst themselves thus raising the open interest under a series of 'gentlemen's agreements'. Volume and open interest mount, and eventually both speculators and the trade can be persuaded to enter the contract — in Japan this is known as 'congratulatory' trading. This method, however, of starting up a contract in the less-wealthy 1990s has not found favour. Trust amongst brokers is not as high as it was and international regulators are not at all sure that they approve of such agreements. They believe that there is a strong argument that such a market is 'false' and a deception to potential genuine clients.

The second possible way of making a market work is by having the client interest built up before the contract is launched, and encouraging clients to participate *ab initio*. This is the method favoured by international regulators and by such exchanges as the NYCE in launching its international cotton contract. This approach demands enormous pre-launch marketing and great expense over a prolonged period, usually about two years. There is no guarantee of success even then, and often some perfectly good contracts fall by the wayside as a result of 'stand-off' behaviour from all potential participants. What is certainly the case is that 'throwing contracts at the wall', especially on an electronic trading system, just because it costs very little to install a contract on an electronic trading system, is not a viable option for an exchange anywhere in the world. London Fox's experience with this kind of approach in 1990–91 should be enough to deter exchanges anywhere else.

New exchanges will undoubtedly be created. The former USSR will be a fertile ground for the development of commodity futures and options, quite probably of a traditional nature, in the late 1990s once some material revival in these economies is experienced. Hungary already has a commodity exchange trading maize and other contracts; an exchange in Spain starting with a navel orange contract is at an advanced stage of research, using MATIF expertise; and there is also research underway in Germany as to the feasibility of a German agricultural exchange.

Notes:

B Savaiko, *Trading in Soft Commodities Futures*, Woodhead Faulkner,1985.

Commodities and major exchange contracts analysis 1990–92

Commodities contracts are usually considered in the five categories shown below.

Commodity traded	Contracts in 1,000s			% of total commodity contracts traded		
	1990	1991	1992	1990	1991	1992
Metals (I)	38,619	45,720	48,481	25.9	30.5	31.1
Energy (II)	43,887	43,395	48,524	29.5	29.0	31.2
Grains (III)	34,027	34,722	35,590	22.8	23.1	22.9
Softs (IV)	23,876	18,513	16,473	16.0	12.3	10.6
Meat (V)	8,445	7,695	6,590	5.7	5.1	4.2
Total	**148,854**	**150,045**	**155,658**	**100.0**	**100.0**	**100.0**

Category I — Metals

Commodity	No. of contracts in 1,000s			% of category I			% of total commodities		
	1990	1991	1992	1990	1991	1992	1990	1991	1992
BM & F									
Gold (o)	n/a	7,453	7,933	—	16.3	16.4	—	4.9	5.1
COMEX									
Gold (f)	9,730	6,800	6,002	25.2	14.8	12.4	6.6	4.4	3.9
Gold (o)	1,932	1,640	—	5.0	3.6	—	1.3	1.1	—
Silver (f)	3,914	4,155	3,016	0.1	9.1	6.2	2.6	2.7	1.9
Copper (f)	1,853	1,640	1,674	4.8	3.6	3.4	1.2	1.1	1.0
Subtotal	**17,429**	**14,235**	**10,692**	**45.1**	**31.1**	**22.0**	**11.7**	**9.3**	**6.8**
LME									
Copper (f)	5,669	6,794	7,338	14.7	14.9	15.1	3.8	4.5	4.7
Nickel (+)	—	—	1,443	—	—	3.0	—	—	0.9
Aluminimum (f)	3,990	5,336	8,226	10.3	11.7	17.0	2.7	3.5	5.3
Zinc (f)	1,389	1,930	4,023	3.6	4.2	8.3	0.9	1.25	2.6
Subtotal	**11,048**	**14,060**	**21,030**	**28.6**	**30.8**	**43.4**	**7.4**	**9.25**	**13.5**
TOCOM									
Platinum (f)	3,269	5,404	4,632	8.5	11.8	9.6	2.2	3.55	3.0
Gold (f)	6,873	4,568	4,194	17.8	10.0	8.6	4.6	3.00	2.7
Subtotal	**10,142**	**9,972**	**8,826**	**26.3**	**21.8**	**18.2**	**6.8**	**6.55**	**5.7**
CATEGORY I TOTAL	**38,619**	**45,720**	**48,481**	**100.0**	**100.0**	**100.0**	**25.9**	**30.5**	**31.1**

Category II — Energy

Commodity	No. of contracts in 1,000s			% of category II			% of total commodities		
	1990	1991	1992	1990	1991	1992	1990	1991	1992
IPE									
Brent Crude Oil(f)	4,083	5,231	6,172	9.3	12.0	12.7	2.8	3.5	4.0
NYMEX									
Crude Oil (+)	23,687	21,006	21,110	54.0	48.4	43.5	15.9	14.0	13.6
Heating Oil (f)	6,377	6,680	8,005	14.5	15.4	16.5	4.3	4.5	5.1
Unleaded Gasoline (f)	4,485	5,509	6,675	10.2	12.7	13.8	3.0	3.7	4.3
Crude Oil (o)	5,255	4,969	6,562	12.0	11.5	13.5	3.5	3.3	4.2
Subtotal	**39,804**	**38,164**	**42,352**	**90.7**	**88.0**	**87.3**	**26.7**	**25.5**	**27.2**
CATEGORY II TOTAL	**43,887**	**43,395**	**48,524**	**100.0**	**100.0**	**100.0**	**29.5**	**29.0**	**31.2**

Category III —Grains

Commodity	No. of contracts in 1,000s			% of category III			% of total commodities		
	1990	1991	1992	1990	1991	1992	1990	1991	1992
CBOT									
Corn (f)	11,432	10,853	10,357	33.6	31.2	29.1	7.7	7.2	6.7
Soyabeans (f)	10,302	9,014	9,000	30.3	26.0	25.3	6.9	6.0	5.8
Soyabeans Meal (f)	4,904	4,498	4,145	14.4	13.0	11.6	3.3	3.0	2.65
Soyabeans Oil (f)	4,658	4,019	4,283	13.7	11.6	12.0	3.1	2.7	2.75
Subtotal	**31,287**	**28,384**	**27,785**	**92.0**	**81.8**	**78.0**	**21.0**	**18.9**	**17.9**
TGE									
Red Beans (f)	2,740	6,338	7,805	8.0	18.2	22.0	1.8	4.2	5.0
CATEGORY III TOTAL	**34,027**	**34,722**	**35,590**	**100.0**	**100.0**	**100.0**	**22.8**	**23.1**	**22.9**

Category IV — Softs

Commodity	No. of contracts in 1,000s			% of category IV			% of total commodities		
	1990	1991	1992	1990	1991	1992	1990	1991	1992
CSCE									
Raw Sugar (f)	5,425	4,269	3,667	22.7	23.0	22.3	3.6	2.84	2.36
Coffee (f)	1,774	1,773	2,152	7.4	9.57	13.1	1.2	1.19	1.38
Coffe (o)	—	—	861	—	—	5.2	—	—	0.55
Raw Sugar (o)	2,393	1,513	849	10.0	8.17	5.1	1.6	1.01	0.54
Cocoa (f)	1,636	1,224	1,397	6.9	6.61	8.5	1.1	0.82	0.90
Subtotal	**11,228**	**8,779**	**8,926**	**47.0**	**47.5**	**54.2**	**7.5**	**5.86**	**5.73**
FOX									
Cocoa (f)	1,702	1,537	1,382	7.1	8.3	8.4	1.15	1.02	0.89
Coffee (f)	1,170	1,196	855	5.0	6.4	5.2	0.80	0.80	0.55
Subtotal	**2,872**	**2,733**	**2,237**	**12.1**	**14.7**	**13.6**	**1.95**	**1.82**	**1.44**
NYCE									
Cotton (f)	1,535	1,614	1,701	6.4	8.7	10.3	1.00	1.07	1.09
O.SUGAR.E									
Raw Sugar (f)	n/a	1,428	—	—	7.7	—	—	0.95	—
TOCOM									
Cotton Yarn (f)	1,866	1,607	2,330	7.8	8.7	14.1	1.25	1.07	1.5
T.SUGAR.E									
Raw Sugar (f)	6,375	2,352	1,279	26.7	12.7	7.8	4.3	1.57	0.82
CATEGORY IV TOTAL	**23,876**	**18,513**	**16,473**	**100.0**	**100.0**	**100.0**	**16.0**	**12.3**	**10.6**

Category V — Meat

Commodity	No. of contracts in 1,000s			% of category V			% of total commodities		
	1990	1991	1992	1990	1991	1992	1990	1991	1992
CME									
Live Cattle (f)	3,797	3,793	3,320	45.0	49.3	50.4	2.55	2.52	2.13
Live Hog (f)	2,241	1,582	1,556	26.5	20.6	23.6	1.51	1.05	0.99
Pork Bellies (f)	1,303	1,005	784	15.4	13.1	11.9	0.86	0.67	0.50
Live Cattle (o)	713	777	561	8.5	10.0	8.5	0.48	0.51	0.36
Feeder Cattle (+)	391	538	369	4.6	7.0	5.6	0.26	0.36	0.24
CATEGORY V TOTAL	**8,445**	**7,695**	**6,590**	**100.0**	**100.0**	**100.0**	**5.66**	**5.1**	**4.22**

Chapter 4: The OTC market

Exchange-traded derivatives try to generate liquidity by establishing homogeneous contracts and encouraging — through the provision of information and a central market-place — the maximum number of people to trade them. Futures contract design is a highly technical skill with the objective to find a contract specification that best combines the needs of the industry. Sometimes the choice is relatively straightforward, as in the selection of the Liverpool 'A' Index for the world cotton contract. Sometimes it is a difficult process of negotiation and compromise between different trade and speculative interest.

All exchanges recognise, however, that no single futures contract can meet every end-user's needs or broker's inclination. One example from the oil industry is that gasoline, diesel fuel and naphtha consumers (such as airlines, shipping firms and plastic manufacturers) are all dependent on oil prices. What they use themselves is subject to a large basis fluctuation from the NYMEX and IPE oil futures market prices. Hedging using the futures themselves can often induce unwanted risk and can even be counter-productive — the futures price can, in some circumstances, actually move in the opposite direction to the price of the oil used.

Financial institutions are increasingly stepping in as intermediaries to reduce this risk. They have created OTC markets in options, swaps, swaptions (options on swaps), collars and caps, to transfer risk where there is basis risk for a commodity against an established exchange-traded market. By creating their own book of OTC products for clients with different needs, OTC issuers seek to establish a risk profile as close to the futures market as possible. They try to lay-off the risk they have acquired on the futures market itself. Take the example of a futures market in pearls. There are two types of pearls: round and oval. The pearl futures market is an index of the second simplest sort: ie, there are two constituent prices and they each count for half the total. Suppose a firm buys 100 oval pearls and wishes to hedge its stock. OTC Ltd grants a put option on 100 oval pearls. Another firm buys 100 round pearls and also wishes to hedge, so OTC Ltd grants another put option, this time on 100 round pearls. Clearly to hedge the options, 200 exchange-traded put options should be bought by OTC Ltd. OTC Ltd makes its profit through the difference in price between the OTC options that it grants, and the price of the exchange-traded options. In practice, such complete laying-off of risk may be impossible to achieve — but that is the principle. OTC Ltd may also seek to lay-off its risk by finding another two firms who are planning to buy round and oval pearls respectively, and selling them call options. An example of this strategy is the jet-fuel index contract. Airlines can buy and jet-fuel manufacturers can sell. The intermediary institutions manage the risk for end-users laying it off. In theory, all end-users could get together and agree exact fixed prices, but, in practice, information constraints make it extremely unlikely that this will ever be achieved. OTC prices therefore reflect information scarcity rather than an absolute increase in the amount of risk taking globally.

For consumers the OTC market does have advantages over the futures market.

- Firstly, basis risk minimisation. Suppose an airline wants a fixed price for its jet fuel. There is no futures market for jet fuel, although there is now the index, so a company with jet fuel exposure cannot hedge its risk directly. One strategy is to use an existing futures markets, hoping that the basis risk would be manageable, even profitable. But not only is there is observable historical basis risk, there is also the possibility that the basis might widen. During the Gulf War, for instance, the basis between gasoil and jet fuel moved from $25/tonne to $183/tonne; this does rather suggest not trusting the futures markets for all 'related' exposures. A simple numerical example can show the risks inherent in this approach. Suppose a company has bought 100 round pearls at $100 each, intending to sell them in six months' time. The futures index for six months' time stands at 120 (a predicted price of $120 for both). The company sells the futures up to the equivalent of 100 pearls. Over the six months, round pearls fall to $80 each, but oval pearls climb to $120. The index remains at 100, being composed equally of each, and the company loses on both the futures and physical markets.

- Secondly, OTC contracts are often available in very large volumes for single transactions. In exchange-traded derivative markets such volume would often not be possible without effecting very significant market movements and would in any event take too long to action. The OTC markets are paper pricing structures where this effect is unlikely to occur, partly through lack of price transparency in OTC markets. Futures markets, therefore, must be seen as only a partial solution to most companies' hedging needs. They are also limited in their time horizons: OTC contracts can extend out over decades, if necessary. There is no theoretical limit, although the risk increases exponentially with time in the same fashion as the area needed to be searched over time.

- The third advantage concerns overheads. On the whole companies prefer not to set up their own trading operations if they are producers, wholesalers or retailers. Using a futures market creates all the costs of futures market trading: an account with a broker; margins to be paid; analysis of the market in question, especially in energy and metals; and many compliance issues; plus the problem that a trading department will start trading rather than hedging. The problem is often how to differentiate the two. An OTC product, by contrast, gives the same economic benefit without margin calls: more working capital is freed up. Of course, the company assumes a credit risk through its exposure to the creditworthiness of the swap partner, which in turn needs to be monitored. The review of major companies' creditworthiness is a sophisticated and relatively frequent business, however, carried out by companies such as Dun & Bradstreet, and much less of a drain on resources than a trading department, although an equal poser for the annual accounts.

Swaps

The definition of a swap (according to Crédit Lyonnais) is, 'A contract between two counterparties to exchange during a given maturity with a given periodicity, a pre-determined fixed price against a floating price noticed for each period, calculated on a defined quantity of the commodity.'

As with most financial innovations since the late 1960s, this form of hedging was introduced to commodities following its introduction in the financial markets. Swaps in currencies and interest rates were traded from the early 1970s onwards, but they have been traded on commodities only since the early 1980s. In essence, a 'swap' involves exchanging price payments streams for a commodity, usually between a fixed price and a variable one. Swaps found an immediate market in commodity trading because commodity prices are volatile, more so than for some financial products. This volatility creates risk, for both producers and consumers of commodities, that needs to be reduced or, preferably, eliminated. Swaps, therefore, are hedging arrangements, used to minimise risk. A swap is a hybrid of several derivatives. It does not incorporate standard terms, it does not allow anonymity, and it is not guaranteed by any clearing authority between the two parties. It is not distributive. A soft commodity swap usually is for one month periodicity, but three and six months are equally possible to arrange.

They are also serial contracts in that an 'exchange' takes place at intervals throughout the life of the swap. For example, an exchange may take place each month on a specified date for, perhaps, six consecutive months.

The maturities for soft commodity swaps range from a few months to several years, although longer than two years is still rare. The larger banks can arrange soft commodity swaps for most producers, wholesalers or retailers' needs.

The exchange is in effect a settlement based upon the difference of a 'fixed' price agreed at the time of the swap contract, and the variable or 'floating' price either when exchange takes place or an average of the floating prices for an agreed part of the period covered. Clearly a degree of sophistication can be introduced here so that, for example, the frequency of the periodicity can depend on the volatility of the underlying commodity's price over the preceding period — a volatility swap. The swaps can also be complicated, for example, by using a sliding scale for prices, or by adding an option for a reduced or increased size of contract depending on changes in the purchaser's demand for the commodity.

At present over 90% of swaps business transacted by banks is energy business. Swaps experts throughout the world, but especially in the US and UK, believe that there is great scope for expansion within the soft commodity markets, especially if reliable price indicators can be found for many more soft commodities, such as tea and rice.

In any case the exchange does not involve the total amount of the contract. It is the difference in price of the fixed and floating components multiplied by the nominal quantity of the commodity in question.

The average prices are calculated for each period by using averages from the relevant futures contract, or, if one is not available, for example for tea, by using an average based on an agreed spot price. It is much more difficult to obtain an accurate price from an often illiquid spot market and this is one of the reasons why swaps also are found much less frequently in these markets. Prices for each type of swap are in the usual quotation for the relevant commodity at the wish of the physical market participant purchasing the swap. So, for example, for frozen orange juice, which is one of the principal soft commodities used for swaps, the contract is expressed in cents per pound or dollars per tonne. Payments are calculated by netting out the difference between the fixed and the floating price.

The contract is settled in cash and, therefore, involves no physical movement of the underlying commodity. The swap is purely to 'fix' the price of a commodity over an agreed period of time.

Taking place concurrently with the swap are the spot (physical) commodity transactions that distribute the commodity whilst the swap offsets price volatility. Buyers continue to procure physical produce from sellers in the 'spot' market at the prevailing price, either paying or receiving cash settlements which equate to and compensate for short-term movements through the swap, but with different counterparts. For instance, the swap buyer continues to procure supplies on the 'spot' market. If the price is above the price fixed he receives, separately from his swap counterpart, the difference in price relating to the quantity concerned. Conversely, if the price 'spot' is below that of the fixed element of the swap, he pays the difference to the swap counterpart. The profit on the swap offsets a loss on the spot market; a loss on the swap offsets any benefit received from buying spot. The price paid by a consumer is therefore fixed at the level of the swap for the duration of the swap agreement.

For the producer, offering a fixed price for the swap is the assurance of profitability of production over time so that he needs to contend with supply issues only. Consumers are able to obtain fixed prices, thereby eliminating the risk associated with price volatility. Similarly, suppliers lock in receipts, also being able to lock in a guaranteed profit margin. Purchasers, whether wholesalers, retailers or consumers, are able to build into their own analyses of costs and revenues the amount they will be paying for certain raw materials over a fixed period.

The more sophisticated strategies based on these principles are used in most commodity markets. These include participations, discounted swaps, swaptions, the establishment of a link with a physical supply of the commodity from one company involved in the derivative transaction, and OTC instruments with such names such as 'rainbows', 'heaven and hell' bonds, range forward contracts, 'knock-out' and 'look-back' options. Many of these instruments contain put or call options, combinations of options, or have option characteristics and are typically quite complex in nature. Rubinstein refers to these instruments as 'exotics' and classifies them into 10 groups including packages, forward-start options, compound options, chooser options, barrier options, binary options, look-back options, Asian options, American exchange options, and two-colour rainbow options. Almost all of these exotics include one or more derivative securities — a product whose value depends on the price of some underlying variable such as a market index or a commodity price.

The most sophisticated OTC market is in jet fuel. Naphtha lags behind: it is a market dominated by a few large petroleum companies, such as BASF and ICI. The gasoline market, by comparison, is characterised by standard forward delivery contracts, with a gradual intrusion of swaps. Major companies involved report that at least 95% of their business is in energy. Ten per cent of their clients are airlines, and the remainder, oil traders and refiners. A similar sort of business exists in soft commodities, but as yet the enthusiasm that exists in energy markets is lacking. OTC energy products have continued to expand even since the Kuwait crisis; they now embrace specialised markets such as Singapore fuel oil, Tapis crude, Gulf Coast residual fuel and Russian gasoil.

The problems associated with the soft commodity markets are the annual crop cycle and the sheer poverty of the producing countries and the associated credit risk. In some cases, wholesale or retail organisations selling soft commodities face relatively inelastic demand curves combined with low profit margins relative to their production quantities: they simply pass on the increased prices to consumers. In addition, the soft commodity trading houses have not yet decided to press ahead with these types of transaction, although they are the companies with the best connections in producing countries. Probably the most significant difference, however, is that many of the companies offering the OTC derivatives, such as Phibro, do so as complementary and sometimes risk-offsetting activity to their physical trade, which enables them both to be intensely knowledgeable about their markets and at the same time very cost-effective and competitive. By contrast in the softs market, Phibro was caught in the 1990 cocoa squeeze and has moved out of the softs market: writing OTC derivatives in it is certainly not a priority.

Exchange-traded contracts *vs* OTC derivatives

The main advantages of OTC derivative transactions over futures contracts traded on exchanges are:

- *Volume*
  derivatives can cover, in one transaction, large volumes that cannot be executed with futures without significantly moving the market against the seller.

- *Maturities*
  derivatives will overcome the poor liquidity beyond the next few months and quotations can be given up to several years.

- *Settlement*
  derivatives will have only one settlement per month. No problem of daily variation margins.

- *Customisation/flexibility*
  derivatives can be structured to meet the producer's precise hedging objectives, combining swaps and options into a single contract, with precisely matched levels of volume, term, and price characteristics.

Almost all such derivative transactions are cash-settled allowing the producer free to market his production in the usual way. The cash flow on the derivative is used to offset changes in sales revenue resulting from price changes.

OTC derivatives do, however, have some disadvantages. The first one is transparency. Counterparties to unfavourable OTC option positions may seek additional payments before allowing 'escape'. On an exchange-traded system, unless liquidity is low this will not be possible as trading takes place anonymously.

Secondly, there is the absence of counterparty risk in using exchange products due to the clearing system. So-called third party risk appears to be increasingly discounted as a criterion in the investment decision as triple A-rated banks become increasingly rare: not a single US investment bank — save J P Morgan (which is, admittedly, very active in OTC energy markets) — has a credit rating above single A. Some managers may now use Japanese or European banks as a result, but most believe that credit is now less of an issue than previously.

This is not necessarily desirable. Regulators in particular, are those who because of it are worried that sudden pronounced movements in interest rates, currency prices or stock markets could expose banks and dealers to much more risk than they have reserves with which to cope. Regulators worry that many products, some of which are designed either by teams of number-crunching 'quants' or, worse, by complex computer programmes, have become so complicated that neither money managers, clients, or regulators understand them or their potential implications.

In turn, this attitude annoys issuers and investors alike. Clearly, there is no gain for regulators if they allow a product that subsequently goes wrong. The relationship of issuer to regulator in many markets, especially in North America, is currently so adversarial as to be counter-productive to the evolution of the market-place. It is probably impossible to ensure that the products coming to market are both innovative and safe. Ultimately, the buyers themselves must exert influence on regulators to ensure that they receive the products they want.

Thirdly, issuers are worried about costs. Whilst the choice of product and issuer must inevitably be that of the buyer, the purchasers of OTC products have to bear in mind a series of costs. One is the cost of legal counsel; another is that of administration overheads: these can often be considerable. For example, a company with an OTC position in the GSCI may find it necessary to monitor all the commodities contained in the index, and will obviously be better able to make decisions depending on how much information the company possesses regarding the performance of its constituent components. Some derivatives experts recognise that, currently, many of the purchasers of OTC products do not completely understand the products they have bought. As a result, a misunderstanding or failure to account for all the factors associated with taking a position in certain products may result in unforeseen financial losses for the buyer. This in turn has caused a certain wariness about these products amongst a certain class of buyer. Wariness, however, is not the same as diminished participation in the market; participation is rising steadily.

Some US exchanges are devising screen-based systems, such as the CBOT's Project A, to abstract OTC business. Project A is a local area network trading system developed by the exchange to provide its members with a low-cost means for trading non-conventional products during conventional trading hours. It was launched on 23 October 1992. Project A currently lists the following contracts: Barge Freight Rate Index futures, Zero Coupon Note futures, Zero Coupon Bond futures, and deferred month US Treasury Bond futures-options. A Ferrous Scrap futures contract, also approved by the membership for Project A, is to be added to the system. The SFE in its 1991 Annual Report said, 'Regarding financial markets, the Exchange is examining new areas, including rule changes, systems changes and product design, which may facilitate interaction between the OTC markets, such as in options, swaps, and warrants and exchange-traded markets. The use of the clearing and guaranteeing capacity of the Exchange has an impact in this research.'

In fact, and substantiating this, the level of default on swaps business is sufficiently low to make this objection of limited force: the International Swaps Dealers' Association (ISDA) estimated that it amounts to only some \$360m annually, less than 0.0115% of the \$4.34trn that OTC business amounts to worldwide, 50% of which is caused by UK local authorities' problems.

It is interesting and encouraging to note, from an exchange point of view, that more volume is showing up on the listed market as offsets to OTC derivative positions purchased by customers. Issuers obviously seek the lowest cost configuration to construct the hedge and therefore lay-off their risk. Frequently, the cheapest alternative is the listed futures and options market. The OTC market has provided extra liquidity for traders who in turn are constructing OTC hedges, and offering them out to clients. Clearly, listed markets benefit from the growth of complementary OTC markets. This is important in that it shows that the two markets complement more than they compete with one another. With increased activity on the OTC side, it is reasonable to expect further business through offsets for the exchanges.

For some, it is crucial to market products exclusively from highly creditworthy organisations with global reach when working with customers who want OTC products. However, when Drexel Burnham Lambert fell, their very large swap book was transferred in a smooth way to other counterparties, with few complaints and no disasters. This is an example of how one part of the broader derivatives market avoided financial disaster very effectively. This competent and orderly unwinding and dispersal of risk over the broad market-place is evidence of the maturity of the OTC derivatives market, as well as to the skill of the users. It demonstrates the errors of regulators who would regulate the market into destruction for fear of disaster.

Indeed, some go so far as to say that the majority of jet fuel business is hedged using the IPE gasoil contract, so that the exchanges' hunt to replace OTC business is likely to prove counter-productive: especially if the upshot (net) of the relatively poor fit between jet fuel and gasoil is that over-hedging is more common than under-hedging. Traders do sometimes run naked OTC positions so that is admittedly unlikely. OTC traders set prices amongst themselves, but value whatever accuracy of strike price and availability of option writers that the exchange possesses.

In general the OTC market is expanding dramatically, with the first such deal apparently done as recently as 1987. Towards the end of 1989 the market began increasing at a tremendous rate and these instruments are now very widely used in the airline, shipping and transportation sectors. ISDA recorded that volumes had increased by almost 50% in both 1990 and 1991. Far less certain though is to what extent OTCs have a role in commodity futures trading. Small specialised futures contracts are declining in importance commensurate with the rise in managed futures trading where liquidity is a prerequisite: but although OTCs are gaining in importance, they do not seem to be taking over from these declining contracts. Rather it seems that some businesses such as oil contain both, and some such as tea, rice and rubber survive without either.

The commodity derivatives departments of some companies suggest that 'futures are one thing, derivatives are another' (we have a terminological problem here; equities traders are firmly of the belief that futures, especially the FTSE-100, are precisely derivatives). Such departments argue that futures involve basis risk, margin calls, have liquidity problems (sometimes), a fixed time horizon and high operation costs. They tend to favour their OTC products whereby exposure can be matched exactly, there is a flexible time period, the risk/reward equation is tailored exactly, and there is simplicity of operation.

The future

Amid concern that the US may be losing its edge in the financial engineering of unlisted derivative instruments to the challenge by global competitors, it is worth noting that other countries are coming into their own as legitimate markets for OTC derivative products. To some extent the deteriorating relative importance of US financial markets may be helping to facilitate this. The global market for OTC derivatives is still increasing dramatically. Asian countries with developed financial markets, such as Thailand, stand a good chance of participating more than proportionately in the growth. As more and more money managers ponder the use of the available products, more national markets are poised on the threshold of full integration.

The three key factions representing the essential dynamic of the marketplace are:

- the buyers (generally large institutions);
- the issuers (mainly investment banks);
- the regulators.

Important to an understanding of OTC markets is an appreciation of the tension that inevitably exists between these forces. There is hostility between the issuers and the regulators as each tries to fulfil their objectives. The issuers are striving to bring products to market that, as a by-product of their innovation, are often complex and difficult to understand. This inspires regulators to resist them, as they are perceived — often accurately — as being fraught with risk, particularly for the less astute buyers who may not fully understand what they are purchasing. *Caveat emptor* aside, the buyer wants prompt, effective attention to his investment needs. Some buyers feel there has been an inadequate response on the part of the providers here.

The accusation is levelled by some institutions, even very large ones, that they are receiving insufficient and poorly targeted service from the issuing banks as part of the deal. The issuers are perceived as having a vested interest in the design of the derivative product. They create the instrument to suit the need of the buyer-institution, but they clearly must aim for profit themselves by hedging out the risk and securing the margin. On occasions products developed reflect the issuers' after-the-fact trading purposes more than they do the market needs of the buyers. It is known, for instance, that the Caisse de Depot et Placement du Quebec routinely establishes auctions with three or four brokers bidding before a given product in order to be sure of an optimal deal. Other buyers have done likewise. It is also known that such institutions have both deep pockets and high financial knowledge of hedging, so buyers have become suspicious. The OTC market itself is perceived to be dominated by the major issuers trading between themselves.

Partly, it is a question of technology available to buying institutions. There are still difficulties in properly evaluating the products. This assessment is borne out by the consensus in Canadian banks, for example, that risk management software currently in use is inadequate as regards cross-product capabilities.

Customised derivatives are undoubtedly finding wider acceptance, and represent a much-needed extension of the commodity, especially soft commodity, markets. Indifferent, suspicious regulators and the oft-heard conservatism of institutional investors are the main problems, but the innovative derivative products available OTC are revolutionising the international investment industry. Examples of the available products include currency, interest rate, and equity-based products — unavailable on any exchange — in combinations of bonds, options, swaps (fixed and floating-rate interest payments exchanged between banks and corporations), swaptions, caps, collars and other derivative structures — some of which lock in prices for up to 25 years. They are attractive to larger institutions seeking to avoid the expense of trading, and to those wanting tailored financing. Part of their allure is that they offer size and longer terms to institutions. Unlike exchange-traded derivatives, the products are usually held to maturity.

That said, it is important to note not only that these products are used almost exclusively in financial markets rather than commodities, but that the business is dominated by a few powerful dealer-brokers in every country. There is perhaps a decade to go before substantial liquidity is achieved in most markets. In Canada, for instance, the four dominant players are said to include the BT Bank of Canada, Citibank, Wood Gundy, and RBC Dominion Securities. Different reasons are offered for the liquidity problem. The corporate financiers who design the products cite lagging education on the part of the investment community and money managers, and a general misunderstanding of 'the art of the hedge' as the main limiting factors. Together with a general suspicion of regulators, there is the belief among the banks (ie, the issuers) that institutional investors are still acquiring the sophistication necessary to employ the products effectively in their portfolios. In addition, risk-aversion on the part of money managers is frequently cited as an inhibiting factor. In other words, risk-averse money managers are unwilling to hedge risk on the grounds that the hedging vehicle looks too risky. Clearly, education is still required.

Credit enhancements from banks may not be sufficient to guarantee the financial integrity of the new players in the energy derivatives markets who lack the requisite financial strength to take their place comfortably in the long 'daisy chains' of paper energy trades. This may reinforce the need for standardised arrangements, and probably some form of clearing systems, for a wide range of OTC instruments — possibly starting with natural gas swaps.

The OTC market has evolved rapidly. There are several interest groups to consider in evaluating how OTC markets can develop needs of their own. On the products side, for many users swaps remain the best package of derivatives available. Swaps do, certainly, have dangers. For example using them at times of greater price volatility. Users do seem unwilling to pay premiums, yet are prepared to take on the exposure associated with swaps. There are always high administrative and back office costs that often go with more complicated strategies. The current situation in the use of OTC derivatives is very varied between companies, and is very likely to continue for the next decade.

There is some truth in the idea that supply is creating demand with these products and once educated as to the merits of the products users do indeed want them. The future of the OTC markets rests largely in the hands of tax-exempt investors, corporate finance people, and the corporations that use the custom-designed products. There is the conflict between the providers and the regulators that must be resolved in a constructive way. The three issues of making suitable products available to clients, credit, and liquidity are ever-present, though all soluble. The development of the OTC markets depends on the resolution of all these issues.

Case study of a new type of market: electricity forward agreements

The electricity forward agreement (EFA) market, is an example of a new UK specific OTC market, run by just one broker, GNI. The construction of the electricity market prior to the privatisation of the UK electricity industry gave rise to the world's first full market in physical electricity, known as the pool. The principal participants in this market are the generators and the suppliers. The function of the pool is to determine the price at which there are sufficient sellers of electricity to satisfy demand. Two characteristics of the electricity market distinguish it from most others:

- Firstly, because electricity cannot be bulk stored, it must be generated at the time it is required; the variation in demand together with the variation in generating capacity permits considerable volatility in the price of electricity. It can vary from below £10/MWh to over £60/MWh or higher.

- Secondly, generated electricity is disseminated over the National Grid, and suppliers and consumers draw it from there. It is therefore impractical to distinguish between different generators or different consumers. Instead, at a given time, all buyers buy at a single price, the pool output price (POP), and all sellers sell at a related price, the pool input price (PIP).

Pool prices are set for each half-hour of the day, giving 48 periods a day. The first step in setting the price is the preparation of the 'unconstrained schedule' at 10.00 each morning, covering the 24 hours from 05.00 the next morning. Each generator submits offers to the grid operator for each plant that is subject to 'central despatch', that is, each plant whose operation can be controlled by instructions from the grid operator. All generators supplying more than 10MW must join the pool. All generating stations with 100MW or more capacity are subject to central despatch, while sets of 1MW or more capacity can elect to be subject to central despatch. The generators' offers detail the availability of each set, its capacity, its operating characteristics and the prices to be charged for its electricity production.

Given the offers from the generators, together with a forecast for the demand and reserve requirements for each half hour, the unconstrained schedule is calculated using a computer-based algorithm. This calculates the lowest price that meets sufficient offers to satisfy the projected requirements — that is, the optimum marginal price, known as the System Marginal Price (SMP). The problem is fairly complicated, and the algorithm has to take into account the characteristics of each generating set to calculate the best arrangement. For example, some sets may offer cheap electricity but start up and shutdown costs may be high; the algorithm must then ensure that these sets are scheduled as far as possible for uninterrupted operation.

Generators are paid at essentially the same rate for generated electricity; the price paid is the PIP (or pool purchase price), and it is equal to the SMP plus an extra margin known as the 'capacity element'. At times of low demand, the capacity element is zero. It increases however, as demand increases towards the point where the possibility arises of generating capacity being insufficient. The capacity element is calculated as:

LOLP x (VLL – SMP)

where LOLP is the loss of load probability, which is calculated by the National Grid for each half hour, varying between zero and one;
and VLL is a figure for the value of lost load, currently set at £2187/MWh; this value is indexed.

The price paid by suppliers for electricity consumed is the POP; it is equal to PIP plus an uplift, covering for example:

- The cost of ancillary services;
- The cost of providing reserve generating capacity;
- Differences between the scheduled and the actual operation.

The uplift is set so cash payments by the pool are exactly matched by receipts, so that the pool's net cash flow for each half hour is zero. The uplift is typically small or zero. Settlement is based on a provisional settlement run 12 days after the trading day, with a final run at 24 days, and payments at 28 days. All payments are made through the pool. Electricity prices in the pool are highly volatile, falling to below £10/MWh at times, and occasionally rising above £60/MWh at others.

Although many large users of electricity and other energy sources are exposed to the electricity price, obviously the main companies at risk are the generators and the retail suppliers, the Regional Electricity Companies (RECs). Given the magnitude of the risk, the generators and the RECs have acted in concert through an industry-wide group to set up a new market in EFA.

The EFA market is a completely open market available to all companies who wish to hedge or trade electricity prices. Dealing is on an OTC basis, giving a great deal of flexibility to hedgers and allowing traders to focus on any particular areas of interest. EFAs themselves are cash-settled contracts for differences, with settlement based on the electricity pool prices, so EFA trading is straightforward even for companies without substantial involvement in physical electricity. Through a competitive tender, GNI was selected as the initial broker for the EFA market by the industry-wide group.

The EFA market was set up to allow electricity market participants to tailor their cover, taking into account the peculiarities of the variations in demand, together with changes in the overall electricity market volumes. EFAs are bilateral outright ('two-way') contracts for differences with settlement weekly based on the average pool price. GNI acts as an OTC broker initiating transactions by matching potential buyers and sellers anonymously over the telephone. Once all details of the trade have been agreed, the identities of the two counterparties are revealed to each other. On acceptance of each other's name, the EFA contract exists between the two parties. GNI has no further involvement in the trade apart from issuing a copy note confirming the verbal details. The market is open to anyone who wishes to trade — although, as in any OTC market, completing a trade is dependent on finding a suitable counterparty who is prepared to take the trader's name. Given that EFAs are purely bilateral deals arranged through a broker with no organised exchange, it would in principle be quite possible to trade any structure of deal required; there is no necessity for standardisation. However, in many OTC markets, although standardisation is not essential, liquidity has tended naturally to focus on particular types of trade. A standard form of documentation therefore generally emerges in a well-developed market; and trading interest typically centres on certain 'benchmark' instruments, such as particular maturities and so forth which are of general interest to the market participants. For the EFA market, the electricity companies have agreed to trade on standard documentation, known as EFA Standard Terms, that set out the characteristics of the trade in general, the settlement arrangements, the events of default, and so forth.

A framework has also been constructed for the type of trade. This framework should be sufficiently flexible to allow a full variety of structures for trading and hedging purposes, while maintaining simplicity. Each day is to be divided into six four-hour periods, numbered 1–6: 23.00–03.00; 03.00–07.00; 07.00–11.00; 11.00–15.00; 15.00–19.00 and 19.00–23.00. Trades will cover one of these contract periods for either both days of a weekend (contract periods WE1, WE2, WE3, WE4, WE5, and WE6), or all the five weekdays of a week (WD1–WD6). WE1–6 and WD1–6 can be traded for a single week, or a strip of weeks as long as is required; one might trade a four or five-week strip to cover a month, or a 13-week strip to cover a quarter, or even a 52-week strip to cover a year.

While the indications are that most interest will be in trading PIP, it will be possible to trade POP, SMP, or spreads between them. The PIP/SMP spread is known as the capacity element, while the POP/PIP spread is known as the uplift. EFAs are cash-settled weekly based on the average value for the appropriate variable (PIP, POP, SMP etc) for the appropriate contract period (WD1–6 or WE1–6) for the week. The fixings for the variables are established by the pool as part of the running of the physical electricity market, and are readily available. PIP and POP settlements are published daily in the 'Companies and Markets' section of the *Financial Times*. The settlement day follows the arrangements for the pool, that is normally 28 days after the end of the week in question. Since settlement is weekly, a contract covering a range of weeks will involve a series of cash flows.

A simple EFA trading operation involves very little overheads. The only essential equipment is a telephone, although if a substantial volume of trading is anticipated, a price screen would probably be useful. GNI uses the ICV Comstock service to disseminate indicative prices for EFAs. The ICV screen pages provide the most visible evidence of activity in the market-place. Pages show last price traded and current bids and offers communicated to GNI by market participants for each of the time periods on each of the variables for certain standard weeks. Early weeks are quoted individually on the screen but later ones are grouped into blocks of four or five or even 13 weeks. Prices for blocks of weeks apply only to that whole block and not to individual weeks. Traders are free, of course, to trade individual weeks or blocks of weeks not showing on the screen as standard dates.

As soon as GNI receives a higher bid or lower offer in any time period, it is shown on the screen and, while the previous price is superseded, the previous bidder or offerer is told that they are no longer showing the most competitive price. If the improved price is removed for any reason (eg, a trade occurs at that price or the price is withdrawn), GNI will check with the previous giver of a price before reinstating it on the screen. The size of the bid and offer will not normally be shown. Volumes traded are not shown and are reported only on a consolidated basis in the weekly summary of trading provided by GNI. Price screens are live only during the 'official' trading times of 10.00–12.00 and 14.00–16.00, although this does not preclude trades outside these hours. Bids and offers received outside these hours will not appear until the beginning of the next session.

Most communication occurs by telephone between participants and GNI. In a busy market, GNI makes use of the message facility on the ICV system. These messages are necessarily brief and are intended to draw the participants' attention to particular contracts of which they might be unaware. In addition, features such as heavy trading of a particular contract may also be highlighted in this way.

EFAs can be traded either by making or taking prices. To make a price, a trader puts in either a bid (to buy) or an offer (to sell) for the appropriate contract at a given price. Alternatively, the trader can take someone else's price by 'hitting the bid' (to sell) or 'taking the offer' (to buy). Normally prices will be for the reference variables; however, other types of price are possible. For example, traders can quote prices for spreads if required. The convention in some other markets when placing orders is to say 'I pay (price) for (size)' to make a bid, eg, 'I pay £17.32 for 1000MW week 40 WD2', and to say 'I sell (size) at (price)' to make an offer, eg, 'I sell 1000MW week 40 WD2 at £17.35'. GNI feels that it would be a useful discipline to adopt this practice in the EFA market, and brokers will repeat orders back to clients in this form.

Other types of order may be possible in EFAs and may eventually evolve over time. The financial markets offer many examples. At this stage, however, it seems unlikely that such orders will be widely used with EFAs, but GNI will try to accommodate individual market users' requirements.

In general, GNI will take it that all orders received are good for the day on which they are given unless cancelled or changed. It may be apparent that some such orders are intended to be good for longer periods of time, but GNI will always check the current validity of such orders before trading commences on a particular day.

Prices given to the broker are regarded as essentially firm apart from the check on the mutual creditworthiness of both parties to a transaction. GNI will always check the details with both parties simultaneously by telephone. The items checked include:

- Buyer or seller.
- Contract variable (PIP, POP, uplift etc).
- Contract week(s) and year.

- Contract time period (WD1–6, WE1–6).
- Number of MW being traded.
- The price agreed.
- Broker identifies 'price maker' and 'price taker'.

Once these details are agreed, the broker exchanges the names of the counterparties. If they are acceptable to each other the transaction is complete and binding.

Source: Gerrard & National Inter Commodities

Notes:

D Rubinstein, *Exotic Options*, mimeo, 1991.

Chapter 5: Risk management and commodity-linked hedging products

The essential problems regarding commodities are summarised below. All will affect the cost of borrowing for the company.

- *Unreliability of supply*
  Commodity hedging of supply reliability can only be undertaken through forward agreements. Insurance and other OTC arrangements are available to protect supply, but it is interesting that the same attention is not paid within the derivatives industry to security of supply as to security of price. The main reason for this is that in the international commodity markets, it is almost always possible to obtain the commodity.

- *Unreliability of quality*
  It is rare to hedge quality specifications. Companies usually place great reliance on the skills of quality inspection companies to ensure that once the certificate has been issued, the necessary quality has been achieved.

- *Unreliability of price*
  This is hedged using derivative instruments. The companies concerned though usually succeed in obtaining good prices and adequate quality during the process of establishing an acceptable price. Exposure to price risk for commodities is enormously varied and widespread.

Companies may be exposed to a variety of different risks, but for a typical company the risk profile resembles the following:

Corporate price exposure

Input exposure	Inflation Exposure	Output exposure
Energy costs	← →	Finished product
Salary costs	← →	Fee revenue
Raw material costs	← →	Tax rate

A pearl sales company, for example, is exposed: to the cost of producing finished pearls in energy terms; to the cost of buying the pearls; to the wages of its own employees; and hence to inflation and relative costs. It is exposed to the demand for, and price of, its output of pearls, and also to the level of tax imposed on it by external agencies, principally its national government.

Some companies, like the above example, are concerned with only one raw material, and so energy costs are restricted to the cost of electricity for an office or petrol for sales force cars. Other companies, such as refiners, are exposed to the price of the raw material of oil as well as the cost of electricity. They are then exposed to the price relationship between input and output. A large company producing a variety of products may well be exposed to a multitude of risks. Some of these risks may well cancel each other out and this highlights the need for an internal risk management team in addition to advice from brokers and providers of risk management services.

The most basic hedge is the straight use of futures by a company exposed to price risk. Imagine a pearl futures market of contract specification 1000 pearls with a current price of $30/pearl. A pearl company aims to profit from rising futures prices, so its market opinion is bullish. Its risk is a rise in prices so its position is to buy futures. Its profit potential is unlimited and its profit point is any futures price above the price at which the position was initiated. Similarly, its loss potential is unlimited (except to the extent that the futures price only can go to zero), and its loss point is any futures price below the price at which the position was initiated. The break-even point is the futures price at which the position was initiated, less transaction costs. There will be margin requirements: the most common way to liquidate such a position is to offset by selling back the same futures contract prior to the last trading day. The delta of the position is 1.00. This is obviously one of the two most basic speculative strategies available in the futures market. The company will make money if futures prices rise, and lose money if futures prices fall. Both the potential profits and losses can be great because of the high gearing provided by futures.

Assume that a pearl company thinks October pearl futures will rise significantly. To take advantage of this possible bull market, the company buys October pearl futures at $30. As long as October pearl futures are above the break-even price of $30 when the company offsets, it will make a profit. If the market falls below $30 at the time the company offsets, the company will lose money on the position.

Long a futures contracts: the bottom line

October futures are at: $/pearl	Profit/loss $/pearl	Profit/loss $/contract
28	2 loss	2000 loss
29	1 loss	1000 loss
30	0	0
31	1 profit	1000 profit
32	2 profit	2000 profit

The following formula can be used to calculate futures profit or loss:

futures profit/loss = futures price (when the position is offset) – futures price (when the position is initiated)

Profits and losses: long futures position

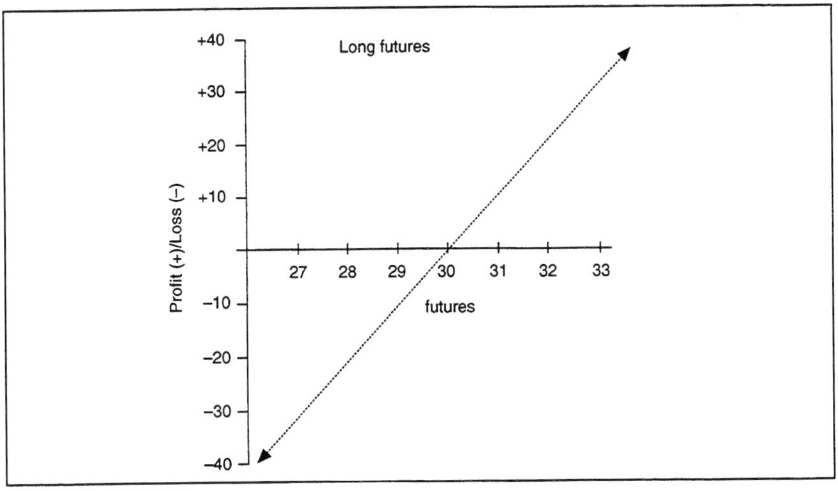

Similarly, if a company risks falling physical pearl prices, it will seek to profit from falling futures prices. Its market opinion is, therefore, bearish and the appropriate futures strategy is to sell futures. Its profit potential is unlimited (except to the extent that the futures price only can go to zero), and its profit point will be any futures price below the price at which the position was initiated. In the same way its loss potential will be unlimited and its loss point will be any futures price above the price at which the position was initiated. The break-even point is the futures price at which the position was initiated less transaction costs. There will be margin requirements: again the most common way to liquidate is to offset by buying back the same futures contract prior to the last trading day. The delta is 1.00. This is the other most basic speculative strategy available in the futures market. The company will make money if futures prices fall, and lose money if futures prices rise. Again, both the potential profits and losses can be great.

Assume that another pearl company thinks August pearl futures prices will fall. To take advantage of this possible bear market, the company sells August pearl futures at $38. As long as August pearl futures are below the break-even price of $38 when the company offsets, it will make a profit. If the market rises above $38 they will lose money.

Short a futures contract: the bottom line

August futures $/pearl	Profit/loss $/pearl	Profit/loss $/contract
36	2 profit	2000 profit
37	1 profit	1000 profit
38	0	0
39	1 loss	1000 loss
40	2 loss	2000 loss

To calculate futures profit or loss, use the following formula:

futures profit/loss = futures price (when the position is initiated) – futures price (when the position is offset)

Profits and losses: short futures position

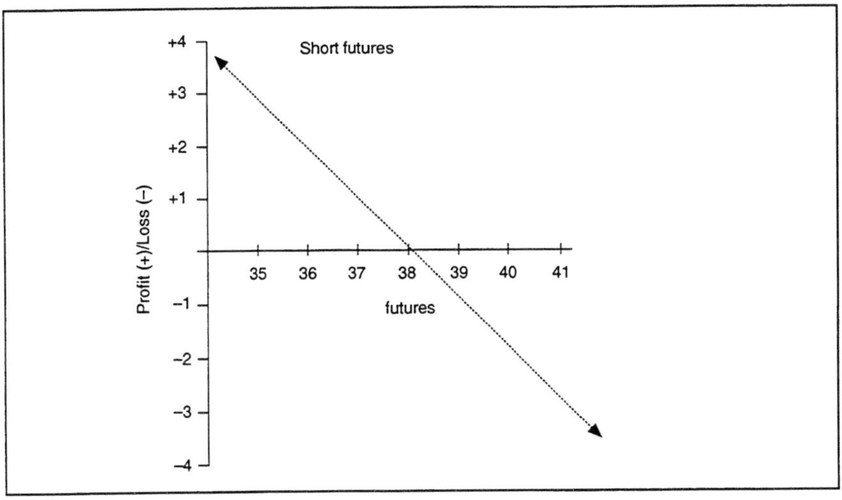

Forecasts

Once the marketing goals are set it is crucial that the target is within reach. A quick method of determining the possible range of prices during the production period is to begin with the existing official or semi-official estimates of the season's average price range for pearls. Suppose the United States Department of Agriculture (USDA) forecasts the range in season average pearl prices to be $143.00–$150.00/pearl. This range should be compared with other forecasts from university studies, advisory services and brokerage firms.

Forecasts are rarely neutral. The USDA, however, for agricultural commodities is one of the best sources precisely because it does not have a vested interest. It also has a world view as well as an understanding of the interrelationship between different commodities' prices. For example, some commodities are substituted in production for one another. A shortage of one agricultural commodity next season may be caused by planting decisions in favour of another one this season. Even the USDA, however, would not claim to maintain a complete global agricultural area allocation analysis as an annual crop year basis, country by country, and crop by crop. Such an immense task would always be complicated by the possibility of bringing marginal land into production when prices look favourable for next season, or similarly taking it out of production if the reverse appears probable.

Production costs

Probably the most important step in planning the marketing of agricultural products is determining what it costs to produce a pound of product. It is impossible to know what price needs to be received for the product unless production costs are known. A market price is meaningless without knowing production costs and derivative markets cannot provide this.

It is important for a producer to review production records for the past three to five years. Keeping accurate records of these costs assists in making future projections. Actual production costs are never known until the process is completed. So, it is necessary, for decision-making purposes, to project, before production begins, the likely break-even cost. This allows a producer to analyse what price is needed to meet to break-even. In most countries services are available to help producers determine the break-even cost.

When calculating production costs, producers must include both variable and fixed costs. Variable costs are those that can be managed (changed) before or during the production period, such as feeder purchases, feed costs, death loss of livestock and wages of seasonal labour. Fixed costs are those that cannot be changed during the production period, such as mortgages on land and buildings, managerial salaries, upkeep of equipment, etc.

Marketing plans

The marketing objective is to take advantage of market prices that conform to profit goals. Futures prices fluctuate in a broad range prior to contract delivery, responding to supply and demand factors that keep changing along the way. Hedgers must take advantage of favourable opportunities, that is, prices at the high end of the market expectations that meet or exceed break-even. Suppose recent futures contracts have traded at some point as high as $5.00/pearl over the top end of the USDA forecast price ranges for applicable marketing periods. That means futures prices could top $155.00 between now and the target sale date, that is, $5.00 higher than the USDA forecast average high of $155.00/pearl. If they do, hedgers must be prepared to take advantage of this, and not to end up paying immense margin calls for unnecessary hedges.

Suppose that the break-even for the operation is $145.00/pearl, and the pearl producer aims for a net price for his pearls of $152.00/pearl to realise a gain of $7.00/pearl. A sensible plan would be to increase sales beginning at or above break-even. Portions of the production can be hedged at various price levels. If the producers want to sell pearls in the cash market at no less than $147.00/pearl and the expected basis is $2.00 under, then the producer could hedge, say, 20% of production when the futures price reaches $148.00/pearl, then hedge 20% more at $149.00/pearl etc.

An example of a pearl marketing plan

The value of this approach is the discipline of studying the producer's costs plus the advantages of monitoring the markets. Even if futures prices never get high enough to enable the producer to complete his marketing plan, he may still be able to hedge a portion above break-even — and that is better than taking a loss on production as a whole.

Portion of production: Hedge 20% Hedge 20% Hedge 20% Hedge 20% Hedge 20% Hedged 100%

At target selling price (futures adjusted by basis) $147/pearl $149/pearl $151/pearl $153/pearl $155/pearl

Futures:$148/pearl $150/pearl $152/pearl $154/pearl $156/pearl

Factor* 148/152 x 0.2 Average price of $152.00

Average price:	$152.00/pearl
Break-even:	–$145.00/pearl
Return:	$7.00/pearl

** Percent of production hedged times target selling price*

Applications for producers and wholesalers

The simplest use of a futures market by a producer is to lock in the price of his product. Take, for example, the case of a rancher breeding cattle. In six months' time his cattle will be ready for market. He does not want to guess the price he will receive when he sells; he wants to know today, so he can plan for tomorrow's investments, purchases, loan repayments, borrowing requirements and income. For this reason, he sells a futures contract at a set price and he knows exactly what he will receive for his cattle in six months' time.

The rancher has hedged — he has protected himself from any potentially adverse price swings in the market-place by establishing appropriate positions in the futures market. Had there been no exchange traders, whether other hedgers or speculators, to assume the risk, the rancher would have had to run the financial risk himself. The speculators assumed the risk that he had wished to circumvent. The futures market, or to a lesser extent the price quoted by OTC writers, give an indication to the producer of what price he might expect to be able to achieve for the product throughout the next year and beyond.

Commodity futures trading has played a major role in the distribution of America's food supply for more than a century. Farmers, agricultural producers, processors and exporters have long looked to futures markets as a way to control major price risk. This frees them to go ahead and concentrate on the efficiency of their own production.

There are many different approaches to hedging. Most of them are appropriate for hedging risk on a single commodity liability or asset and some relate to hedging a portfolio, protecting an institution from a change in the slope of the yield curve.

If a producer, wholesaler or other trading company happens to be holding a stock of a commodity, and determines that hedging is likely to be a more profitable strategy than selling the crop or stock on the spot market, then an appropriate amount of futures will be sold to effect the hedge. In practice, most hedges are usually placed in the nearby, or at least most liquid, contract. Theory would suggest though that the hedge should be placed in the contract month or months in which the producer expects to make a sale. However, some measure of trading speculation enters into these calculations. For example, the company's assessment may be that the December contract will be weak relative to the nearby July, so following the maxim that the successful risk manager will always wish to put on hedges in the month or months he expects to be the weakest, the hedge will be deposited in December instead, gaining more profit the stronger the hedge becomes.

Spreads

The most important influence on the spreads is the fundamental supply and demand for the cash commodity. Spreads are generally less sensitive to daily market volatility caused by fund position shifts, rumours, and technical trading. In most commodity markets, evidence suggests that spreads strengthen (the nearby month becomes more expensive relative to others) in bull markets and weaken in bear markets. A 'bull spread' is selling higher prices deferred futures against nearby cash or futures. This guarantees a price differential, allowing for example a wholesaler to concentrate on earning basis appreciation. If the company uses a bull spread when the market is close to 'full carry', the market is effectively paying for storage and interest on the stored commodity. Country wholesalers may want to use a bull spread to lock in carry at only 60–80% of the delivery point's full cost of carry; typically country elevators carry grain, for instance, at a lower cost than terminal elevators as their storage rates are lower. Another spread trading tactic is the 'bear spread'. These are used when stocks are high and basis levels are weak. During periods of increasing grain stocks or slack demand, spreads will tend to reduce. A production or holding company hedging during such a period will want to keep hedges in a more nearby month than would be conventionally indicated, expecting the weaker basis prices to rally the basis as the expiry date approached. Then, as the spreads approach full carry, the bear spread rolls the hedges into a more distant month, collecting the profit in the process.

Such spread tactics can be carried out between markets, although the risks are clearly greater. They may be between cash and futures, altering the futures contract sold so as to take advantage of perceived differences in relative price. For example a coffee merchant may choose to hedge in New York against a Brazil shipment in the belief that the basis will widen. A futures hedge may be taken in CBOT wheat futures rather than KCBT because of a belief that soft red wheat is overpriced relative to hard red winter wheat.

Exchanges themselves suggest that commodity futures can be used by the following types of institutions, although derivative markets can be used by companies active in the physical markets whether as producers or consumers.

Producers

Futures markets trade higher volumes than the comparable physical markets. This is something of a guide as to the degree to which the trade uses the market — cocoa futures, for example, are a much larger market than the physical cocoa market. Futures volume is also an indication of where the prices are actually made. Cotton prices, for US cotton at least, are in practice made on the New York Exchange. They very much reflect physical conditions outside, but the actual striking of bargains on the Exchange floor is what sets prices that are then followed as guidelines, with accepted premiums, discount and basis, by traders conducting physical deals. Rice futures prices, however, are dominated more by what is happening in the physical market — this applies to all futures markets with low absolute liquidity and especially to those with a large spot market as well.

Correlations have been calculated by Goldman Sachs for their GSCI for a number of key commodities. The Goldman Sachs calculation however overlooks the fact that some commodities have futures markets elsewhere; cocoa and the oil contracts which are also traded on the IPE as well as the NYMEX contracts included by Goldman Sachs. Generally, and with the noticeable exception of soyabeans, the agricultural and oil contracts trade a smaller percentage of world trade than do the metals. It is expected that these percentages will continue to exhibit the falls that have been seen in 1990–91 for at least several years. Speculative interest is declining both because of regulation and the worldwide recession that has reduced, quite dramatically in a number of cases, the amount of money that is available for investment into futures markets. This reduction has also made it more difficult to launch futures markets as initial liquidity cannot be generated to order by broking houses.

Producers throughout the production chain have an interest in maintaining steady input costs. Raw material costs form a large part of final production costs (20–40% of the finished product in most cases). For raw material producers, though, 100% of their income can be derived from a single commodity. Whether they use a 'producer hedge' or a 'consumer hedge' depends on their exposure with respect to the commodity, not their own commercial activity. For example, a manufacturing company is a producer — but for property, metals, or electricity it will need a consumer hedge. A retailing company consumes raw materials, but it may take advantage of a producer hedge to protect the value of raw material stocks that it holds. Such companies are rarely directly represented on exchange floors. They act through selected brokers or they may become associate members of an exchange in some instances.

Exchange of futures for physicals

An EFP is the exchange of a futures position for a physical position, and this facility is available on all contracts listed on the IPE. In an EFP, two parties agree to either swap cash and futures positions or to establish opposite positions with each other in both the cash and futures market. In this way futures are being used, not only as a financial instrument for hedging, but as a vehicle for separating the pricing from the supply function.

At the Exchange's request, buyers and sellers are required to present documents to substantiate the change of ownership of the cash commodity. A futures contract established through an EFP is the same as any other, and will be marginalised in the normal way. It is worth emphasising that in an EFP, the buyers and sellers search out and negotiate with each other (unlike Standard IPE Deliveries and ADPs) to tailor contractual agreements which suit each party's particular needs. The two parties will often be regularly involved in trading with each other, and may have a long standing business relationship. This is one of the principal benefits of an EFP. EFPs have become an innovative flexible source of supply and well accepted vehicle for physical energy transaction.

Executing an EFP

There are three examples cited here: an EFP to liquidate positions where both parties are in possession of opposite cash and futures positions; an EFP to transfer a position where one party holds a futures position; an EFP to initiate a position when neither party holds a futures position.

Open interest declines in the first example; is unchanged in the second; and increases in the third. As stated above, the pricing of both transactions of an EFP are negotiated and the basis accounts for the difference in quality, timing and location between the contracts. After executing the transaction, the resulting futures positions are marked to market in the normal way.

An EFP can be agreed at any time (24 hours a day), but must be executed on the market floor prior to the cessation of trading in the futures contract (in the case of gas oil or unleaded gasoline, however, EFPs may be registered up to one hour cessation of trading of the relevant contract). To execute the EFP, each party instructs their broker of the transaction. The transaction will be cleared and posted on the Exchange as an EFP, at the specified price regardless of the market price.

EFP to liquidate position

A refiner needs to acquire physical crude oil. How can he purchase crude oil on a regular basis and maintain the flexibility of pricing crude oil at his own discretion? At the same time a producer may also wish to dispose of his equity crude on a regular basis, but price the crude only when it is favourable, without being at the mercy of a volatile market.

1 January Refiner is short physical crude oil. He wishes to begin pricing this oil as it is purchased. He buys 100 March Brent crude contracts at $18 per barrel.

2 January Producer is long physical crude oil and wishes to begin pricing his sale and sells 100 March Brent crude contracts at the now more favourable price of $19 per barrel.

8 February The two companies in discussion agree to transfer their physical positions and transact an EFP of 100 March crude contracts for 100,000 per barrel (100 contract equivalents) of physical crude. The refiner agrees to purchase physical oil at a transfer price defined by IPE's March Brent settlement price of 8 February.

The refiner transfers his long futures position through his broker to the producer. The refiner has therefore exchanged his original short physical position to being long crude with no futures position. The producer has disposed of his long physical position, and the short 100 March futures position has been netted off against the long future position he has acquired through the EFP from the refiner.

The futures positions are exchanged at the IPE settlement price of 8 February. Concurrently, Alaskan North Slope crude (or any other suitable crude) is delivered to US Gulf Coast from producer to refiner at the IPE settlement price of 8 February less a pre-arranged differential, of say, $1.

Irrespective of the settlement price, the realised purchase price and sales price remain the same for each party. Let us look at the balance sheet for both parties now, using three different IPE settlement prices $17, $18, and $19:

	8 February IPE Settlement Price	$17	$18	$19
Refiner	Long Futures	$18	$18	$18
	EFP-Sells Futures	$17	$18	$19
	Hedge P&L (Futures)	–$1	$0	+$1
	EFP-Physical Price (IPE–$1)	$16	$17	$18
	Realised Purchase Price	$17	$17	$17
	Net Futures Position (Zero)	—	—	—
Producer	Short Futures	$19	$19	$19
	EFP-Buys Futures	$17	$18	$19
	Hedge P&L (Futures)	+$2	+$1	$ 0
	EFP-Physical Price (IPE–$1)	$16	$17	$18
	Realised Sales Price	$18	$18	$18
	Net Futures Position (Zero)	—	—	—

EFP to transfer position

A distributor makes regular contracts for the purchase and sale of gas oil but, again, would like to have the flexibility in timing the pricing of his material. At the same time, he would like to reduce his storage charges without running his stocks too low.

1 January A distributor is short physical gas oil for March delivery and buys 100 February gas oil contracts at $315.

8 January A refiner is producing physical gas oil and has not yet priced his oil. The distributor and refiner agree to EFP 100 February gas oil contracts for 10,000 tonnes of in-tank gas oil. EEC quality gas oil is transferred in-tank from refiner in Rotterdam to the distributor at the IPE settlement price of 8 January less an agreed differential of, say, $3 per tonne. The distributor transfers his long futures position to the refiner. Let us look at the balance sheet for both parties:

	31 January IPE Settlement Price	$310	$320	$330
Distributor	Long Futures	$315	$315	$315
	EFP-Sell Futures	$310	$320	$330
	Hedge P&L (Futures)	–$5	+$5	+$15
	EFP-Physical Price (IPE–$3)	$307	$317	$327
	Realised Sales Price	$312	$312	$312
	Net Futures Position	—	—	—
Refiner	No Futures Position	—	—	—
	EFP-Buys Futures	$310	$320	$330

Net Long Futures Position	100	100	100
Hedge P&L (Futures)	undetermined		
EFP-Physical Price (IPE–$3)	$307	$317	$327
Realised Sales Price	undetermined until he sells his long future position.		

In the example three different settlement prices are used; $310, $320 and $330. The distributor's realised purchase price is fixed at $312 per tonne, irrespective of the physical or future market level. On the other hand, the refiner has maintained his inventory by holding a long gas oil futures position, and therefore his effective sales prices remains undetermined until he liquidates the position. If he thinks prices will rise, he can hold onto the futures position in order to benefit from this. Conversely, he can liquidate the position immediately if he thinks that the market will weaken during the next few weeks.

EFP to initiate position

8 February A producer is long but still believes the physical price will increase. At the same time a refiner who has a contrary view believes the physical market will begin to fall. Despite this, both parties are interested in either disposing of or acquiring some physical material, yet want to retain the flexibility of taking advantage of a subsequent potential market move in their favour. Both parties therefore agree to EFP 500 March Brent crude contracts for 500,000 barrels of physical crude oil. Futures positions are exchanged at the current prevailing market price (12 noon) on 8 February.

Concurrently, Oseberg or any other grade of crude oil is delivered to Rotterdam from the producer to refiner at the IPE market price at 12 noon on 8 February less a suitable discount (eg, $1).

In this example, three different transfer prices are used: $35, $36 and $37. Irrespective of the 8 February transfer price, the realised purchase price for the refiner and the sales price for the producer remain separated from the actual supply function of the physical oil and can be determined independently by each party at a later date.

	8 February IPE Settlement Price	$35	$36	$37
Refiner	No Futures Position	—	—	—
	EFP-Sells Futures	$35	$36	$37
	Net Short Futures Position	500	500	500
	Hedge P&L (Futures)	undetermined		
	EFP-Physical Price (IPE–$1)	$34	$35	$36
	Realised Purchase Price	undetermined until his short futures position is brought back		

Producer	No Futures Position	—	—	—
	EFP-Buys Futures	$35	$36	$37
	Net Long Futures Position	500	500	500
	Hedge P&L (Futures)	undetermined		
	EFP-Physical Price (IPE–$1)	$34	$35	$36
	Realised Sales Price	undetermined until he sells out his long futures position		

The refiner can buy back his short futures position and the producer can sell out his long futures position independently. Therefore each party can determine their respective purchase and sales prices separately from the supply of the physical oil. The refiner's position is immediately hedged by the EFP, yet his acquisition cost for the cargo of Oseberg will not be determined until the futures position is closed out.

The producer has been able to sell his production into the market whilst at the same time being able to wait for the market to move up, in order to then take full benefit of a high realised sale price. Buy using this technique, he would also be able to avoid the situation of becoming a distressed seller in the market.

Note: Although the outright prices for both the sale and the purchase of the cargo of Oseberg has not yet been fixed, and therefore both the refiner and the producer retain this flexibility, the risk to both parties has not been entirely eliminated. If the differential between the price of Oseberg and the price of IPE Brent (the basis) changes during the remaining period, then the profitability of the trade will change.

If the basis increases beyond $1 under the futures, say to parity with IPE Brent, then the producer will have foregone this potential basis gain, whilst the refiner will have profited by being able to acquire the crude at the reduced differential, ie, one at a discount to Brent.

Conversely, if the agreed basis were to subsequently fall to an increaed differential to Brent, say $2 under IPE Brent, then the refiner would have foregone the opportunity of acquiring the crude at a cheaper discount to IPE Brent whilst the producer has achieved a better differenital than would have been possible were he to have waited to sell the crude on the spot market.

Exchange of futures for swaps

As an example, a company may agree with Oil Co. plc to grant to them a 10,000 tonne swap at $195.00/tonne against the monthly average price for March 92 jet fuel cif North West Europe. This represents a straight swap deal between the two counterparties.

However, it may suit the two firms to agree a basis for jet fuel against IPE March gas oil of $24/tonne and to exchange the swap for a March gas oil position.

- The company is short jet fuel swap for March and long 100 contracts of March gas oil at $171/tonne.
- Oil Co. plc are long jet fuel swap for March and short 100 March gas oil at $171/tonne.
- Both firms have a balanced position (albeit with a basis risk) and are poised to take advantage of trading opportunities.

For example, Oil Co. plc may grant a jet fuel swap to an end user and close out the futures position, ideally at a profit, and may let the position run or trade against it in a variety of ways.

The price agreed of $171/tonne for the exchange of the IPE gas oil futures, however, will not necessarily be the IPE market price, since it depends upon the jet fuel price and basis agreed between counterparties.

It will be seen, therefore, that the EFS is exactly parallel to an EFP in that both require a futures transaction to take place at a pre-arranged price.

Wholesalers

Such companies make their profits from buying and selling both the physical and the derivative markets in particular commodities. Some trading companies are full or associate members of exchanges, but these companies in some of their physical business and all of their futures business usually operate through brokers. Global Rice, for instance, has never been a member of a rice futures market and has no intentions of being so, even if the CBOT were to launch a global rice futures contract. They may use CBOT rice futures, however, and if so they would go probably through a US broker directly. Richco is one of the world's largest and most successful trading companies but their trading activity is usually carried out through a number of different brokers and they do not advertise in advance which markets they intend to use.

Potential difficulties for hedgers

Delusions of omniscience

Some individuals who have been involved in, say, the pearl business for many years feel they have a good insight into where the price of pearls is going. This is the type of individual who might put on a 'Texas hedge' (buying pearl futures contracts when he already owns pearls). He will increase the risk, not cut it. He becomes a speculator in the very commodity in which he is already at risk.

Straight speculation

An individual may also become a speculator by hedging his pearl production, but cannot resist what he thinks are good price moves in the pearl futures. If the producer is buying or selling pearl contracts without producing pearls, he is speculating, whatever his broker may say about price correlations and commodity interrelationships. This is indisciplined.

Aimless trading

Some individuals want to hedge but do not know their production costs. In order to use the futures markets successfully, a producer must accurately know his costs. Without costs, the producer will not know whether it is sensible for him to hedge or not.

Jitters

Another type of producer finds it tough to stand day-to-day fluctuations in the market; margin calls upset him. This type of producer may be more comfortable with cash forward contracting or options.

Premature bailing out

A producer may give in to the temptation to offset and profit from a short hedge after a market decline, but before his production is marketed, anticipating that prices will rebound. But the market keeps falling, and he is now without protection. Another producer may hedge at an acceptable level, but seeing the market rally, causing margin calls that he (or his lender) finally cannot stand, he offsets the hedge at a loss, only to see the market drop so that he suffers a cash market loss as well. This kind of producer would be better off to hedge only a fraction of production, use cash forward contracts or use options.

Failing to take advantage of arbitrage opportunities between physical and futures prices

For example, when a contango is in operation — which often happens on the LME, for instance, the differential can be such that it produces a higher guaranteed yield than can be obtained from interest rates on traditional money exchanges. The way to do this is to buy the spot metal and sell the same quantity at the same time for redelivery at a forward date.

Another example is arbitrage between futures exchanges contracts for the same commodity. It is, however, worth pointing out that although producers may have unique knowledge of the specialist difficulties that apply to the relationship between their own physical production and futures prices, this is unlikely to extend to a better global understanding than, for example, the USDA. Arbitrage opportunities are usually, therefore, the prerogative of specialised and export traders.

Financing

When a commodity trader or company, or an investment fund, hold warrants that they do not wish to sell but need to release cash for a period, the broker can arrange the sale of the warrants and the simultaneous purchase of a forward position. This is known in LME parlance as 'lending' enabling the client to maintain their position whilst releasing funds.

The most important commodity-linked product used as a hedge is the option, whether exchange-traded or OTC. For example, consider the pearl trading company. When it competes for a contract in a fixed price tender by an international jeweller, for example, it is taking on the risk of the cost of the pearls that will be used in the finished jewellery. The trading company does not know whether their tender will be accepted. If the pearls the company will need for the tender fall in price, the company will be liable on the futures market for the loss. If the company does not hedge and the tender is accepted, the pearl price might rise and the company runs the risk of making a loss through having under-priced the pearl content of the tender.

The problem can be overcome through the proficient use of options. The company can purchase call options as a hedge, with the premium costed into the tender. If the tender is rejected, the company may have the opportunity to trade against the option and may even make a profit. If the tender is accepted, on the other hand, he can take up his option and enter into a conventional futures hedge.

Another example would be a pearl producer who needs to hedge production in the futures market to guarantee a price level. One possible option for the producer is to sell short and become committed to either buying back or delivering the pearls on the expiry date. But a put option would be perhaps better, especially when the market is in backwardation. If the market price for pearls rises by the time that sale time for production has arisen, the option can be abandoned and the premium is the total cost of the hedge. If the option has some time left to expiry it can be sold, perhaps recouping a sizeable percentage of original outlay. If the market price has sold the option can be exercised, providing the producer with a short futures position at the strike price of the original option contract.

Risk management using options

There are four fundamental ways to trade options:

- buy or sell calls;
- buy or sell puts.

All other strategies evolve from these four basic options. They can be combined to take advantage of numerous perceived market positions and risk profiles.

Of the four simple strategies, the point of *buying a call* is that risk is limited and profit unlimited. The maximum amount that can be lost is the original premium. If the option falls to or stays out-of-the-money, then it will expire worthless. If however, the price of the underlying physical commodity rises, then the option can either be closed out or exercised, producing a profit. Calls tend to be bought when investors are bullish about the underlying, but either do not want to take an unlimited risk for accounting or other investment reasons, or when there is perceived to be a finite risk of some factor that could drive down prices rapidly. For example, a perceived 80% chance of a rise in prices by 20% and a 20% chance of a fall by 40%. Generally, the more bullish the market perspective, the more out-of-the-money the strike price should be — it will be cheaper, the more out-of-the-money it is.

Conversely, *selling a call* brings immediate income but unlimited risk. The maximum profit to be made is if the options expires worthless. Although selling a call can be offset by buying another at the same strike price, the reason for selling is that the investor believes the market price of the underlying commodity will not be rising. The more confident the investor or institution is of the market not rising, and perhaps even falling, the closer to at-the-money or even in-the-money options can be sold. Any sale of options brings unlimited or effectively unlimited risk and must therefore be watched closely to see if it itself needs to be hedged, either through the OTC options market, through the futures market, or simply through an offsetting exchange-traded options contract.

Buying a put option, another strategy with a limited risk/high profit profile (limited only by the fact that the commodity's price cannot fall below zero), should be bought if the investor believes that the market will fall. Once the option is in-the-money, ie, the underlying commodity is trading at a lower price than the strike price of the option, then the investor can sell the option or exercise it. Clearly the more bearish the investor is, the more out-of-the-money the option should be. This position gives the maximum leverage in a falling market, with limited risk.

Conversely again, *puts are sold* when investors believe that the market is not going to fall, at least to the level of the strike price of the option. The more convinced the investor is of the unlikelihood of a fall, the closer to an in-the-money put can be sold. In order to avoid making a loss on selling an in-the-money put, the price of the commodity must not fall by more than the premium received.

There are however other factors to consider about a commodity market other than the direction of prices. There is the question of volatility. Does the trader believe that volatility will rise, fall or is he not sure? There are appropriate options trading strategies to combine each of these outlooks with a view on the direction of prices, and also with a particular position held on the futures market itself.

1 Buying calls

Unlimited profit potential, with risk limited to the premium paid. A bullish strategy, the further out-of-the-money the more bullish but the lower the premium. Break-even is at the strike price plus the premium. It is important to recall that the storage cost for a commodity may well equal or exceed the option premium. Moreover, by storing, the owner of the commodity remains exposed to downside price movements eliminated by a call option. The lower interest rates are, the more attractive storage becomes.

However, every commodity owner must assess his own cost of storage in order to make a fair comparison between the alternatives of storing, selling the cash grain and buying options or selling the cash grain and buying futures.

2 Buying puts

Unlimited profit potential, limited at least only by the price falling to zero, with risk limited to the premium paid. A bearish trade, the further out-of-the-money the more bearish, but the lower, the premium. Break-even is at the strike price less the premium.

3 Buying straddles

The purchase of puts and calls at the same strike price, to be used when a price breakout is expected but the direction is uncertain. Profits are unlimited; break-even is when the price breakout exceeds the double premium cost.

4 Buying strangles

The purchase of out-of-the-money puts and calls with the same expiry date. Similar to a straddle, it is used when markets are stable and a price breakout is expected but the direction is uncertain. Profits in either direction are unlimited; loss is limited to the total premium paid and is maximised if the price does not change ie, is in between the two strike prices. Break-even is at the strike price of the put less the total premium or of the call plus the total premium.

5 Bull call spread

The purchase of calls at a price and the sale of calls at a higher price. A bullish trade, although less bullish than straight call purchases, and less costly. Profit is limited to the difference between the strike prices less the net cost of the options. This is the most popular bullish option trade and accounts for a number of call option writers' activity.

6 Bear put spread

The purchase of puts at a higher strike price and the sale of puts at a lower strike price. A bearish trade, but less bearish than straight put purchase, and less costly. Profit is limited to the difference between the strike price less the premium. This is the most popular bearish trade and accounts for a number of put option writers' activity.

7 Buying put options for protection against lower prices

(Source: CBOT)

7.1 Example:

It is May, the crop has just been planted, and the farmer is concerned that between now and October there may be a sharp decline in prices. The farmer would like to have protection against lower prices without giving up the opportunity to profit if prices increase. At the present time, the November futures price is quoted at $7.50/bushel. The cash market price in the area during October is normally $0.25 under the November futures price, so the local basis is $0.25 under. Thus, if the November futures price in October is $7.50, local buyers are likely to be offering about $7.25.

Premiums for November put options with various strike prices are presently quoted as follows:

Put option strike price $	Put option premium $/bushel
7.00	0.11
7.25	0.19
7.50	0.30
7.75	0.44
8.00	0.60

Action: After considering the various options available, a decision is made to buy the at-the-money put — strike price of $7.50 — at the premium cost of $0.30/bushel.

Result: If the prices decline, and assuming the basis remains steady, the farmer will receive a minimum $6.95 total net return for the crop. That is the option strike price ($7.50) less the basis ($0.25 under) less the premium paid for the option ($0.30).

7.2 Example:

Assume the November futures price has declined to $6.50 and that local buyers are paying $6.25 (futures price less the basis of $0.25 under).

With the futures price at $6.50, the put option with a strike price of $7.50 can be sold for its intrinsic value of $1.00. Deducting the $0.30 paid for the option gives a net gain of $0.70. That, added to the total cash market price of $6.25, gives a total net return of $6.95.

If prices *increase* the logical course is to allow the put option to expire, because the right to sell at $7.50 when futures prices are in excess of $7.50 is worthless. The net return will be whatever amount local buyers are paying for the crop less the premium the farmer initially paid for the option.

7.3 Example:

Assume the futures price when the farmer sells the crop has increased to $9.00, and local buyers are paying $8.75 (futures price less the basis of $0.25 under).

The farmer allows the option to expire. The net return will be $8.45 (local cash market price of $8.75 less the $0.30 option premium).

Regardless of whether prices have decreased or increased, there is an easy way to calculate the net return on the sale of the crop:

Futures price on sale of crop:

– Local basis when crop is sold

– Premium paid for option

+ Intrinsic value of option (if any)

= Net return

The following table compares the alternatives and illustrates the potential net return under several possible futures prices.

If November futures price in October is	Purchase $7.50 put for $0.30 premium	Hedge or forward contract	Do nothing
	Net return on sale of crop		
$	$	$	$
6.00	6.95	7.25	5.75
6.50	6.95	7.25	6.25
7.00	6.95	7.25	6.75
7.50	6.95	7.25	7.25
8.00	7.45	7.25	7.75
8.50	7.95	7.25	8.25
9.00	8.45	7.25	8.75

Depending on what the futures price is at the time, and assuming the October basis of $0.25 under has been correctly estimated, the second column shows the net return if the farmer were to sell his crop in October, as a result of buying the put. A minimum selling price of $6.95 for the crop would be established, and at the same time the farmer could take advantage of increases in the market price.

The third column shows the net return if, rather than buying a put in April, the farmer was to lock in a definite selling price by futures hedging or forward contracting (based on a November futures price of $7.50). In this situation, although the selling price would be locked in the farmer would be protected from the decrease in prices, but would not be able to participate in the price increase.

The fourth column shows the net return if nothing were to be done. Note that in this circumstance, while a price increase would yield a higher return than buying a put (by the amount of the option premium), there would be no protection against a price decrease.

The results in the table are shown graphically in the chart below in dollars and cents.

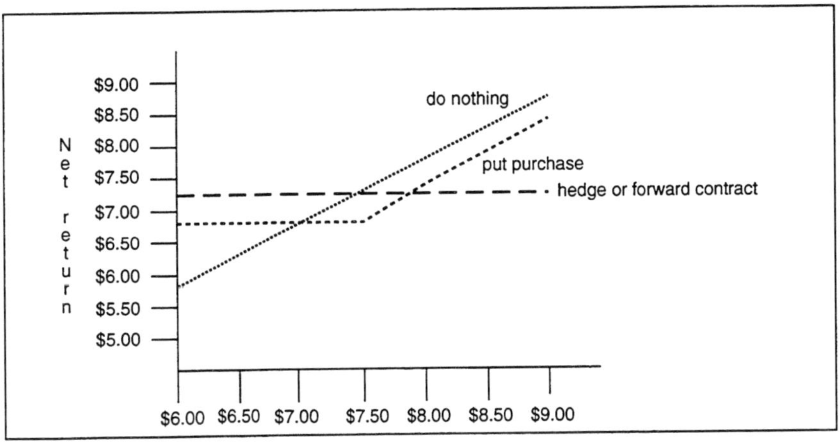

8 Buying put options for 'price insurance' when crop is stored

(Source: CBOT)

It is not harvest time, there is available storage space and the farmer would like to hold his crop until spring or summer in order to profit from an unexpected price increase. Unforeseen events — such as weakness in export demand — could result in lower, rather than higher, prices. The farmer would like to have protection against such a decline if it could be achieved without giving up the opportunity to benefit from rising prices.

The July corn futures price is presently quoted at $2.80/bushel. Based on past experience, the farmer estimates that the cash price of corn in the area during June will be $0.10/bushel below the July futures price.

The currently quoted premiums for put options with various strike prices are as follows:

Put option strike price $	Current put option premium $/bushel
3.00	0.15
2.80	0.10
2.60	0.08

Action: The first step should be to calculate how much 'price insurance' each of the various options would provide, ie, the minimum local selling price that the option ensures. This is easily computed: simply subtract the option premium and the estimated basis from the option strike price. The figures are as follows:

Assume a decision is made to purchase the out-of-the-money put with a strike

Buying a put with this strike price $	Premium $	Amount assured by option at least* $
3.00	0.15	2.75
2.80	0.10	2.60
2.60	0.08	2.42

* Assuming the local basis in June is $0.10 under.

price of $2.60 at a premium cost of $0.08/bushel. The reasoning is that the farmer is basically bullish about the price outlook and wants protection only against the possibility of a 'major' price decline. It is obvious that the less the farmer pays for the option, the higher his net effective selling price will be if, as he anticipates, the price of corn increases.

Note: In choosing which put to buy, he may want to select an option with a strike price that assures him of a return at least equal to his production cost. Or he may want to pay a higher premium for an option that guarantees production cost plus some amount of profit.

Result: Depending on the July futures price when he sells his crop in June, the table below shows what his net effective selling price would be (1) if he had purchased a put with a $2.60 strike price for a premium of $0.08, and (2) if he had not purchased the put. In both cases, it is assumed the local basis in June is $0.10.

If July futures price in June is $	Net effective with put $	Selling price without put $
2.15	2.42	2.05
2.30	2.42	2.20
2.50	2.42	2.40
2.60	2.42	2.50
2.80	2.62	2.70
2.95	2.77	2.85
3.20	3.02	3.10

Summary

Note that if prices increase between harvest and June, having bought the put will reduce the farmer's net effective selling price by only the cost of the option (in this example, $0.08/bushel). If prices have decreased, however, having bought the option will substantially increase his effective selling price. This option will have served its purpose of providing 'price insurance'.

9 Buying call options at harvest to profit from a winter/spring price increase

(Source: CBOT)

An increasingly popular practice among farmers involves 'paper farming'. Rather than place their crops in storage at harvest, they sell the crop in the local cash market and purchase futures contracts for the same number of bushels. This provides immediate cash for their crops. The money can be used to pay off loans and reduce interest expense. It also eliminates the physical risks of crop storage, while providing the opportunity, through the purchase of futures contracts, to profit from a price increase. Although a speculative strategy, buying call options could be a better alternative than the purchase of futures contracts, for two major reasons:

- buying a call involves a known and limited risk — the amount of the option premium — whereas buying futures contracts involves potentially unlimited risk and unlimited margin calls.

- whereas the buyer of a futures contract may be forced to liquidate his position (in order to avoid further loss) if there is a price decline, the buyer of a call has 'staying power'. Since his maximum loss is the option premium, he can afford to hold the option in the hope that the price decline will prove temporary and that the price will eventually increase.

Assume the farmer produces corn and it is now November and the July futures price is quoted at $2.80/bushel. The premium for July at-the-money call options (a call with a strike price of $2.80) is quoted at $0.10/bushel.

Action: The corn should be harvested and sold. For every 5,000 bushels of corn that he sells in the local cash market, he instructs his broker to purchase one July $2.80 call at a premium of $0.10/bushel.

Result: If prices decline, his maximum loss, no matter how steep the price decline, will be $0.10/bushel — the premium paid for the call.

If futures prices increase and he holds the call option until expiry and sells it, his net profit will be the amount by which the July futures price exceeds the $2.80 strike price (its intrinsic value) less the $0.10 option premium.

Depending upon what the July futures price is when the option expires in June, the accompanying table shows his profit or loss (1) if he had bought a July $2.80 call at a premium of $0.10, or (2) if he had bought a July futures contract at a price of $2.80.

	Net gain or loss if the farmer	
If July futures price in June is $	Bought call	Bought futures contract
2.15	.10 loss	.65 loss
2.40	.10 loss	.40 loss
2.60	.10 loss	.20 loss
2.80	.10 loss	No gain or loss
2.90	No gain or loss	.10 gain
3.00	.10 gain	.20 gain
3.40	.50 gain	.60 gain
3.80	.90 gain	1.00 gain

As previously mentioned, the buyer of a call achieves 'staying power' which can be very valuable. To understand why, assume that one farmer buys a call with a $2.80 strike price, and that another farmer buys a futures contract at $2.80.

Further, assume that, after several weeks, the July futures price drops sharply to $2.50. To avoid further loss if prices continue downward, the farmer who bought the futures contract liquidates his position at a $0.30 loss. The farmer who bought the call, on the other hand, knows that his maximum loss is limited to the $0.10 premium that he paid, so he continues to hold the option. Should prices eventually turn upward, he is still in a position to realise a profit.

Although producers can possibly sell their crops at harvest and buy call options to profit from a winter/spring increase, this is a strategy that is usually used by those seeking to protect themselves from this type of increase.

10 Buying call options for short-term protection against rising prices

(Source: CBOT)

Buying call options is a strategy that can have a variety of uses. For example, a processor of soyabeans may anticipate making a substantial purchase of soyabeans in the cash market over the next several weeks. On the one hand, he would like to have temporary 'insurance' against a sudden price increase. On the other hand, he would also like to be able to save money if the prices decline. Or, perhaps a livestock feeder may need to buy a large quantity of feed ingredients over the next few weeks and is worried that prices will increase before he is able to complete the purchases.

The following shows how a strategy of buying call options can be used in the short run as protection against rising prices.

10.1 Example:

For the sake of simplicity, we will assume that the processor wants protection for a period of two weeks against an increase in the cost of buying 50,000 bushels of soyabeans. This can be achieved by buying call options and then selling them when the need for protection no longer exists.

Assume it is March and that the July soyabean futures price is quoted at $7.50. The premium for an at-the-money July call — a call with a strike price of $7.50 — is currently $0.30/bushel.

Action: The first step in buying call options for short-term price protection is to determine the number of calls to buy. An allowance must be made for the fact that a given change in the futures price may not result in an equal change in the option premium. The increase or decrease in the premium could be less. Accordingly, it is necessary to purchase a larger number of options to achieve an effective hedge.

10.2 Example:
If a \$0.20 increase in the futures price can be expected to produce only a \$0.10 increase in the call option premium, it is necessary to buy two call options for every 5,000 bushels to be hedged.

Since the 50,000 bushels to be hedged represent 10 futures contracts, it is necessary to buy 20 calls. If the premium is \$0.30/bushel, that is a cost of \$1,500 per call (\$0.30 x 5,000 bushels).

Result: Assume the futures price increases from \$7.50–\$7.80 (an increase of \$0.30/bushel) before soyabeans have been purchased in the cash market.

If the call premium during this period has risen by \$0.15/bushel — from \$0.30–27\$0.45 — each of the calls will be worth \$2,250 (\$0.45 x 5,000 bushels) when the processor sells them. That is a net profit of \$750 per call. This profit, multiplied by the 20 calls purchased, equals a total net profit of \$15,000, which offsets the increase in the cash market cost of buying 50,000 bushels of soyabeans.

Consider the example of wheat. In 1990, producers 'hung on' to their stocks hoping for a price rally. When prices did actually fall, by \$1/bushel, they lost out heavily. In 1991, they did the reverse and saw prices at harvest rise by nearly \$2. For the 1992 crop year, some marketing experts for wheat in the US Midwest said that the right strategy, as of mid-year, was to sell at harvests, because basis levels were strong, but to retain ownership by purchasing call options in order to capture expected price rallies before the end of the year. This strategy, as an example of how to use the agricultural option markets, has two objectives. Firstly, the producer sells cash grain at beneficial basis levels and, secondly, the call option provides the possibility of benefiting from future price rises. Factors such as the size of stocks and the expected volatility of the cash price determines the expected cost of such operations. The alternative strategy would be to buy futures, which allows for full participation in a price rally but would expose the producer to downside risk. Clearly if market conditions were the reverse with low basis then a put option would be desirable.

Another option for wheat producers is what is known as a Minimum Price Contract (MPC). These are effectively OTC options granted by the elevator owners. MPCs guarantee a specified base price when the wheat, or other commodity, is sold, whilst still allowing the producer to take advantage of price increases. Frequently, the MPC involves selling the commodity at harvest and writing the contract then. For a fixed cost, the producer has a set time during which he can participate in a market rally as if the wheat were still owned — the cost, a one-off fee to the elevator, will include the option premium, any brokerage commission paid by the elevator and his service charge. MPCs, as distinct from exchange-traded options, do not respond in time value in the same way. With an MPC, the producer only gains if the futures price moves above the strike price of the MPC. In other words an MPC has zero time value.

The existence of a continuous market means that options initially bought can be quickly sold, and options initially sold can be quickly liquidated by an offsetting purchase. This provides the opportunity to rapidly respond to changing circumstances or objectives.

For example, if a farmer paid $0.014/pound for a soyabean oil put option with a strike price of $0.23, and after several months the underlying futures price declines to $0.18, the put now has an intrinsic value of $0.05. By selling the option at this price, the farmer can assure a net return of $0.036/pound at the time the oil is sold regardless of what happens to the price in the meantime ($0.05 is the intrinsic value of the put option minus the $0.014 premium). This could be an attractive strategy if, at $0.18, the price decline has run its course and prices are likely to rise.

11 Options in combination with hedging or forward contracting

As the farmer increases his understanding of options, he may well discover potentially worthwhile ways to use puts and calls in combination with hedging or forward contracting, either simultaneously or at different times.

For instance, assume a local buyer offers what the farmer considers an especially attractive price for delivery of his crop at harvest. As a result, he would sign a forward contract. But he would also like to benefit if prices at harvest turn out to be substantially higher. This can be accomplished by buying a call. Buying the call has the effect of reducing his downside protection by the amount of the premium while allowing him to fully profit from any price increase greater than the cost of the call.

12 Short hedging using puts and calls

Puts and calls also can be used in combination, without hedging or forward contracting, in order to establish a floor and ceiling price to hedge a long cash market position. To establish a short hedge, one must buy a put and, at the same time, sell a call.

For example, suppose December corn futures are at $2.71/bushel. A combination position can be established by buying a $2.70 put at $0.21 and selling a $3.10 call at $0.12. The total cost for this combination is $0.09 ($0.21 – $0.12). Since the farmer is selling a call, he will be required to post margin. By executing this position he has set a floor of $2.61 ($2.70 – $0.09) and a ceiling of $3.01 ($3.10 – $0.09) assuming a zero basis.

How can the floor and ceiling remain in tact in the face of volatile markets? Suppose the futures price increases to $3.40/bushel. The person who bought the call from the farmer could exercise it. Now, with a short futures position at $3.10/bushel, the farmer could deliver and collect $3.10. Remember, the position was placed at a $0.09 debit, making the net profit $3.01. However, prices could have gone the other way to $2.50/bushel. In this case the farmer would exercise the $2.70 put and again subtract the $0.09 debit, for a net price of $2.61.

A long hedge using option combinations also can be established by buying a call and, at the same time, selling a put. For example, suppose May corn futures are at $2.80/bushel. A combination can be established by buying a $2.70 call at $0.16 and selling a $2.50 put at $0.07. The total cost for this combination is $0.09 ($0.16 – $0.07). Since the farmer is selling a put, he will be required to post margin. By executing this position, he has set a floor of $2.59 ($2.50 + $0.09) and a ceiling of $2.79 ($2.70 + $0.09), assuming a zero basis.

13 Covering production risk

If the farmer has experienced a short crop in past years when under a forward contract agreement, he may be interested to know that one way to cover production risk is to buy a call option. For example, suppose a producer has entered into a forward contract to deliver 10,000 bushels of corn at $2.60 in November. He simultaneously buys two December $2.60 corn calls at $0.15/bushel. A floor price for the crop has been established at $2.45.

Suppose it was a long, dry, hot summer and production fell short of expectations. The call option could be used to replace the forward contract commitment. The call could be exercised, and once assigned a long position remain there to receive delivery. The delivered grain could be used against the forward contract agreement.

14 Futures vs options

A summary of key differences between futures and options on futures is as follows:

	Futures	Options on futures
Risk on purchase	Unlimited risk on long and short positions	Defined and limited of puts and calls
Price protection	Establishes a 'lock in' price	Establishes floor or ceiling price
Margin calls	Possible on both long and short positions	No margin calls on purchase of puts
Hedging strategies	Limited hedging strategies	Multiple hedging strategies

The premium the buyer of an option pays for the rights conveyed by the option represents the most he can lose on the option transaction. On the other hand, trading futures contracts involves potentially unlimited risk if the futures market moves against his position. Whereas the person with a futures position may be forced to liquidate his position in order to avoid further losses, the holder of an option has 'staying power' — since his maximum loss is the premium already paid, he can afford to continue holding the option in the hope that the futures price may eventually move in his favour. Hence the second major difference between futures and options.

When futures prices do move against a futures position, the holder of that position is subject to unlimited margin calls until he closes his position. There is no margin requirement for the buyer of an option; the premium that he pays is the most he will ever have to deposit with his broker, even in the face of adverse futures prices. Note that if the option holder subsequently exercises his option and assumes a futures position, he will be required to put up initial margin for that futures position in accordance with the rules of the exchange.

Another fundamental distinction between futures and options is how they are used for hedging purposes. While futures permit hedgers to 'lock in' a specific price, options allow them to set a particular floor or ceiling price. Since a hedger assumes a futures position opposite to his cash position, he effectively offsets any cash market loss and profit. However, by taking a long put position, a hedger can establish a floor price and by taking a long call position, a hedger can establish a ceiling price — and still retain the ability to participate in favourable price movement.

The matching of different options with different strike prices and maturity dates gives tremendous flexibility in tailoring a hedging strategy to match a particular objective at a given time.

15 Writing call options to achieve a higher effective selling price for a crop that is stored

(Source: CBOT)

Prior to the start of trading in options, farmers storing their crops at harvest had two options open to them. They could:

- speculate on a price increase (which left them vulnerable to a price decrease);
- hedge in futures or forward contract (which eliminated the opportunity to profit from a price increase).

Options provide additional alternatives. One such alternative, as already explained and illustrated, is the opportunity to buy put options (which provide protection against lower prices without giving up the opportunity to benefit from a price increase). Another alternative is to write (sell) call options. Writing call options can be an effective marketing strategy if it is anticipated that the futures price will remain relatively stable.

A written call option indicates a neutral or bear market bias. The gains on a short call are limited to the proceeds of the sale. If the market goes up, the writer of a call option can incur unlimited losses. An in-the-money call is more bearish than an out-of-the-money call.

Since a short in-the-money call is more bearish than a short out-of-the-money call, it is less flexible in terms of coverage if the price of the underlying instrument rises. The out-of-the-money, on the other hand, provides more slack on the upside. This difference in coverage is reflected in the premiums of the short calls, where the in-the-money call is greater than the out-of-the-money call. With the in-the-money call premium, the writer is at a higher risk of being exercised than with the out-of-the-money call premium.

If the prices are expected to remain essentially unchanged, the strategy could be to write an at-the-money call.

This is how a strategy of writing call options would work. The farmer produces soyabeans and it is now November and the July futures price is quoted at $7.50/bushel. Premiums currently quoted for call options with various strike prices are as follows:

Call option strike price $	Call option premium $/bushel
7.25	0.43
7.50	0.30
7.75	0.20
8.00	0.13

The farmer estimates that the basis in his area in June is likely to be $0.20 under (ie, the local cash price will be $0.20/bushel below the July futures price).

Action: Before taking any action, the first step is to calculate the net return per bushel that each of the various options provides, depending on the level of the July futures price when the option expires in June.

If the futures price at expiry is above the call option strike price:

- the call option holder will exercise the call option.
- the net return will be the call strike price less the basis plus the premium.

Net return if

If futures price at expiration	Write call with strike price of (1)				Hedge or contract (2) at $7.50	Buy put with $7.50 strike price (3) at a premium of $0.30	Do nothing (4)
is:	7.25	7.50	7.75	8.00			
	premiums						
	.43	**.30**	**.20**	**.13**			
6.50	6.73	6.60	6.50	6.43	7.30	7.00	6.30
7.00	7.23	7.10	7.00	6.93	7.30	7.00	8.80
7.50	**7.48**	7.60	7.50	7.43	7.30	7.00	7.30
8.00	**7.48**	**7.60**	**7.75**	7.93	7.30	7.50	7.80
8.50	**7.48**	**7.60**	**7.75**	**7.93**	7.30	8.00	8.30

(1) Emboldened figures indicate the option will be exercised by the option holder. Net return will be the strike price less the basis ($0.20) plus the premium.

The remaining figures indicates the option holder will not exercise the option. Net return will be the futures price less the basis ($0.20) plus the premium.

(2) Taking a basis of $0.20 under into account, the net return will be $7.30, regardless of the futures price at expriaton.

(3) Net return is the futures price less the basis ($0.20) less the premium ($0.30 premium assumed) plus the intrinsic value of the option at expiration (if any).

(4) Net return is the futures price at expiration less the basis of $0.20 under.

If the futures price at expiry is below the call option strike price:

- the call option holder will allow the call option to expire.
- the net return will be the futures price less the basis plus the premium.

To compare the arithmetic of the various options (options with different strike prices and different premiums) as well as other marketing alternatives, it is useful to prepare a table similar to that on page 129.

'16 Write a call' — exactly what happens?

The answer to this question depends on what happens to the underlying futures price. If the underlying futures price at expiry is below the option strike price, nothing happens. The option holder will allow the option to expire worthless, the crop will be sold in the local cash market for whatever it will bring, and the broker will be instructed to write his client a cheque for the option premium. The net return is thus increased by the amount of the premium.

16.1 Example:
A farmer has written a call option with a strike price of \$7.50 at a premium of \$0.30, and at expiry the futures price is \$7.00. Assuming a \$0.20 basis, the farmer can sell his crop to a local buyer for \$6.80. Adding the premium to the cash price increases his net return to \$7.10. The option thus added \$0.30 to the effective selling price of the crop.

If the underlying futures price at expiry is above the call option strike price, the option holder will exercise his option and the farmer will be assigned a short futures position at the option strike price. By simultaneously selling his crop in the cash market and having his broker liquidate the short futures position (by buying an offsetting futures contract), the farmer's net return will be equal to the option strike price plus the premium (less the local basis).

16.2 Example:
The farmer has written a call option with a strike price of \$7.50 at a premium of \$0.30 and at expiry the futures price is \$8.00. The option will be exercised and the farmer will require a short futures position at the strike price of \$7.50. This position will have a built-in loss of \$0.50 (because the futures price is \$8.00).

The next step would be for the farmer to sell his crop to a local buyer (if the basis is \$0.20 under, he will get \$7.80), and instruct his broker to liquidate the short futures position. The net return will be \$7.60, computed as follows:

$7.50 strike price

– 0.20 basis

+0.30 option premium

= $7.60 net return

It should be kept in mind that at the time the farmer wrote the call option, the futures price was $7.50. Assuming a basis of $0.20 under, the local cash price is equivalent to $7.30. As writing the option provided a net return of $7.60, it can be said that writing the option enabled the farmer to add $0.30 to the net effective selling price of the crop. Granted he would have made more money ($7.80 against $7.60) if he had done nothing, but doing nothing would have given him no protection against lower prices.

Note: writing options is a much more complicated and risky strategy than buying them, because the writer will be obliged to perform if the option is exercised. This type of strategy should only be used by producers completely familiar with this market and with a full understanding of the risks involved.

Which strategy?

To grant options, the company or fund must have a definite objective in doing so and the necessary resources to support the plan until the option expires. Option granters run all the unpredictable risks associated with commodity markets, and do not know whether — or at what time in the case of tradable options exercisable at any time before expiry — or when the option will be exercised. Funds and companies can protect their positions as option granters by holding the physical commodity or a long futures position. But the granter of a call option, for example, runs the risk that the value of the cover he has may fall below the original cost of the commodity, less the premium he has received for writing the option. This is the risk taken by the granter. Moreover, even if the long futures position is then reversed, producing a naked option, the producer is at risk should the market turn around and the value rise to above the strike price.

Selling options, some exchanges point out, is similar to running a naked futures position. The writer is responsible for margin calls and has unlimited risk. Profit potential, unlike futures, is limited to the amount of margin received. So the advisability of writing options depends on expectations — as with all derivative positions. For example, if the producer expects the market to remain flat or even decline after harvest and then rally early the following year, then writing a call whilst holding the commodity makes sense. If the analysis is correct then the commodity owner gains the premium and is able to sell the commodity at a higher price next season. The cost of storage and interest must be included and the risk is of course that the market will increase before next season with the result that the loss on the options position will outweigh the gain in the price of the cash grain. The rally will be missed and the final price will be lower than the harvest price because of the storage, interest and commission costs. The same problems exist in reverse for expectations about market falls.

There are a number of situations in which granting options is a more likely trading strategy than simply entering a market to write naked options. For example, when a trading company holds a stock of pearls for which there is no immediate outlet and whose value needs to be hedged. One alternative is simply to sell on the futures market; another might be to sell a call option. If the option is declared, the position is the same as that on the futures hedge but a premium has been received: if not, then the premium offsets the loss in value of the stock. Another case where writing options is a plausible strategy is against a long position in a futures market or with a call option already bought. This does eliminate the guaranteed profit from selling against the original position but it does give the investor a potentially higher price if the option is called or the premium is abandoned. Finally, selling options can be considered as a form of speculation. For example call options can be sold at the current strike price if the granter believes that the market will fall, or vice versa: but this is precisely the risky strategy that prudent investors will avoid. The potential loss will be reduced by the size of the premium. If the options are declared then the granter can cover his loss by buying or selling a futures contract. If the option is abandoned, the granter's profit is restricted to the premium.

In practice, the fundamental conditions of the market determine what hedging strategy is appropriate for any given situation in the physical market.

Other hedging strategies

It is also worth noting that the complexity of most companies' exposure and the sophistication of available products makes it extremely unlikely that the extent of their commodity price risk management strategy would be confined solely to exchange-traded futures and options. For many agricultural producers though with a single exposure (or even a clutch of exposures) to agricultural products the closest they need get to such a strategy is a relationship with a futures broker which amounts to little more than a mutual evaluation of when and how many futures or options contracts to sell or buy. Production and trading companies, by contrast, face complex exposures.

Consider the pearl trading company, Oyster Corporation. It buy pearls from a series of suppliers. It buys both round and oval pearls internationally on a variety of terms and it sells pearls internationally. Oyster Corporation's raw material costs, in common with the majority of such companies, amount to some 30% of its total costs. In fact, it buys approximately $50m of pearls annually. In the long term, any price increases can be passed on to pearl purchasers, but in the recession the particular risk is that substitute products, synthetics for example, could destroy traditionally inelastic demand curves (ie, unresponsiveness of purchased volume to price). Moreover, Oyster Corporation would like to agree to sell pearls to US retail outlets, but the US retail outlets demand constant price forward agreements. The hedging objective is to enable long-term sales agreements to be reached, to guarantee a maximum price for the raw material and to enable sales prices to be maintained in the event of sudden price increases in pearls.

Oyster Corporation's solution is to approach its bankers, and get them to construct an index of pearl prices in dollars for the structure of raw material demand required. The next stage could be to purchase, for example, a pearl price collar. With this structure, Oyster Corporation would receive payments from the bank if the average price offer at the specified time was above the agreed level, and pays the bank if it falls below a certain level — a payment offset by the lower cash payments Oyster Corporation would have to pay for the pearls. The effect of the strategy was to guarantee both a maximum and minimum raw material cost for the volume of purchases covered by the collar. In the short term, specific price agreements might be reached with the bank to cut uncertainty even further.

Exactly analogous principles could be constructed for Pearl Fisher Inc., a pearl production company. Here the company's price risk would clearly be on the downside, and the strategy employed would be to guarantee a range of output (sales) prices. Clearly, the financial intermediaries concerned try to rely on informational uncertainties — the fact that Pearl Fisher and Oyster Corporation do not know or trust one another — and different risk/reward profiles to promote their own business. In a world entirely full of stable forward contracts there would be no need for OTC commodity hedging products because the forward transactions themselves would fulfil that role.

Commodity swaps

Although 'swaps' in currencies and interest rates have existed since the early 1970s, equivalent swap contracts have been traded on commodities only since the latter part of the 1980s. In essence, a 'swap' is an exchange of obligation, typically referring to that between a fixed price and that of a variable nature. They were adapted from financial swaps, but found immediate acceptance in commodity based transactions in view of the traditionally high level of commodity price volatility. Indeed, the average price volatility over time of several commodities can be double or more that of financial products. This inevitably introduces an element of risk for both producers and consumers of commodities which needs to be reduced, if not eliminated. Futures markets provide a partial solution, but have limitations: limited time horizons, standard contract terms and limited variety. So, an alternative and additional hedging medium was welcome.

Swaps, therefore, are hedging arrangements, used to minimise risk, but differ from traditional futures contracts in that no delivery is made. They are also serial contracts in that an 'exchange' takes place at variable intervals dependent upon the prevailing price throughout the life of the swap. For example, an exchange may take place each month on a specified date for, perhaps, six consecutive months. The exchange is in effect a settlement based upon the difference of a 'fixed' price agreed at the time of contracting and the variable or 'floating' price either when exchange is due to take place or an average of the floating prices for the period concerned. But, in either case the exchange does not involve the total amount of the contract. What it does represent is the difference in price of the fixed and floating components multiplied by the nominal quantity of the commodity in question. The contract is thus settled in cash and involves no physical movement of the underlying commodity. The swap can, therefore, be considered to be a mechanism purely to 'fix' the price of a commodity over an agreed period of time.

Concurrent with the swap are the separate spot or physical commodity transactions which continue to perform the distribution function. The swap, meanwhile, offsets price volatility. For, in effect, buyers continue to procure physical produce from sellers in the 'spot' market at the prevailing price, but either pay or receive cash settlements which equate to and compensate for short-term movements through the swap, but with perhaps entirely different counterparts. For instance, the buyer of the swap, normally a consumer, would continue to procure supplies 'spot' and should the price be above the price fixed, he would receive, separately from his swap counterpart, the difference in price relating to the quantity concerned. Conversely, should the 'spot' price be below that of the fixed element of the swap, he would pay the difference to the swap counterpart. Accordingly, the profit on the swap offsets a loss on the spot market, while a loss on the swap offsets any benefit received from buying spot. In this way the price is assured at the level of the swap fix for the duration of the swap agreement.

The benefit to the producer offering a fixed price for the swap is the assurance of profitability of production over time. He needs only, therefore, to contend with supply variances only. Consumers in the meantime are able to secure a fixed price, which in so doing eliminates price volatility risk. *Ipso facto*, suppliers lock in receipts over time while simultaneously assuring themselves an acceptable profit margin. Consumers lock in payment flows and can build, into budgets and cost analyses actual costs for certain raw materials over a specified period of time.

Key participants in the swaps markets are companies such as J P Morgan, Crédit Lyonnais Rouse and Mitsubishi. In London there is also increasing participation in the metals and softs markets from such companies as Eurobrokers and Intercapital. In metals, the market's development has exceeded the ability of ISDA to impose a standardised market agreement. Metals dealers, in particular, are concerned to avoid the impact of the default clauses which under conditions of restricted liquidity could hamper the development of the market. In the metals markets competition already exists, but there are as yet few substantial deals in the soft commodity markets.

Using commodity swaps

A commodity swap arranged with a major bank allows a producer to hedge its production sales price. The producer specifies the reference quotation, the settlement periods, the duration of the contract, the quantity per period, also the preferred currency in which to deal, and any other particular aspects of the contract. The bank takes on the price risk that the producer wishes to avoid. So, for example, suppose that the producer wants to hedge 1000kg of pearls per month of next year's production. A fixed price of $1000/kg is agreed between the producer and the bank. The reference could be a pearl futures contract, or a spot market quotation, with an unequivocal reference written into the swap contract to a price for pearls agreed by both parties. The floating price is either the spot price or the nearby of the futures contract (or the second nearby after the first position enters the delivery month). Usually, as noted, it is the average of daily settlement prices that is taken as the floating price.

Types of swaps

Double-up swap

A double-up swap is a contract between two counterparties to exchange during a given maturity with a given periodicity, a pre-determined fixed price against a floating price for each period, calculated on a variable quantity of the commodity. For each period one counterparty has the right, but not the obligation, to double the volume on which the swap is based. Against this right, the other counterparty, the producer, will receive a more advantageous fixed price. The usual periodicity is one month (three or six months are possible). Maturities can be from a few months to several years. Floating prices are calculated for each period by averaging the daily prices for the nearby future contract of the commodity. Prices are usually expressed in cents per pound or can be converted in $ per tonne. Cash payments are made by netting the floating and the fixed price; there is no physical exchange of the commodity.

A double-up commodity swap allows a producer to hedge the price of its production at a price above the prevailing market level. The best way to clarify the mechanism of a double-up is to take a simple example from the frozen orange juice market.

A client is looking to hedge 1000 tonnes per month of its 1993 production. The solution could be a double-up swap with the following characteristics:

Period:	January–December 1993
Volume:	2,204,600 pounds (1000 tonnes) per month
Fixed price:	165 cents per pound (market level for ordinary swap 155 cents)
Reference:	FCOJ (frozen concentrated orange juice) future contract listed on the NYCE
Floating price:	Daily average computed monthly of the nearby FCOJ contract, or second nearby contract when first contract is in delivery month

Mechanism

From January 1993, at the end of each month, the fixed price (here 165 cents) must be compared with the average of the daily settlement prices of the nearby contract of the NYCE. For the month of January 1993, the average of the daily settlement prices of the March contract must be computed. If this average is less than the fixed price the client is paid the difference between the two prices for the volume concerned. If the average settles at 1.4935, for example, the issuing financial intermediary pays the client (1.65 – 1.5935) x 2,204,600 = US$124,559.90.

If the average is above the fixed price the opposite occurs, but for a double volume. For example, if the average settles at 170, the client will pay the financial intermediary US$220,460. In February and for the other months, the same procedure is repeated.

Collars

A collar is a contract between two counterparties to exchange, during a given maturity with a given periodicity, the difference between the floating price if above the upper limit of the collar or below the lower limit of the collar for each period, calculated on a defined quantity of the commodity. The usual periodicity is one month (three or six months are possible). Maturities can be from a few months to a couple of years. Quantity can accommodate most needs. Floating prices are calculated for each period by averaging the daily prices for the nearby commodity contract where it exists. Prices are usually expressed in what is usual for the commodity. Cash payments are made by netting the floating and the fixed price. There is no physical exchange of the commodity.

Example

A commodity collar will allow a producer to hedge the price of its production within a pre-defined price range. The best way to clarify the mechanism of a collar is to take the following simple example.

A client looks to hedge 1000 tonnes per month of its 1993 production. The solution could be a collar with the following characteristics:

Period:	January–December 1993
Volume:	2,204,600 pounds (1000 tonnes) per month
Upper fixed price:	170 cents per pound
Lower fixed price:	145 cents per pound
Reference:	FCOJ future contract listed on the NYCE
Floating price:	Daily average computed monthly of the nearby FCOJ contract, or second nearby contract when first contract is in delivery month

From January 1993, at the end of each month, the average of the daily settlement prices of the nearby contract of the NYCE is compared with the upper and lower fixed prices. For the month of January 1993, the average of the daily settlement prices of the March contract is calculated.

If this average is less than the lower fixed price, the producer is paid the difference between the two prices for the volume concerned. For example, if the average settles at 139.35, the producer is paid (1.45 – 1.3935) x 2,204,600 = US$124,559.90.

If the average is above the upper fixed price, for example 175, the producer will pay the issuing financial intermediary (1.75 – 1.70) x 2,204,600 = US$110,230.

If the average is between 145 and 170, no payment will be made. In February and for the other months, the same procedure is repeated.

Caps and floors

The buyer of a cap (floor) gets the right, during a given maturity with a given periodicity, against the payment of a premium, to receive the difference between a floating price for each period and a pre-determined fixed price when this floating price is above (below) the fixed price, for a defined quantity of the commodity. In effect, this is a series of call options. The usual periodicity is one month (three or six months are possible). Maturities can be from a few months to some years. Quantity can accommodate most needs. Floating prices are calculated for each period by averaging the daily prices for the nearby futures contract. Prices are usually expressed in what is usual for the commodity. Cash payments are made by netting the floating and the fixed price. There is no physical exchange of the commodity.

Mechanism

A commodity floor will allow a producer to hedge the price of its production. The best way to clarify the mechanism of a floor is to take a simple example:

A producer is looking to hedge 1000 tonnes per month of his 1993 production. The solution would be a floor with the following characteristics:

Period:	January–December 1993
Volume:	2,204,600 pounds (1000 tonnes) per month
Strike price:	155 cents per pound
Premium:	3.45 cents per pound
Reference:	FCOJ future contract listed on the NYCE
Floating price:	Daily average computed monthly of the nearby FCOJ contract, or second nearby contract when first contract is in delivery month

Immediately after the transaction, the producer pays the financial intermediary the premium amount which in this example is 0.0345 x 2,204,600 x 12 = US$912,704.40.

From January 1993, at the end of each month, the fixed price (here 155 cents) is compared with the average of the daily settlement prices of the nearby contract of the NYCE. For the month of January 1993, the average of the daily settlement prices of the March contract is calculated.

If this average is less than the fixed price, the producer is paid the difference between the two prices for the volume concerned. For example, if the average settles at 149.35, the producer is paid (1.55 – 1.4935) x 2,204,600 = US$124,559.90.

If the average is above the fixed price, no payment will be made by the producer. In February and for the other months, the same procedure is repeated.

Price protection through OTC options

The purchasing company specifies a reference quotation, the duration of the contract, the settlement periods and the quantity per period, the preferred currency, which is usually dollars, and the ceiling price. Another supplying company specifies the premium that it intends to charge for the guarantee that the purchasing company will have to pay no more than the ceiling price. The principal advantage to the purchasing company is that it retains all the benefits of a price fall; the advantage to the supplying company is that it benefits from receiving the premium in addition to the sales revenue.

So, for example, suppose a purchasing company wanted to protect its exposure to fuel oil prices for the whole of a year, whilst retaining the opportunity to benefit from falling prices. Such a course of action is frequently sought when the estimation of future price developments is '80-1/20-2' — an 80% chance of a fall by one and a 20% chance of a rise by two. With this analysis, which will determine if replicated in the treasury of the supplying company, the price of the OTC option it is clear that the OTC option is attractive for the purchasing company. With the same reference quotation and the same amount to be covered of 20,000 tonne, and with a maximum that the purchasing company wants to have to pay for its oil monthly is $100, the supplying company enters into a contract with the purchasing company for a fixed premium of $10/tonne. The purchasing company pays the supplying company $10 x 20,000 x 12 = $2,400,000.

If the mean Platts NWE Cargoes for one month is $90, the purchasing company receives all the benefit of the lower fuel oil prices. If the Platts quotation selected is, for example, $110, then the supplying company would pay the purchasing company $110 – $100 = $10 x 20,000 = $200,000. If the contract were for physical delivery, a customer might pay Platts + $5 each month for its product up to a maximum of $105/tonne. So whatever happens to prices, the purchasing company pays only $105/tonne maximum.

A number of more complicated types of option are available, combining different types of assets and strategies.

Better of two assets options

An option paying out on the better performing of two underlying instruments, eg, an option that pays out the better performing of two stock markets.

Chooser options

A chooser option offers purchasers the choice after a predetermined period between a put and a call. The pay-outs are similar to those of a straddle but chooser options are cheaper because the purchaser must choose before expiry whether he wants the pay-outs of a put or a call. They can be a useful tool for a fund manager who anticipates that forthcoming information will be an important determinant of changes in a market but does not know the direction those changes will take.

Debt-equity swap

Debt-equity swaps are often used by heavily indebted countries. Instead of being paid interest or principal, creditors are given equity in such a country's companies. They are also used for company refinancing and are largely inapplicable to commodity markets.

Difference options

These are options that pay the price difference between two assets. The strike price provides the initial reference point for valuing the option. Buyers' profit or loss will depend on how the current price differential between the two assets compares with the differential when the option was launched. Such an option would be useful, for example, if an investor thought that the performance of different indices will differentiate.

Conclusion

It is important to conclude this chapter with some caveats. Some companies, including agricultural producers with relatively straightforward price risks, insist that they do not wish to hedge the price of their primary output. Once convinced of the merits of price hedging, however, they carry it out too enthusiastically. This type of 'Texas hedge' actually increases rather than diminishes risk. Inadequate attention to production costs and therefore to minimum required sales costs, causing losses to be made by settling for too low prices, is another typical mistake. A third type of mistake with futures positions is to buy and sell too frequently in order to avoid margin calls. A further mistake is to pull off hedges as soon as the situation is attractive, only having to return to the market, thereby incurring extra costs as soon as it becomes unattractive again. Another mistake is to value liquidity above all else, failing to pay the necessary premium, for example, for an OTC contract which would be much more suitable. Indeed, the failure to accept premium payments as a legitimate form of insurance is one of the main factors preventing the growth of the options market. A final mistake is to hedge an input but not an output when they are closely related. All these are symptoms of a failure to approach the risk management issue as an integrated whole: to identify all the risks (and which cancel each other out), all the available strategies, and then to implement them all consistently and together. In an international recession of the magnitude seen in the 1990s, the tremendous ensuing benefits of stable profits are almost certain to be prized by investors, managers, and bankers alike.

Chapter 6: Managed funds and derivatives

Apart from hedging existing portfolios, the next most important use of derivative products for fund managers is as part of a planned investment strategy. Managed futures have seen dramatic growth; the doubling of funds under management to $20bn in 1990, and the rise to $25bn in 1991, was partly due to an estimated $6bn flowing in from European and Japanese financial institutions. Before 1990, investment in managed futures was mainly confined to the US, but the increased internationalisation of managed futures investors suggests that fund managers now take it very seriously as a method of investment. Managed futures are gaining regulatory ground worldwide. In May 1992 the Commodity Futures Trading Commission (CFTC) granted its approval to implement average pricing procedures. This allows single average prices to be received on orders that are so large that they may need to be executed at multiple prices. This is also in accordance with the raising of position limits and the relaxation of its closure requirements for investors with over $2m in securities and $200,000 in initial margin.

The most important recent development however was the relaxation, in May 1992, of the rules governing managed futures investment in Japan. Trading in Japan — especially for overseas investors — was previously limited by high deposit rates, and scepticism of the single price session system in operation. Funds totalling Y300bn have already been invested in a series of funds organised by local partnerships, leasing companies and foreign experts. Hong Kong is following, and Taiwan, Malaysia and Thailand will join Australia in making the Far East the centre for managed futures investment. It is indeed conceivable that in the long run — just as happened with the service industries servicing Asian manufacturing — Asian funds will demand that the futures industry that services them repatriates its profits to Asian countries and not to the US or Europe. The establishment of Asian futures exchanges and collaboration projects with western exchanges is likely to be the first evidence of this trend. Managed futures business for the SFE, for example, increased by 100% in 1992.

With funds under management of $25bn, managed futures when compared with conventional fund management (including the use of all derivative markets) may appear insubstantial. When gearing is taken into consideration however — using futures exchange initial margins as a guide to its extent — exposure is well in excess of $500bn. Managed futures funds need liquid contracts. Their future development will require greater transparency and efficiency for OTC products as well. At that point it can be expected that managed futures will themselves invest in OTC and swap funds specifically created to profit from the efficiency of the departments of the banks concerned in managing, for example, energy transactions. It must be noted however that the majority of effort for managed futures goes into financial futures and not commodities. It is likely that the considerable liquidity difference between most financial contracts and their commodity counterparts will be self-perpetuating, and that this disparity of effort, both in terms of investment and analysis, will continue.

Portfolio theory, pioneered by Markowitz showed that by increasing the number of stocks held in a portfolio from one to four, portfolio risk, as measured by the standard deviation of average return, was reduced by 69%. These theories have been further advanced by experts in managed futures who argue that the inclusion of an allocation of managed futures within a diversified portfolio, alongside equities and bonds, increases market return for a reduced level of risk. Managed futures performance does not depend on a constantly rising market for capital appreciation. This is a use of the ability to short derivative markets and to alter positions cheaply. Managed futures also enhance portfolio diversification. This is particularly evident during periods of great market uncertainty, when advantage can be taken of all market fluctuations — with over 100 distinct futures contracts traded worldwide (under half of these contracts being commodity contracts).

The marketers of funds usually act only as intermediaries sourcing investments from retail investors and institutions. The trading managers design the investment programme, commonly structured as publicly quoted investment funds; offshore private placements; or pooled accounts for individual retail investors. It is also the managers' role to select and appoint trading advisers to the programme. The trading managers, having established a programme, will continue to monitor the trading advisers' on-going performance and ensure that the fund remains true to its original investment policy. The trading adviser, known in the US as a commodity trading adviser (CTA), advises on the particular investments in the futures markets with the aim of returning, through his investment skills, the maximum return possible, given the trading parameters dictated to him by the trading managers.

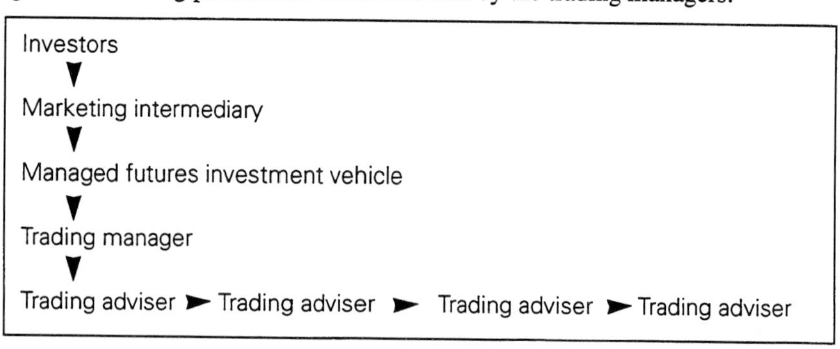

Selecting the right investment

It is difficult, perhaps even impossible, to discuss a universal method of selecting the right managed futures investment, as each investor naturally has different investment criteria. Successful futures fund management is a specialist technique requiring a highly active and disciplined approach. Trading managers and advisers must be fully aware of how futures markets operate. Experience is the key element in judging potential rewards and inherent risks. It is crucial therefore to identify the best trading manager before selecting a suitable investment vehicle.

Many other factors need to be carefully assessed. The four key areas to consider are, whether the fund is:

- diversified by market, to expose the investment to the markets available worldwide? Is it diversified by trading method and by trading application?

- managed by specialists, who have proven performance over different trading cycles?

- properly administered and controlled, including daily monitoring of the advisers' performance over different trading cycles?

- subject to rigorous money management rules, whereby strict trading guidelines, gearing ratios and draw-down limits are set and adhered to?

It is also important before making an investment to:

- Understand the fee structure and, particularly, the commission charge in relation to the trading activity, the level of management and performance fees and whether there are entry or redemption charges.

- Make the right product choice. For example, the investor can select a multi-adviser product, covering all the commodity and financial futures markets, or at the other extreme, select an individual adviser who specialises in specific markets.

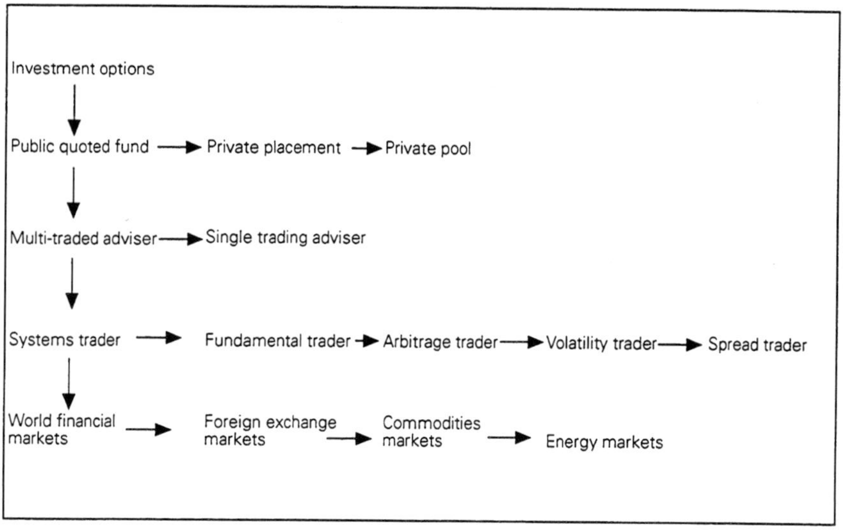

The managed futures industry is developing quickly, and with it the percentage of open positions in commodity futures markets held by managed futures increasing. In Europe, for example, the use of derivatives is now permitted by practically all European countries. The EC is currently being lobbied to give an EC passport for even geared futures and options funds that can be expected as a corollary of 1992 integration. The UK now has legislation in place to permit the establishment of unit trust futures and options funds. However, most of these funds are being injected into financial, not commodity, derivatives. The benefits for investors are clear and because of the perceived reduced risk, there is broader credibility than straight futures investment. Most financial institutions, including many of the top 100 universal banks, are investing in managed futures. Other holders of institutional funds, such as pension funds, have also begun to invest, as have several major multi-national corporations. Managed futures will increase their share of the investment market in the 1990s. They are making steady advances on the regulatory front too. The CFTC is currently considering relaxing the stringent disclosure and reporting requirements for futures funds.

Fund managers

All fund managers hold a stock of assets, the return from which they seek to maximise subject to whatever legal, political, administrative, tax, accounting, management risk or other constraint may be imposed on the portfolio. The return of an asset, stock or portfolio, can be calculated from the value of the portfolio over time:

rate of return over (t – t1) = value at time t – value at (t – 1)/ value at (t – 1)

The return of a portfolio comprising a number of different assets is the average individual return, multiplied by the relative initial capitalisation of each element of the portfolio — which itself changes according to the period chosen, because the ratio between the capitalisation of the different assets (in the absence of any draw-down) changes with the value of the different assets, and fund managers are concerned about the future return of the portfolio. In order to calculate this, future price changes, the date of receipt of returns, and risk, must all be taken into account.

Asset risk is the possibility that asset returns may not be constant. Conventionally, this is divided into two elements:

- market risk — systematic, non-diversifiable risk caused by the existence of the market itself;
- specific risk resulting from characteristics of the assets themselves, which is amenable to diversification.

In practice, the distinction is far from clear. The boundaries between market and specific risk are not absolute. The more diversified the asset stock, the less specific risk the fund manager will be taking. There is a decreasing return to scale on asset diversification. Increasingly the old discipline of the need to diversify between discrete asset classes — for example between property and commodities — has become outmoded as markets interlink both internationally and between commodities. In particular in the recession of the early 1990s it has been strategically incorrect and, therefore, difficult to find any sector that is consistently outperforming others. Mathematically, this distinction is measured by the beta factor which measures how sensitive a particular asset is to changes in the market (ie ß = covariance of asset return with market return/market return variation) and if it is less than one, the asset fluctuates less than the market and *vice versa*. The problem, of course, is the question of how wide the definition of 'the market' is to be.

Every fund manager selects and maintains their asset portfolio in terms of a combination of risk and reward factors, for example, to maximise return subject to a given risk level, or demand a certain rate of return and seek to minimise risk. Full diversification gives the fund manager a rate of return exactly equivalent to the market (ie, a ß of one). In order to optimise the risk/return ratio however, 'dynamic portfolio management' is necessary, this necessitates constant alterations in the balance of assets within the portfolio. During periods of rapid market increase, high ß stocks tend to be preferred, and *vice versa*. As with all dynamic hedging, such a strategy entails high transaction costs, and the problem of liquidity which may be encountered in respect of some assets. Obviously, it may prove a great deal easier to enter desired markets than to exit undesirable ones, producing a permanent skew in the attractiveness of the strategy.

Individual or institutional investors — if they have an opinion about the direction of commodity prices or inflation — are therefore well placed to use derivative markets. The sole aim of the investor as speculator is to profit from correct judgements. Speculators/investors can take open ('naked') positions in the futures markets, either for long periods or overnight. Bearish speculators can use the high gearing provided by futures contracts to generate high profits: but open positions also carry the risk of equally high losses. Initial margins — which are themselves calculated precisely on the average risk of trading — can be less than 10% of the overall value of the contract. An initial deposit of 10% produced gearing of 10, which means that a 10% fall in prices destroys the entire investment, and a 10% rise doubles it. If the position is liquidated within one day, the trade is called a 'scalp'; there would be no margin payments payable because no overnight position is held. Profitable scalp trading depends on the trader's skill in anticipation, and the ability to execute orders sufficiently quickly and effectively throughout the day to create profits.

Taking futures market positions is a route to high risk exposure, so fund managers have developed certain more sophisticated methods. For example, much differential trading is done. This is exactly the same as spread trading by speculators. The fund manager uses the same contract but not necessarily in order to benefit from a change in the differential between them. The majority of users of this trading strategy are not risk managers at all, but speculators. Differential trading is often used in soft commodity markets, especially those with physical delivery where some market participants may have reasonable cause to believe that deliverable quality of the commodity might suddenly become scarce, or abundant. Clearly the main advantage of this strategy is its risk neutrality in respect of overall price level change. Consider the example of a trader who wishes to take advantage of a belief that the October/December spread in the pearl index futures market is too narrow. He buys October and sells December. Suppose he buys October at 100 and sells December at 120. In one month of the two legs of the switch (or straddle) being on, the differential widens: October stays unchanged but December falls to 115. He then sells October and buys back December at a profit of five. If he had believed the differential was to widen, the opposite strategy would have been adopted: sell October and buy December. Either way, if both October and December had risen or fallen by the same amount, the profit from one leg of the switch would have exactly counterbalanced the loss on the other, so the trader is protected from overall price movement.

The basic differential trading strategies are as follows:

Market Situation	Expectation	Strategy
Discount October/December	Narrow	Buy October/Sell December
Discount October/December	Widen	Sell October/Buy December
Premium October/December	Narrow	Sell October/Buy December
Premium October/December	Widen	Buy October/Sell December

The same approach is taken to trading the differential between two different futures contracts, for example between wheat and rice, or between gasoil and crude, or between cotton and cotton yarn, based on information about the historical differential between them and also expectations of future changes. A familiar spread trade is between New York and London cocoa or between NYMEX heating oil and IPE gasoil. In each case the exact equivalencies will depend on currency conversion, usually between one contract in dollars and another in local currency, as well as matching the contract specifications and the implications of them. Often a differential between two apparently similar contracts can be explained by the implications of, for example, allowable delivery ports. So although reduced initial margins are usually available for differential trading because of the reduced overall risk, this concession does not usually apply to inter-contract trading.

Spread trading involves less risk because it involves the simultaneous sale and purchase of two commodities, or two months of the same commodity. The trader takes a view on the relative price movement. A straddle can be either bullish or bearish. If the futures market is seen as being at a premium to the spot market, the trader can sell the near month and buy the far month, expecting the near month to decline faster than the far month. Conversely, a bullish or long straddle occurs when the spread trader buys the near month and sells the far month, expecting that the near month will rise, because it is currently at a considerable discount to the physical market.

By extension, differential trading can be and is used by risk managers as an approach to trading where the company is involved in both the physical and futures markets. In a premium market, a widening differential suggests the selling of futures and the buying of physicals, for example. Physical traders are therefore able to make profits out of their hedging operations, by trading the differential/basis between physical and futures prices. Such a basis may be unattractive to the hedger in the first instance and so the relatively more risky practice of separating out the legs of the hedge must be undertaken. Another approach is known as the purchase or sell on call. A physical market participant, say a pearl trading company, has bought in pearls at $100/kg in January, intending to sell them on in June. The company's risk clearly is that pearl prices will fall between January and June. Currently the futures market is saying that the price in June will be $110. Suppose that the potential buyer of the pearls believes that the price will fall from $110. The pearl company offers the buyer a deal of June futures (or any futures month, even one after delivery) minus $5. The company also offers the buyer the right to choose a time at which the pearl company's short position is closed out, in order to minimise the buyer's costs. Suppose that the price falls to $95, and the buyer decides to close out the futures position of the pearl company and take delivery.

Physicals	Futures
S 110	B 100
B 95	S 90
+ 15	–10
Net Profit: $5	

The buyer has bought the pearls cheaply and the pearl company has locked in its basis profit of $5. Clearly this is a method of distinguishing and isolating the physical supply mechanism from pricing itself, and helps trading companies in their relationships with their bankers enormously.

The opposite is equally feasible. Buyers can hedge through a decision of their preferred basis and finding sellers to fix the price by selling futures for the buyer's account at the agreed differential. This may be done exclusively through the brokers of the counterparties, when it is known as a 'give-up', passing the futures trade from the buyer to the seller's broker in this case. The two positions of buy and sell on call can be combined, for example by a trading company which is accustomed to buying and selling pearls in the marketplace. The company sees in January, for example, that the market is trading at a discount with the physicals cheaper than the futures. The trading company buys pearls at June–5, price fixing at the seller's discretion. The trading company then finds a buyer at June–3 with the buyer given the opportunity to choose the date of closing out. The trading company has locked in the basis ($2/kg in this example, whatever happens to prices. A numerical example may make this clearer:

Physicals	Futures	
S 105	B 100	Basis –5
B 94	S 91	Basis –3
Profit: 11	Loss 9	Basis –2 = net profit

Clearly had prices fallen the trader would have made the same amount of profit, but through the futures rather than the physical trades.

Traders may use the possibility of basis trading to avoid some of the problems associated with trading illiquid commodities with highly specific and technical specifications. They may agree to use the basis of a liquid futures contract of the nearest specification to their own traded commodity and trade that rather than using a forward contract based on the relatively illiquid market of their own commodity.

Since the 1980s attitudes in government especially in the UK, but also in the US and to a lesser extent throughout the world, have changed towards the discouragement of private and especially small-scale private investment in futures markets. Many brokers find small accounts unprofitable, and certainly a large number of commission houses simply decline approaches from private individuals, directing them instead towards managed futures. The tough regulatory measures now governing the marketing of futures to private investors are often cited as the bureaucratic impediment to more involvement by private individuals. In the UK some individuals are able to become local members of exchanges by putting up capital — they are called independents in the US.

By proprietary traders who are looking for an improvement to their investment yield through capturing price changes and/or volatility in options.

By arbitrageurs, seeking to trade the spread between different futures and options contracts. For example, traders might seek to arbitrage the GSCI against its 18 different constituent commodities, according to the precise, detailed shares of the index that each contract represents. The arbitrage equation for this contract is

$$X = (WPA/NC) \times 250 \times N / CS$$

where x = number of underlying futures contracts to offset GSCI contracts;
WPA is the world production average;
NC is the normalising constant (5,123.065 at present);
250 is the size of the contract multiplier;
N the number of GSCI futures positions to be arbitraged;
CS the contract size of the underlying futures contract.

For every 100 GSI contracts, rounded even to two decimal places, for example 21.99 live cattle contracts are required, and a total of 213.81 commodity futures contracts. It is unlikely that any traders attempt, or will attempt, to hedge precisely against the GSCI. What is much more plausible is that the GSCI can be used to hedge out a general movement in commodity prices, allowing the investor to take advantage of a specific contention about the relative change in commodity prices.

By commodity trading advisers and other commodity pool operators in the US, who profit from price movement or who wish to establish fully diversified commodity exposure with one trading decision. By extension, any index represents a good profit hedge for commodity firms generally, who do very much tend to make money when commodity prices generally are rising and volatile. A spread hedge and some options on the GSCI, depending on the exact rate of increase/volatility: profit equation would lock in profits.

By pension fund managers and other institutional investors who want a portfolio exposure to liquid real assets to diversify away from stocks and bonds, and who again want to make a single investment decision to do so, as opposed to managing a series of different commodity derivative trading operations.

Commodity index futures attract investors wishing to adjust the ß coefficient of their portfolio without operating in spot markets, where there are often high transaction costs and liquidity problems. Using an index, investors are able to set the ß level of the portfolio to correspond to expected market evolution. For example, an investor can sell contracts in proportion to the ß and value of his portfolio in order to receive a return exactly opposite to the return on his spot asset portfolio. The value of the portfolio will effectively have been frozen and the ß of the asset portfolio and the index future taken together will be approximately zero. Clearly the period over which the hedge is to occur and the costs of transactions and margins add to the complexities of evening out ß correlations between an asset portfolio and the futures index.

It is also arguably easier to anticipate the general direction of commodity futures markets than of an individual futures contract. Such anticipation can also relate to inter-month spreads, or the relationship between the GSCI and a specific market that the trader is following.

Portfolio managers with a stock of commodity assets, whether in futures or physicals, can hedge their stock through a single decision, with a range of correlations depending on the exact breakdown of the stock.

By investing in commodities, portfolio managers are obtaining access to 'real assets' within their portfolio, whether they do so through the GSCI index or through the futures contracts directly. Investment in property is another example of a real asset investment. These investments balance within a portfolio the financial assets of bonds and financial derivatives such as interest rate options.

Portfolio diversification is a common requirement for asset managers and they have sought in the past to use a range of derivative contracts to enable them to do so. Why commodities? Available evidence shows that the GSCI index is negatively correlated to the S&P 500 and US government bonds (over the period 1970–91, –.32 and –.18 respectively, rising to –.4 and –.44 between 1986–91). For example, the GSCI rose in late 1990 through the same period that the S&P 500 suffered a serious fall.

An extension of the principles of commodity-linked financing and OTC products providing a stream of payments, however structured, based on the value of an asset, is that fund managers are able to create synthetic commodity portfolios and to place and remove hedges on a variety of physical and equity assets. This is especially important for fund managers seeking diversity of returns. Notably, for example, physical or paper oil has been a good hedge for stock and bond prices and inflation. This is logical — high oil prices deflate expectations but contribute to inflation. In energy and metals markets, the tendency to backwardation has resulted in investment institutions being able to take advantage of both the diversification implicit in owning energy assets — without any of the difficulties inherent in owning the physical assets — and simultaneously getting the benefit of the backwardation. This is especially significant for investment institutions with particular restrictions on the type of investments they can undertake. More sophisticated versions of the same strategy allow investors to benefit in part from both commodity and financial changes, for example, combinations of interest rate and oil price changes (and volatilities), or exchange rate and natural gas prices. Energy-linked notes of this type are a more direct entry into the energy market than equity purchases, and they can be varied to resemble fixed-interest bonds, equities or any other form of investment. The benefits are the administrative efficiency and price participation, plus probable tax benefits and customisation — to include collars, charge levels and volumes. There is, of course, a certain credit risk, and the set-up costs may be high relative to the straight purchase of assets.

Risk management and commodity-linked hedging products

It has been strongly argued that derivative instruments themselves, especially when used in conjunction with computer programme trading, create market price volatility. Most notably, it has been argued, the October 1987 Stock Market crash demonstrated the interaction between spot and futures markets so far as stocks and stock indices were concerned. Since then there has been agreement between the CME and the New York Stock Exchange to take coordinated steps should wide variations occur in the Dow Jones or the S&P 500. Similar steps have been taken in other countries. There has been a wide variety of studies made of the impact of derivative instruments on traded prices, most of them posting conflicting results. There is little evidence, anyway, to suggest that those commodities with active futures markets have less volatile prices than those without; nor, equally importantly, is there any evidence to suppose that the particular types of commodities with active futures markets are less or more volatile than other types without them: US versus world cotton, or world white versus US rough rice. Hodges (1990) summarises the issues well:

> If a number of large institutions act simultaneously in a similar way, albeit unconsciously, we can expect to see big price changes. When these occur, should we blame the computers or analysts that trigger the trades, should we blame the derivatives that they choose to trade in, should we blame the inadequacies of the markets in which they trade, or should we blame the structure of financial holdings that puts so much money under the control of so few hands?

(Do Derivative Instruments Increase Market Volatility, FORC, University of Warwick, November 1990)

Options and funds

Options have been traded on the LME since the Exchange began in 1877, and are now traded on most exchanges worldwide. There was some business during the inter-war years, but it was only when prices began to demonstrate much greater volatilities during the 1970s that options trading became more prominent.

Fund involvement in options is admittedly limited, with a small fraction of available monies from derivatives funds being placed in them. Most traders suggest that this is likely to continue at least until the year 2000, unless the tax treatment of options in any way is made different from that of futures in major markets — which is very unlikely. The relatively low use of options by fund managers is not because options are inherently of no use to fund managers, but there are two central problems perceived by them. Firstly, stop loss positions are thought to be a cheaper way of achieving the same objectives, and secondly, liquidity in many options contracts is by no means as substantial as it could be to the satisfaction of fund managers. The cost of using options was the main reason that brought the clampdown on options trading in the late 1970s — trading was banned altogether in the US from June 1978 until 1981. This was caused by the practice of reselling options, purchased on exchanges, to the general public at exaggerated prices. In addition, margining systems were not properly established for different option contracts.

Those funds that participate in options markets prefer trading options. Before the 1980s, the only options available were simple options. In the case of the LME these had prompt dates rather than months. Premiums were priced according to time value only. The granters of such options were always completely uncovered until the delivery date, and the buyers could never recover any premium. These have been superseded by traded options, where prompt dates and strike prices are limited, thereby concentrating liquidity and enabling tighter quotes to be made. Traded options therefore give funds the ability, at least in theory, to cover any option risk during the life of the contract — but only to the depth of liquidity that is available from the market-maker.

Option market-makers are sometimes criticised as responsible for this lack of liquidity, which is especially unfair since they are in many cases the only people standing between the exchange and a blank screen filled by Black-Scholes estimates rather then real quotes. Paul Shuman of Mees Pierson ICS, one of the key users of options on the LME, points out that 'market-making is a business in itself and should not be approached by those who are not willing or able to devote the necessary time or resources to the task'. The main difficulty in establishing the necessary liquidity in the traded options markets is the problem of determining volatilities accurately with only historical volatilities as evidence. Added to this complexity is the fact that almost all futures markets, especially in commodities, do not trade 24 hours, seven days a week and it is often difficult for options market-makers to take account of bid-offer spreads in the futures market. One made criticism frequently made of options during the 1980s is that they are used to creating 'artificial' tightness in markets by accumulating sizeable options positions for specific prompt dates. Options traders insist that this is unlikely, in practice, to occur. The very lack of liquidity in options contracts makes it so. Another criticism that has been made is that call options with a strike price above the current market price can be declared, in order that those who have sold those options are forced to take cover. To achieve such a move, though theoretically possible, would require a tremendous and risky investment. Companies selling options at any strike price run the risk that the option will be declared, and this may certainly be unexpected. Another criticism brought against options markets in commodities is that the size of open positions is not widely known and that this may have an affect on futures prices around the prompt date. Professional options traders do use the futures markets to protect themselves against the risk of an option being exercised, and if sufficient companies thus operate the market price can be affected: however, options business only accounts for a very small percentage of total business — about 7% on the LME, for example. The percentage has risen from about 5% in the late 1980s but the rise is very gentle. Moreover only a small percentage of the total options business is actually hedged on futures market and it is also possible to discover factual information about the size of open options positions; exchanges have the power *in extremis* to bring any untoward situations to a point of acting upon them. In addition, options traders point out that squeezes on derivatives markets occur because of material shortages. Call options do get bought to cover risk — but had these options not existed or been available at attractive prices, traders would have bought the physical commodity, thereby creating a greater squeeze than with options, because actual shorts in the market have a greater risk attached than option shorts until declaration. Expert option traders believe that options can be used to reduce wild swings in futures markets. Physical traders can use options to hedge, or trade products which combine risk limit and profit potential.

It is certainly true that options trading is resilient to the lack of liquidity and constant attempts at regulation. Some companies such as Rudolf Wolff on the LME have operated options programmes for their clients for over a decade, and as a results is responsible for a large part of total options turnover, but these client are rarely funds — more likely specific market hedgers. This is despite the fact that because options are priced in terms of their premium and that the premium is payable immediately upon having bought the option, profits and losses can be quantified on a cash basis irrespective of the prompt date of the option. Option market-makers are committed to market-making in all of their quoted options at all times when the LME is open for futures and options trading. Although software to manage options exposure is available, options contracts worldwide have not achieved the volumes predicted a decade ago.

Options traders themselves do not see funds using options as a replacement for futures trading but as an adjunct, as part of a sophisticated investment strategy. There are times when options are not desirable instruments — for example, when premiums are low by comparison to how the market is expected to move or has recently moved, it would be ill-advised to sell a call or put. Conversely, when premiums have reached an historical high in relation to historical volatility, purchasing options is not to be recommended. They all want the market to broaden, with an increase in the number of players and consequently narrower bid offer spreads. It is the usual problem: the market-makers from the brokers are looking for investors, but the investing institutions want to make markets themselves, to maximise profits if they use the market at all. In London, fund managers in derivatives are relatively reluctant to discuss the use of options in any depth, as they believe that the disadvantages generally outweigh the benefits.

Chapter 7: Commodity-linked financing

The problem

Companies need to borrow and lend money for their operations and the cost of these operations will depend on the cost of borrowing money. The cost of borrowing the money however, will depend on the interest rate applicable from the lending institution according to the terms of the agreement (either varying with respect to national interest rates, or a fixed rate, or perhaps some combination of the two using caps, collars etc). Whichever approach is taken, it is extremely unlikely that variations in the interest rate are going to correspond with the cash flow experienced by the company concerned. Numerous factors influence a company's ability to service its debt. Ideally a company would like to borrow money that would be repayable according to its own cash flow potential. A company selling pearls would like to pay out more on its borrowings when it can afford to do so ie, when pearl prices are high and demand is plentiful, and correspondingly face reduced borrowing costs when demand and prices fall.

The cash flow of some companies critically depends on the price it has to pay, or will receive, for a single commodity or a group of commodities. These companies' returns depend on high levels of risk that ensure that investors require a premium before they are prepared to invest and which indeed cause the companies' borrowing costs to be increased by risk-averse bankers. The form in which the finance is raised is almost irrelevant whether through equity, debt, or some form of bond or project-related finance; the outcome, in terms of increased cost for the associated risk, will always be there. The very volatility of commodity prices means that companies face oscillations in income, with static costs, considerably greater than the variations in interest rates on their borrowings, and certainly not timed to coincide with them. For companies that do not need to borrow substantial amounts, this is not as serious a problem. For any company however, intending to make an impact in the world of the commodity concerned, significant borrowings are almost certainly inevitable.

The unfortunate effect of this is that the success of the company, and certainly the path described by its profits, become dependent to a greater extent on the relationship between borrowing costs and the price of the commodity to buy and sell, rather than the efficiency of the company's operation itself. Companies actively attempting to provide derivative products to serve as a means of overcoming these problems have repeatedly stated that treasury departments in these companies seem more concerned with the exact costings of plans rather than the long-term prices to be obtained from the operations and deposits themselves. This results in those long-term capital projects — planned either on no assumptions at all about future commodity prices, or on some straight-line assumption that, of course, fails to transpire — being disrupted when prices fall dramatically. Staff numbers are often cut and postponements made throughout the company. Stop-go becomes the order of the day. The rate of return on the project therefore becomes lower than it needs to be. Companies that are dependent on commodity prices therefore have a poor reputation.

The problem, therefore, is the oscillation of commodity prices compared to financial obligations in specific currencies. The logical solution to this problem — given that derivative products can be used to lock in prices for almost any commodity over any reasonable period (the rarer the commodity and the less liquid the associated futures market, the more expensive the hedge) — must be to lock in input (and output, where possible) prices to avoid dependence on market volatility. Then it makes greater sense to concentrate on achieving low costs and efficient operations, in the knowledge that borrowing costs have been structured around the price of the commodity, ensuring a stable cash flow, especially over the period when the project is starting up and is crucially dependent on a profit margin. In most of the cases studied by the companies providing this type of commodity finance, the locking in of prices is more of a determinant of company profit than any efficiency gains. Companies, however — especially those run by people experienced in commodities — are often reluctant to take steps that lock in asset values and thereby build margins of great appeal to both the banker and the investor. They prefer to run risks rather than operate companies with steady, guaranteed profits and low risk portfolios. Evidence from the past decade suggests that financial investments have proved more lucrative than investments in major industries such as oil, so this approach is certainly flawed.

Product marketing and finance

Two questions arise from the previous section. Firstly, why does this happen? Secondly what products are available and how are they currently marketed?

The first reason is that company executives regard pearls, gold, or even oil as 'their business'. Business development officers in exchanges are familiar with the refrain, 'we're in the business of mining gold/selling tea/investing in property and we don't want to stop ourselves making profits when the market looks up/recovers/breaks out from the 50 cents mark'. The only answer to this problem is to educate the companies and bring the Treasury derivative experts into closer contact with the production and sales staff. The marketing executive needs to continually demonstrate, with the assistance of worked examples, why it always makes more sense to lock in prices. The problem, according to such executives, is that having spent days working on the company in question to establish the legitimacy of the case, the company will then seek other competitive quotes. A possible solution may be to get structured finance recognised as a division of the planned Futures Industry Association (FIA) in the UK and similar organisations elsewhere. The benefits of such operations, as well as hedging through the direct use of the markets, can be explained generically to potential users through education programmes funded by the industry rather than by individual companies.

Some institutions, such as commodity funds, are much more frank in their intention to directly expose the investor to movements in commodity prices. Such organisations in providing, either explicitly or implicitly, a return to their shareholders always emphasise that they will lock in margins for commodity purchases only when they deem it sensible to do so. The investor does indeed invest in the commodity price, depending on the company's degree of exposure, and the way in which the market discounts future changes in the commodity price in the share price. Some funds and companies suggest that when the portfolio of shares and commodities, to which the investor is exposed, is quite wide then such exposure actually offsets the reduction in the value of other investments that will be affected by inflation. Using commodities as an inflation hedge, however, is not entirely sensible; it is rather crude, with correlations that are unimpressive at the best of times.

The message for large companies is quite clear: share prices closely follow the returns obtained on their major commodity operations. For example, RTZ's profit since 1982 has been largely dependent on the international copper price — although the company itself mines a wide variety of minerals. Closer investigation would most likely reveal that there is in fact a particular combination of mineral prices that would reflect the profitability of the company even more closely. The earnings of companies such as RTZ demonstrate substantial volatility, which in turn reflects the commodity prices as major determinants. The company's expertise therefore, in large-scale buying coupled with the ability to lock in margins, would be highly likely to improve rates of return and thus provide a more stable profit level so improving the attractiveness of the company to investors. Logically the principal responsibility of company managers is to get the best return on assets — to sell the commodity at the highest price whilst paying as little as possible for it. A company that operates without proper structured finance and hedging is, in effect, gambling on the commodity markets.

Consider the following simple example. A company sets out to establish a pearl fishing operation and borrows $100,000 over two years from Bank Z to finance the project. The pearls are valued at $100 each. The company expects in its initial business plan to use 1000 pearls (out of a total production of 3000 expected over two years) to repay the capital monies borrowed. With interest rates fixed at 10%, payable on initial year balances, the total interest cost would be $10,000 plus $5,000 in year two, a total of $15,000. A total of a further 150 pearls must be incorporated into the business plan. Clearly, if the price of pearls falls dramatically, to $50 for example, the number of pearls required to pay back the loan rises from 1,150 to 2,300 — only 700 short of total production. In this dramatic example, it is quite likely that the company would go bankrupt.

With commodity-linked finance (the ability to pay for funds according to the price of commodities rather than specific currencies), Bank Z agrees, in advance, to accept a certain number of pearls in exchange for the loan. The number of pearls demanded will depend on the current futures price, or at least the bank's forecasts, for pearls, averaged over the repayment period. Clearly, the bank will be able to hedge the price of the pearls it receives instead of cash, thereby locking in the cash value of the repayment stream. If the average futures price for pearls over two years is $125, then the bank would only require 920 pearls plus its profit margin, perhaps a further 30, for the organisation of the hedge. Both the company and Bank Z benefit in stability and profits.

How are the transactions that are currently carried out organised? Some industries have historically made major efforts to hedge their future produced assets, the gold industry is a good example. The first company to make use of the gold loan was Pancontinental in 1983 to finance the development of the Paddington mine. In the past, the banks tended to integrate the asset hedge into the structure of the loan. The deals were driven, understandably, by the need for finance rather than an intention to lock in the future rate of return on assets. The hedged quantity was usually the amount of gold deliverable against the loan, adjusted for time value and the spread of the lender, rather than as part of the gold company's long-term asset management plans.

The gold loan provides both finance and a guaranteed future sale price for the company's gold. The company borrows the gold that it in turn sells to raise funds and which it repays with gold from its own production. Under these terms, the company locks in the current spot price for gold, and receives zero cost financing. The quantity of gold will be adjusted to accommodate the lender's spread. The zero cost financing is made possible by the bank's ability to sell the gold forward that it is to receive from the producer at the price above spot reflecting, in general, US dollar yields.

Although this gold commodity loan was a straightforward and convenient means of raising funds, the company was usually exposed not only to problems and variables associated with future gold prices, but also to the fact that the net present value (NPV) of the asset was affected by interest rates and currencies. It is usually more convenient to separate the provision and timing of funding from the actual output hedging process. For example, if a gold producer is prepared to take a dynamic position in the hedging of the future gold assets he will probably be able to benefit from attractive price cycles as they occur, rather than lock them in at the bank's convenience.

As an example we can take the case of the Refugio mine project in Chile. The project has a US$75m gold loan, linked to a $25m lease and purchase agreement priced at Libor +25% and a $39m equity finance shared equally by Bema Gold and CMR. It was expected to operate at a cost of $128/troy oz, producing 256,000oz/year. At gold price levels of $350/oz, the venture projected a margin of $200/oz. The total output of gold would be reduced by the repayment of gold to the bank that provided the loan. Further deductions of 8.1875% (Libor +5%) on the lease and purchase arrangement of $25m would account for a further $2.047m per year, or about $8/oz on the total output. The figures available suggest that the output of approximately one year will be repaid to the bank against the gold loan, compared to a total mine life of 9.4 years. The first gold from the mine is currently expected to be produced in 1994, two years after the conclusion of the financing.

Structured finance affords the opportunity to lock in the gold price at an appropriate time, rather than in response to temporary financing needs. These types of loans however are the basic form of commodity financing; borrow a fixed amount of dollars and repay the debt in a fixed amount of gold. The lender has obviously taken on board the risk and must therefore take the decision as to how much of the future gold supply he wishes to hedge. The futures markets provide the lender with an opportunity to do. The alternative for the gold producer is to hedge the gold supply into dollars to the extent of the loan repayment schedule, and avoid the inevitable premium that the lender will impose for the organisation of the loan. In this example if the company Treasury is equipped to run numerous hedging positions, and alert enough to ensure that hedges cancelling each other out are lifted, the net cost will almost certainly be less through direct hedging by the company concerned.

The Hydro-Quebec example

Fourteen percent of Hydro-Quebec's (HQ) 127bn kW/h annual output is linked to risk and sharing contracts. The link is based on original base prices of both electricity and aluminium. The base prices used in the example, for illustrative purposes only, are $30mW/h for electricity and $2000/tonne for aluminium. The exchange rate differences between the C$ and US$ have been assumed to be hedged away. HQ claim that reductions in expected profitability due to aluminium-linked sales contracts are running at C$300m for 1993 compared with C$200m for 1992. Without these contracts however it is not certain whether HQ would have been able to make the sales at all.

Using the base prices as indicated, with aluminium prices broadly indicative of the last two years, the September 1990–91 losses on the notional aluminium position would have been $128m by comparison to the base. The equivalent figure for 1991–92 would have been $195. These figures are broadly in line with those supplied by HQ. This would suggest that their notional aluminium position amounts to 266,000mts per annum, or 22,225mts per month. The second table shows the total change in income per month compared with the change in aluminium from the base price. This exposure is equivalent to that of a medium to large aluminium smelter.

MwH base price: 30 — Aluminium base price: 2000

Month	Actual	Indexed	Elect. price	Change price per Mw	Quantity MwH/Mnth	Change in monthly income
09/90	1773	0.8865	26.60	–3.41	1,481,667	(5,045,075)
10/90	1920	0.9600	28.80	–1.20	1,481,667	(1,778,000)
11/90	1830	0.9150	27.45	–2.55	1,481,667	(3,778,250)
01/91	1652	0.8260	24.78	–5.22	1,481,667	(7,734,300)
02/91	1574	0.7870	23.61	–6.39	1,481,667	(9,467,850)
03/91	1535	0.7675	23.03	–6.98	1,481,667	(10,334,625)
04/91	1441	0.7205	21.62	–8.38	1,481,667	(12,423,775)
05/91	1341	0.6705	20.12	–9.89	1,481,667	(14,646,275)
06/91	1313	0.6565	19.70	–10.31	1,481,667	(15,268,575)
07/91	1331	0.6655	19.97	–10.04	1,481,667	(14,868,525)
08/91	1292	0.6460	19.38	–10.62	1,481,667	(15,735,300)
					Total 1990/91	**(127,749,300)**
09/91	1250	0.6250	18.75	–11.25	1,481,667	(16,668,750)
10/91	1186	0.5930	17.79	–12.21	1,481,667	(18,091,150)
11/91	1171	0.5855	17.57	–12.43	1,481,667	(18,424,525)
12/91	1132	0.5660	16.98	–13.02	1,481,667	(19,291,300)
01/92	1194	0.5970	17.91	–12.09	1,481,667	(17,913,350)
02/92	1284	0.6420	19.26	–10.74	1,481,667	(15,913,100)
03/92	1313	0.6565	19.70	–10.31	1,481,667	(15,268,575)
04/92	1332	0.6660	19.98	–10.02	1,481,667	(14,846,300)
05/92	1333	0.6665	20.00	–10.00	1,481,667	(14,824,075)
06/92	1313	0.6565	19.70	–10.31	1,481,667	(15,268,575)
07/92	1329	0.6645	19.94	–10.07	1,481,667	(14,912,975)
08/92	1333	0.6665	20.00	–10.00	1,481,667	(14,824,075)
09/92	1313	0.6565	19.70	–10.31	1,481,667	(15,268,575)
					Total 1991/92	**(194,846,575)**

Month	Change in aluminium price	Total change income	Notinal aluminium mts short/month
09/90	227	(5,045,075)	(22,225)
10/90	80	(1,778,000)	(22,225)
11/90	170	(3,778,250)	(22,225)
01/91	348	(7,734,300)	(22,225)
02/91	426	(9,467,850)	(22,225)
03/91	465	(10,334,625)	(22,225)
04/91	559	(12,423,775)	(22,225)
05/91	659	(14,646,275)	(22,225)
06/91	687	(15,268,575)	(22,225)
07,91	669	(14,868,525)	(22,225)
08/91	708	(15,735,300)	(22,225)
09/91	750	(16,668,750)	(22,225)
10/91	814	(18,091,150)	(22,225)
11/91	829	(18,424,525)	(22,225)
12/91	868	(19,291,300)	(22,225)
01/92	806	(17,913,350)	(22,225)
02/92	716	(15,913,100)	(22,225)
03/92	687	(15,268,575)	(22,225)
04/92	668	(14,846,300)	(22,225)
05/92	667	(14,824,075)	(22,225)
06/92	687	(15,268,575)	(22,225)
07/92	671	(14,912,975)	(22,225)
08/92	667	(14,824,075)	(22,225)
09/92	687	(15,268,575)	(22,225)
			(533,400)

An electric generating company with varying cost inputs could have carried out a swap with a financial institution to eliminate the associated risk, exchanging aluminium (notionally) for a fixed cash supply or even a fixed supply of gas or oil. In addition, or as a complex alternative, HQ could have organised a series of cash/aluminium swap deals, providing them with the necessary cash to buy their inputs. Such instruments would allow HQ to enter into further contracts with their aluminium customers, assuming new base levels were entered into for both prices, and they could again swap to protect them from falling aluminium prices. The fixed swap price of the aluminium should then be used as the base price for the electricity supply contract, matching all the forward deliveries and adjusted for different weightings per period.

A deal was originated by HQ, which had a large quantity of spare energy that it was anxious to sell. HQ approached the aluminium smelters and ensured electricity sales by agreeing to receive aluminium prices instead of electricity prices. HQ did not benefit from the sale in 1991. They claimed that the shortfall on electricity sales was C$160m and that the figure rose again in 1992 as the percentage of their electricity consumed by the aluminium smelters increased again. Each tonne of aluminium produced demands between 13–14.5,000kW/h of electricity, depending on which smelter was used.

When HQ started their contract, aluminium prices were trading at between $2600–$3000/tonne. By late 1991, the price had fallen to almost $1000/tonne. HQ runs an annual aluminium position of roughly 80,000 tonnes. Naturally, the power generation company does not wish to be exposed to primary metal prices in this way. It must therefore go short the aluminium futures market itself, or at least obtain an option, in order to neutralise the effect of changes in the base metal price. This would lock in the value of the cash received from the aluminium smelters. The risk gets passed along the chain and at each point there is a financial institution picking up a profit either from taking on the risk itself or from broking a contract. The alternative strategy, as mentioned above, would be for the aluminium smelter to have accepted the risk associated with electricity prices and to have sold the aluminium forward or to have hedged the sales price on the futures markets.

Ideally, but as yet impossible in the absence of efficient cheap forward markets for electricity, the aluminium smelter would lock in the cost of the electricity by buying the electricity futures, or a call option at least, and locking in the sales price of the aluminium through forward sale agreements or by using derivative markets — provided that the margins thereby derived are satisfactory. The company can then concentrate on the real task, of improving efficiency and making its product sell.

In the HQ case, the deal was mainly motivated by the smelter's wish for cheap electricity, rather than the ability to lock in attractive sales prices for the aluminium. What has actually happened is that HQ have undertaken to sell power at what is below market cost. Any additional supplies locked in would similarly just increase their exposure to aluminium. This would of course be in their interests if aluminium prices increase, unless they hedge that advantage away. If they do not, then they run the risk that prices will in fact trade lower. If their own input costs then rise in price, their position could become extremely difficult — as 14% is a sizeable element of their total production to be unprofitable.

The aluminium smelters have locked in the sale price of part of their production, at rather unpromising levels. Financial companies recommend that firms try to deconstruct, to isolate, all the risk elements in the balance sheet. A risk element can be defined in two parts:

- firstly, it must be an input or output, or a component element or determinant of the price of one, which cannot be controlled in respect of its price by the company concerned;
- secondly, it must be a price that can be hedged.

Structured company finance groups believe that every risk that is a risk element should be neutralised and then hedged according to the particular hedging requirements of the company. There is an obvious caveat to this; clearly, there is no need to hedge offsetting risks. In general, however, it makes good sense to disaggregate such issues as commodity, currency, exchange rate and interest rate risk. The 'price' thereby agreed would reflect the most efficient hedging method and would also ensure that companies which are not in the business of a particular commodity do not, as a result of a commodity financing transaction, find themselves inadvertently in that business. Otherwise their return on capital will change in distribution from their own business to that of the inputs.

By carefully and intelligently using these financial instruments and by developing the necessary expertise companies can place a cash value on the stream of future assets that they are likely to accrue. They can lock in income in domestic, or any other, currency by using swaps. Returns for shareholders — which according to financing companies are the main objective — are thus maximised and borrowing costs should be reduced due to the increased security for the lender. It is likely that exchanges will eventually act as guarantors for this type of financing. This would improve the credit risk position which, at present, depends on the financial position of the institution offering the commodity-linked financing. Even public financing can now be linked to commodity values — evidenced by the issue in 1991 of the Finnish Export Credit $100m Eurobond linked to the movement of the GSCI.

Source: Louise Rowsell, Mitsubishi Finance International plc

Conclusion

The largest expansion of OTC transactions is due to their application as part of structured finance transactions. The purchasing company ensures that its repayment schedule is linked to the value of their principal income. Many of these transactions have been carried out for companies in developing countries where producers need development finance. The most frequently transacted base metals as the basis for these structured finance transactions are copper and aluminium but the transactions throughout the range of commodities stretches out to five years. Participants in the US do not yet have regulatory permission to operate in these markets, except for energy. Leading firms offering these services are Mitsubishi Finance, Citibank, Goldman Sachs, Banque Paribas and Bankers' Trust. The key to all such transactions is the transference of the hedging function from the producer, purchaser or inventory holder to the specialised company providing the commodity-linked financing.

Finally, it is important to note commodity trade financing. Letters of credit from banks are short-term guarantees to trading companies. Providers of letters of credit may require hedging strategies to be put in place, or they may simply enact a hedging strategy themselves and charge the client.

Chapter 8: Traders and approaches to trading

Deciding on likely price movements is central to decision making by traders, governments, hedgers and speculators on futures markets. Traders make profits by buying cheap and selling dear, and speculators will only take up a trading position — providing valuable liquidity to the market — or trading companies purchase or sell stocks of a commodity — if they have a definite view of what is going to happen to prices. Hedgers are risk averse, but they may not want to hedge substantial components of their portfolio if they believe that prices are set to rise substantially.

Commodity traders usually rely on their own and their colleagues' experience to trade their preferred commodities. They are reluctant to trade any other commodities (whether on the physical or futures markets) even when the market for their own is in decline. In all the commodity markets, an appreciation of not only the direction of price movement but both its extent and likely duration is knowledge that is at a great commercial premium.

Much trading and judging of prices is indeed experience, especially when balancing risks and rewards and deciding the precise time of entering a trade and closing it out. Apart from experience and personal contacts, there are two other basic methods used, fundamental analysis and technical trading — especially in the futures and options markets where there is an available 'track record' of prices. OTC price databases are available although only to the issuers from their own sales information. Although all futures markets follow spot prices to some extent — and where they are physical delivery markets it takes very little liquidity to create quite accurate pricing — there is a difference between markets. For example, these methods are important for cotton futures; due to the volume of transactions both the New York and the Tokyo markets are relatively liquid — price movements are reasonably reliable estimates of opinion and change. Much the same applies for cocoa, coffee, sugar, the metals and the oil and oil derivative markets traded on the exchanges. However, the CBOT rice futures market, the European naphtha forward market, physical markets in metals such as lead, zinc or palladium, and many others are usually not very liquid at all. There is therefore no one homogeneous market price.

Fundamental analysis

Fundamental analysis relates price movements to changes in supply and demand conditions and is therefore the type of price analysis with which economists are familiar. Since long-term prices always relate to supply and demand conditions, fundamental analysis is highly advisable for participants in futures markets as well as the physical market. Demand tends to vary throughout the year, but there are also longer-term considerations — such as the attractiveness of synthetic substitutes and growth in real incomes and consumer tastes — which have an impact on cotton prices. Complex econometric equations exist linking gross domestic product (GDP), consumption, and commodity prices, especially energy prices. One key problem with these models is the degree of segmentation that exists within the markets. Where does one market stop and another begin? Another problem is the impact of macroeconomic and political considerations upsetting the market.

Physical commodity markets are often illiquid and lack accurate price information. Futures markets, at least, are usually different. For each commodity and delivery period there is a price spread quoted reflecting the price as determined by all the participating players. In some cases, as a result, price quotations from the physical market when its futures counterpart is closed, are impossible to obtain. Since futures markets tend to be more liquid than their physical counterparts, they tend to react more quickly to any news relevant to the physical commodity and, despite the fact that there are day-to-day changes particular to derivatives markets (causing arbitrage opportunities) in general, the physical price is based on the true supply and demand and is not fixed by futures.

Physical commodity prices themselves react to changes in supply and demand, exhibiting a cyclical pattern of over-supply and shortage. This is caused by the substitutability of agricultural land between numerous different crops. If there is an over-supply of a crop relative to demand, the price will fall. Producers will then switch to another more profitable crop. Demand may pick up, due to the price fall, and then there will be a shortage caused by the producers' switch to another crop, The price then rises again. The producers then decide to grow more of the original crop, and the cycle repeats itself. Given the time lag between planting and harvesting, and the lag in demand reaction to price change, it is not surprising that it is impossible to achieve a sustainable balance in only one crop cycle. Non-agricultural commodities suffer these problems too. In petroleum, for example, milling, refining, spinning and other processing schedules are planned long in advance. So there can be a shortage of one product (the glycol shortage in 1988–90 is a good example). It is the case, therefore, that at most times derivative markets are in the process of adjusting to change, whether with bullish or bearish implications, and this causes a contango market with varying degrees of acuteness or, in the extreme, a backwardation in the market.

Fundamental analysis begins with the detailed examination of market fundamentals. For example, cotton traders study the supply and demand characteristics for cotton worldwide. They are familiar with drought conditions in China if they exist — such factors will affect whether China needs to import or can export. They will study monsoon times and insect pests. Their analysis is comprehensive and thorough although usually unaccompanied by any formal econometric models. Inflation and the growth in real incomes, the steady increase in world population, the relatively fixed areas available for cotton cultivation, foreign exchange reserves, currency values and other economic variables have all had their effect on long-term cotton prices. There is little doubt that fundamental analysis is a worthwhile exercise.

Official and quasi-official publications giving information on production, yields, acreage sown, trade, and forecasts of these and other statistics are vital to all commodity derivative traders. For example, in the US, energy is covered by the Weekly Petroleum Status report, published by the US Department of Energy every Wednesday. The American Petroleum Institute (ADI) issues a complementary statistical bulletin every Tuesday. Similarly the 'USDA numbers' are crucial for cotton traders. When the world cotton contract is started, the daily release of the Cotton Outlook spot price (as it will become known) will affect prices. USDA numbers are released monthly. For grains and oilseeds, crop production figures are released in the US on a monthly basis similar to the USDA, although the exact days of release differ. Crop progress reports are issued every Monday during the growing season, which is between April–December. Grain stocks information is released at the end of September, as is information on hogs and pigs. For livestock, similar information is issued at the end of July, and cattle feed and livestock slaughter data is published monthly. The Bureau of Mines of the US Department of the Interior publishes its Metal Industry Indicators and Mineral Industry Surveys monthly. So, the majority of commodities (rice and naphtha being notable exceptions) are the subject of such factual reports. The reports may be bullish, bearish, or neutral in their effect on the market. All participants who are considering entering a market for the first time need to know the frequency, timing, and usual significance of regular demand and supply news.

Sometimes, as in the case of the API figures, the release of information is timed to occur outside market hours thus ensuring that the news is properly understood before the market reacts. Of course, reports and news can reach the markets at any time. The market can turn over dramatic volume — often three times a typical day or more — in response to just one rumour. Market participants protect themselves against or to exploit the change caused by the news or rumour. In the oil markets, production problems caused by fires, storms and explosions (Piper Alpha, for example) have an immediate and dramatic impact. Trading desks, therefore, have full access to news agency screens such as Reuters. Traders develop a market oriented attitude to news — their first reaction to news of any magnitude or relevance is 'how will this affect my market?'

Demand information is more elusive and indefinable. This may involve subjective analysis of the general economic conditions that underlie demand for oil, metals and soft commodities. In general, economic growth generates a proportionately rather greater consumption growth, and the determinants of economic growth are investment, present consumption, government policy — especially with regard to taxation and expenditure, and the balance of payments. The huge errors made by dedicated economic forecasters, however, who use complex econometric models to predict demand conditions, demonstrate the extreme difficulty involved in this kind of work.

What is generally true about commodities is the equation:

$$ST(t) = S\{t/t - 1 - D\{t/t - 1 + ST(t - 1)$$

Stocks at time t are equal to stocks at the previous time point, plus production over the period less consumption over the period. No objective analyses of these 'world supply and demand balances' exist, although many are published by the USDA for agricultural commodities, and by some private companies, for example, F O Licht for coffee. Moreover, each commodity market is segmented and imperfect in its transmission of price and other information. However, such calculations, based on information currently known about the fundamentals of a market, are the basis for further analysis.

In some countries, rice and wheat are, to some extent, substitutes for one another and patterns of rice demand may sometimes be partially explained by reference to the wheat/rice price ratio. The use of fertilisers is an essential factor in production growth, and therefore in the fundamental analysis of rice prices. There are other shorter-term fundamental factors. The most noticeable is seasonality, due to the new harvests in both hemispheres that affect prices.

The US typically raises 40–50% of the world's corn, so any changes in US crop prospects can have a major impact on prices. China accounts for about 15% of global production, the European Community around 10%, the Eastern European countries which together account for 5–10%, and the CIS with nearly 5%. The growing season in the southern hemisphere is out of sync with the northern hemisphere by six months. The major players in the southern hemisphere are Brazil with about 5% of total world production, and Argentina and South Africa, each with 2–3%. In these countries, planting occurs in October and November (instead of April and May), pollination takes place during January (rather than July), and most of the harvesting is done in April (compared with October). These timing differences give the southern hemisphere far more importance in the world corn market than the production figures might suggest. For this reason, growing conditions in these countries are closely monitored by the market and can have a major impact on prices.

Informed traders also monitor conditions around the world that can affect the production of other crops that compete with corn. These include other feedgrains like barley, oats, rye, and milo (grain sorghum); tropical crops such as cassava (tapioca); and various food grains including wheat.

Since US corn accounts for such a large share of world production, US production schedules are responsible for the seasonal price patterns often observed in the corn market. Corn moisture levels are influenced by the amount of humidity in the air, so autumn weather conditions determine the rate of harvest progress. Excessive rainfall can delay harvest and cause mould, spoilage and other weather damage to standing, or unharvested corn. For this reason, dry autumn weather usually improves grain quality. In an average year, US corn prices are typically lowest following harvest, usually between October and January when supplies are largest relative to demand. Prices often remain under pressure until April or May when planting gets under way, and then move steadily higher through the July–August pollination period. At that point final crop size has been established, so prices usually turn lower until harvest, when the cycle begins again.

This sequence is generally regarded as the 'normal' course of events. Unexpected weather developments, however, either favourable or unfavourable, can quickly alter this pattern and cause wide, and potentially profitable, price swings. The direction of those price swings depends to a large degree on expectations: what actually happens compared with what the market expects will happen. For example, if the market is expecting a drought, a period of rain and cooler temperatures could send prices lower as crop prospects improve. In other words, prices often fall if growing conditions turn out to be better than expected. On the other hand, suppose there is the possibility of an early killing frost. This might cause prices to rise as growing conditions become worse than expected.

There are numerous varieties of rice with different characteristics and harvest times — November/December in the northern hemisphere and April/May in the southern hemisphere. With intermediary crops in some areas rice continually comes to market. However rice cannot be stored for a long time in view of its high degree of hydroscopy and poor storage conditions in most growing areas. The main harvest takes place in the northern hemisphere between October and January and prices are likely to follow seasonal patterns: high prior to harvest and low just following the harvest. The production and stocks in the three largest producing/consuming countries, for example China, India and Indonesia may alter the seasonal pattern. Rice consumption by livestock, for instance, is higher in the winter months when pasture is not available. To the extent that these seasonal patterns conform to market expectations, there will be no substantial market response.

For cotton, new harvests in both hemispheres affect prices. There are many dozens of types of cotton with different characteristics and harvest times — November/December in the northern hemisphere and April/May in the southern hemisphere. Consequently there are two major seasons when cotton initially comes to market, although cotton can be stored from year to year. The main harvest takes place in the northern hemisphere between October and January and prices are likely to follow seasonal patterns: high prior to harvest and low just following the harvest — not so much because of the availability of the cotton itself as the increased certainty of its availability. The production and stocks in the three largest producing/consuming countries, China, the US, India and Pakistan may alter the seasonal pattern. To the extent that these seasonal patterns conform to market expectations, there will be no substantial market response.

Traders always pay close attention to all weather factors. The amount of rain that falls during the main growing season is crucial in determining the annual crop level of almost every crop. For example, cotton growing areas, in particular in Asia, frequently experience periods of drought or floods, although this can also happen in the US. Even after the main crop is harvested, weather continues to play an important role. World weather is sufficiently disparate that congenial climatic conditions on one side of the world can be matched by equally unfavourable conditions elsewhere. Cotton traders will always pay close attention to the weather conditions in the US Delta, because this may determine the availability and quality of the next year's US crop. Part of the reason for not adopting complex econometric models is this very difficulty of incorporating climatic factors.

Annual carryover stocks are also important contributors to price levels for all commodities; they affect import demand and hence price levels. The size of stocks and their location between countries and organisations also affects price levels. The stock/consumption level plays an important role in determining prices although the absolute level of stocks is not important. The government stocks of rice held by numerous countries — but most importantly for world trade prices India, Pakistan and Brazil — have a different and more substantial effect than the smaller stocks held by private companies. The International Cotton Advisory Committee (ICAC) state that their price forecasts are based 'on the statistical relationship in the last 19 seasons between the Cotlook 'A' Index and the ratio of ending stocks to consumption.' The equation used also takes into consideration changes which are expected in, for example, government stocks of cotton held by numerous countries — but most importantly for world trade prices in China.

International organisation and national policies, especially of the US and Thai governments are major determinant of rice prices. This explains in large measure why rice traders are very concerned to be close to these governments. Government decisions can have an effect in both the short and long term. For example, the Thai government's continued export support policy has encouraged revenue for the Thai exporters, but has also had a generally lowering effect on international prices. In the short term, announcements of the World Market Price by the US Government have a substantial effect on short-term trading conditions. Many traded commodities have an extremely important national and international economic role and therefore have tremendous political significance.

Rice is an especially important commodity internationally and access to political decisions is crucial. There are several key policies which rice traders watch;

- Firstly, the US export policy — PL480, EEP and other export shipments. What does the US Government want from its rice farmers? How much rice does it want planted, and how much exported? Rice traders know that the US agroindustrial complex is so interrelated with government that what happens in Washington is every bit as important for determining rice prices as events in Arkansas or Texas on the rice farms themselves.

- Secondly, Thai Government policy — does the Thai Government intend to support their rice farmers by buying intervention stocks, and if so, to what extent? They provide assistance including fertiliser subsidies, free irrigation for producers, favourable credit terms for both producers and exporters and government-to-government deals.

- Thirdly, the EC agricultural policy and the convertible adjustable preferred stock (CAP) — does the EC intend to bring down its intervention price barrier to imports, and if so, over what time period and to what extent?

Governments may take unexpected actions that drastically affect the price of rice in the open market. Imports or exports may be restricted by means of bans and/or taxes or encouraged by means of subsidies. For example, both China and Indonesia strive to keep their crop yield secret so that other countries will not know the size of their import demand or export surplus. At the end of 1988 China surprised the world trading community when they secretly purchased a large amount of rice from various traders, out of which about 1.4m tonnes was actually delivered. By buying before the arrival of the harvest they caught most traders short and pushed prices up during the first half of 1989. In this context it is important to recall that since rice tends to trade by cargo, and prices reflect specific trades, even one deal done can move prices by several dollars per tonne.

Like rice prices, cotton prices are also susceptible to international organisation and national policies, especially of the US Government. This explains why cotton traders are concerned to be close to the US Department of Agriculture and the US Foreign Agriculture Service. US Government decisions can have an effect in both the short and long term.

Wars and the threat of war are other good examples of price determinants. The supply of a commodity can often by blocked. Such events in areas not actually critical to production, distribution or consumption can also have an effect. The implications of such tensions may be convoluted. They may be felt in a reduction in the value of the dollar, or in a change in other relative prices. This will affect commodities priced in certain currencies, such as LCE's sterling cocoa contract, or the dollar commodities such as oil and precious metals.

Domestic interest rates also affect trading strategies (and thus prices), especially those involving expensive stockholding such as cash-and-carry operations. This especially affects US agricultural markets such as grain and soya. Some speculative players forsake the relatively risky forum of derivative trading, leaving their money on deposit instead.

Such news has an often unclear impact, with equal bullish and bearish interpretations. Derivative markets can move on news that has no bearing on the physical market whatsoever. Rumours themselves do undoubtedly affect prices as well. Exchange markets, especially the actual floors, live off rumours that spread like wildfire. Many, of course, are started by the market participants themselves who are trying to benefit their own positions — starting a bullish rumour when they are long is an obvious example. Some rumours are based on uncertainty rather than fabrication but rumours that cause large price changes hurt the reputation of exchanges. It is usually impossible to locate how the rumour originated. Because rumours are usually bullish in nature, and as the market is likely to sink back in price once the truth is widely known, traders often say, 'buy the rumour, sell the fact.'

Cotton analysts and traders are sensitive to both national and international policy, too. Cotton is another important commodity internationally and again access to political decisions is crucial. Cotton traders closely watch the following:

- Chinese export policy.

- The policy of the US Government: how much cotton does it want planted, and how much exported? Traders know that the US agroindustrial complex is so interrelated with government that what happens in Washington is every bit as important for determining cotton prices as events in Arkansas or Texas on the cotton plantations themselves.

- The EC agricultural policy and the CAP — does the EC intend to bring down its intervention price barrier to imports, and if so, over what time period and to what extent?

The accuracy of information collected through the analysis of these economic and political factors is essential for the prediction of the future direction of prices and a successful trading strategy.

Short-term fundamental analysis

The problem with fundamental analysis is translating the general principle — that demand and supply conditions are the determinants of prices — into short-term trading instructions. Commodity traders are still sceptical of the statistical techniques that can be used to quantify the impact of administrative changes, but they tend to work better in predicting long-term changes. Indeed, for long term forecasting, there is no alternative to statistical methods. Long-term modelling is however no use if short-term margins — in a highly geared instrument such as futures — work against the trader; or if the specific deal the trader intends in a physical market does not work because of loading problems, quality failure on inspection, or worst of all, failure to pay.

For the short-term analysis of markets, especially those that are illiquid or segmented, it is virtually impossible to build a model that is sensitive to daily changes in supply and demand conditions. Commodity traders use econometric models, if at all, to provide background analysis of long-term trends. Given that variation margins are taken daily, traders operating on fundamental analysis stand to suffer serious cash flow losses if short-term trends move against them on the New York futures — especially if the short-term factors are peculiar to the New York market. It is clear, that in the short term, expectations change so rapidly that the construction of statistical models incorporating them for commodity prices has not been attempted. All traders are sceptical, anyway, of economic forecasting.

Technical analysis

The alternative to fundamental analysis is *technical analysis* which is based on the evaluation of prices themselves. It is used by some participants on the New York markets and is closely followed by cotton analysts in the major US cotton trading companies, though not apparently by any in the European physical cotton markets.

Individual traders employ a variety of strategies, but their tactics fall under one of three headings:

- Position trading — a position trader buys or sells based on a specific market opinion.
- Spreading — a spreader tries to take advantage of changes in the price relationship between one contract and another.
- Scalping — a scalper, in effect makes the market, trading for small gains by establishing, then quickly closing out, long (buy) or short (sell) positions.

Technical analysis is more commonly used for short-term trading and there are a large number of different systems in operation. Arguably, markets can be observed performing distinctive patterns in the evolution of their prices: the market price is revealed by the pattern of previous price movements. The price link between futures and physicals is often weak. Historical physical prices caused by fluctuating demand and supply are important, but technical analysis is concerned with the movement of futures prices in isolation. The statistical deductions arising from this sort of analysis encourage trading on the basis of mathematical probability rather than long-term fundamental changes in the demand/supply balance.

Suppose that pearl prices fall to \$140/pearl, where there is 'buying strength'. The price, unable to fall below \$140, may rise slowly, falling back later and again meeting buying strength. If this continues, technical charts will show this support level. If the price falls below \$140, it is usual that the fall will then be considerable; firstly, because as there was substantial buying done at the \$140 level, there is likely to be less at lower prices and, secondly, it is now probable that speculators will short the pearl market to take advantage of the fall, thereby intensifying the magnitude of the fall.

Technical analysts examine whatever trends can be detected in an attempt to establish what is likely to happen next. Technical analysis can also be combined with cyclical theory. Sometimes technical patterns can be constructed through the interaction of cycles in price series. Technical analysis further assumes that prices follow patterns that do not require external economic considerations. Technical traders use other data from the markets, such as trading volume, open interest, price spreads between contract months and the equivalent data from options contracts.

The key difficulty is always to establish that the patterns can be validated, which is why experienced technical traders usually put in stops at crucial price points that would invalidate their reasoning. Technical traders contend that all fundamental factors have already been incorporated into the current price of the security — for example a cotton future — and that changes are instantly discounted. The high liquidity of the cotton futures market in New York is an incentive for technical traders. It provides an incentive for speculators to become involved, and technical analysts place great store by liquidity itself as this smoothes out price distortions caused by individual orders that may be irrational. As far as the NYCE cotton market is concerned, there is little doubt that the cotton price interacts with the spot market price. New York prices respond to all three sets of stimuli:

- fundamentals impacting the physical market, what one might like to call 'quasi-fundamental' factors;
- reports, analyses and comments on the market which quickly become incorporated into short-term market psychology;
- technical factors also monitored by the NYCE.

The NYCE publishes market volume and open interest statistics on a daily basis. Although there are in theory an infinite number of potential traders in a market, in practice this data provides some evidence of why prices are evolving in the way that they are. For example, if both price and volume figures rise together, this is probably because of fresh long positions in the market, so that once volume begins to fall, price is very likely to follow suit. Again, the higher the open interest the more vulnerable a market becomes to sudden changes, especially given that because of the very high volumes involved in the market, individual contract months on the NYCE can become subject to 'squeezes' where there appears to be insufficient cotton to meet the necessary deliveries.

If a market is bearish and the speculators are, therefore, going short, the price often rises just before the market closes. Jobbers, locals and small investors, wishing to day trade to avoid carrying risk overnight, often close out their trades briefly at the close of trading so the price may rally. This often happens at the close of trading, especially on Friday afternoons, and ahead of a long holiday weekend, for similar reasons. This is known as 'short covering'.

In bullish markets, speculators will close out taking their profits by selling, causing a downturn in the price at the close of the day and at weekends. This is known as profit-taking or long liquidation.

The automatic triggering of stops by price movement can create a self-fulfilling prophecy in the market. For example, if the price moves down from \$160 to \$150, it may trigger stops at \$150, forcing the market down to \$140.

More stops are triggered at this level, in turn forcing the market lower. Day traders often try to 'hit stops', but in liquid markets it is difficult to move markets effectively in the hope of establishing such a self-fulfilling effect. When it does occur it causes a further fall. Futures markets often have their own momentum, independent of developments in spot markets. Similarly, in a rising market speculators can seek to find buying orders and trigger them.

There are a number of computer programmes available (particularly in the US), that advise traders and even execute orders according to technical factors based on historical data inputted. Futures markets do not generally, with the possible exception of some fund operations, contain computers executing orders. In the aftermath of 1987 crash, computer trading, in the sense of the automatic execution of orders, was blamed for the speed of the equity crash. The possibilities for the integration of programme trading computers with electronic trading systems are limitless. Exchange guidelines often prohibit it, but in practice PCs could be networked easily to allow it. This is a problem that will not go away and is certain to occupy the minds of international regulators in the next century.

Relative Strength Indicators (RSI) can be used to forecast markets. An RSI is a momentum oscillator that measures in index form the velocity of price movement. An RSI indicates the strength of speculative selling and buying by evaluating the strength of the price, and the velocity of movement. Even when long-term price trends are clear, short-covering or long profit-taking can be indicated and forecast by RSIs.

RSIs are calculated by dividing the average of up-closes by the average of down-closes for a given period (which is likely to be five, nine, or 14 days). For example, suppose gas oil (second delivery month) closes over nine days as follows:

Friday 140	Monday 138 - 2	Tuesday 137 - 1
Wednesday 136 - 1	Thursday 135 - 1	Friday 138 + 3
Monday 135 - 3	Tuesday 136 + 1	Wednesday 134 - 2
Thursday 133 - 1		

The total value of up-closes is four and the total value of down-closes is 11. These figures are then divided by the number of days, in this case nine. Then the up average (4/9) is divided by the down average (11/9):

4/9 divided by 11/9 = 4/11 (0.36)

So 0.36m is the relative strength (RS). To achieve the index figure, the following equation is used:

Index = 100 – 100/RS + 1

Thus, if we apply the figure of 0.36:

Index = 100 – 100/1.36 = 100 – 73.53 = 26.47

RSIs below 50 indicate an oversold situation. In this example the market is shown to be heavily oversold, and a reversal in the price trend is due. RSIs above 50 indicate an overbought situation; a figure of around 50 indicates a balanced (and often quiet) market. To update a nine-day average, the up and down averages are multiplied by eight, the next up or down figure is added to the respective figure which is divided by nine for the new averages, and then applied to the formula.

Other technical indicators are essentially ways of following trends and changes in trends. Identifying a trend can be simply a matter of looking at a bar, point or figure chart and relying on visual inspection. A more complex way is to calculate moving averages (averaging the sum of a predetermined number of daily closing prices — as a new closing price is added to the total, the first price is subtracted), which reduce the extent of variation caused by a single day's trading. These can be taken across different time periods, for example over nine or 15 days. The longer the period taken, the less distortion and the more information about rates of change of price, but also the less information of sudden change that is likely to emerge from the analysis. Similarly, momentum indicators can also be used. Chart analysis is perhaps the most commonly used method, however. Chart analysis involves graphing prices (which would otherwise be seen as a mere list of statistics) on a bar chart, where each day's highs and lows are written, with a line connecting them and a horizontal line showing the day's closing price. These charts can show the evolution of prices over time very clearly, and changes in trends — identifying support and resistance zones — are often thought to be signalled by characteristic chart patterns. One of the most famous is the 'head and shoulders' formation, in which prices over a curve, fall back, rise again above the top of the first curve to form the 'head', and then repeat to form the second shoulder. Technical analysts see this as a bearish signal. Other patterns that are looked for are 'downtrend channels'; 'double tops'; 'wedges'; 'flags'; 'triangles' and 'pennants'; 'island tops' and 'island bottoms'; and 'key reversals'. Once prices emerge from a depressed state they tend to trade in a channel, where declines towards the uptrend line are buying opportunities and stops can be placed outside the trend line; areas of price resistance or 'support' (below which the market is unlikely to fall) and 'overhead resistance' (the opposite) are especially important.

Charts are studied going back decades to establish significant trends in the market. Most traders study long-term charts on a monthly and weekly basis so they are able to spot potential longer-term price reversals before analysts looking only at daily prices. Considerable scepticism attends all these contentions, mainly from those who believe that the markets follow, albeit imperfectly, the basic fundamentals of the underlying cash market, and that the technical patterns reflect just a process of adjustment by the market to changes in outside conditions. That is not to say, however, that individual traders cannot make substantial profits out of this lack of correlation: they can.

Chart analysis provides a pointer to future trends. In a falling market, as noted above, there may be a support level. In a rising market, the price may reach a resistance level at which there is considerable selling, and should there be a breakthrough, a sharp rise will follow if it is indeed a resistance point.

Many different chart patterns have been identified; each must be interpreted in view of the particular commodity's market. A number of commercial organisations specialise in providing market participants internationally with support services — Knight-Ridder, Reuters, Telerate, for example.

Currently the largest funds in derivatives rely to a great extent on technical analysis, trading on market trends, and they do tend to make considerable profits, although they are primarily used in financial rather than commodity futures. Technical analysis is no longer dismissed by many analysts and traders. The problem technical analysts face is telling the difference between a change in price due to daily fluctuations and a change due to a trend.

The many aspects of technical analysis can be combined into a trading system used by traders and fund managers. There are many successful trading systems in existence, but they are not publicly available; the suspicion is that a measure of competent intuition is allowed to disrupt rigorous technical instructions from time to time. Comparing technical and fundamental analysis as trading tools, it is clear that fundamental analysis is very limited in advising the initiation of trades and is poor at predicting the effect of sudden shocks. Technical analysis can reveal something of market psychology, but can also generate a mass of conflicting price indications. When both technical and fundamental analysis point in the same direction, they are very likely to be correct.

Chapter 9: The regulation of futures trading

As with other financial business and market activities, futures trading is regulated by the designated authorities of the country in which the market is situated. Although nowadays the actual location of a market is no longer an easy question to answer (especially with Globex). The time may come when a single PC will be linked to several different exchanges. Apart from the difference in contract specifications and administrative procedures, one important difference that will occur when a different screen is called up is that a different set of national regulations will be in force. Trading is becoming subject to a number of different sets of rules and laws:

- those of the country in which the trader is;
- those where the trade nominally takes place (the exchange's host country);
- those of the client's country.

True internationalisation of futures and options markets is, however, hampered by language difficulties and the lack of information about foreign commodity markets. It has to be admitted that international derivative regulations are increasingly falling into line with what can be described as a central model. This central model is as follows:

Ministry of Finance

▼

Central Regulatory Authority (devolved powers from Ministry of Finance under Futures and Options Act 198X)

▼

Self-Regulatory Organisations for brokers Exchanges

▼

Confusion over OTC markets

(Currently, for example a committee of the ISDA is developing a Master Commodity Price Swap Agreement which would be of great use for bankruptcy and other legal disputes — but this is not yet promulgated).

There are naturally enormous differences between markets but the brief country-by-country analysis below demonstrates the increasing homogeneity between different national regulatory regimes.

All national regulatory authorities are constantly issuing new rules and regulations concerning issues such as compliance rules and capital adequacy. These new rules are made available to members of the self-regulatory organisations and can also be obtained by individuals on application. Individual compliance officers within broking firms are usually kept up-to-date by the regulators through mailings although it is impossible for them to know everything.

International regulation is like a club, and just as most regulatory organisations recognise each other internationally, so the individuals speak at each other's conferences and compare their budgets for size. For example, the SFE is recognised by the US regulator, the CFTC, as an exchange, although agricultural contracts are excluded. In reality, agricultural futures are far from being as international a business as financial futures anyway, and few US traders would want to use either the Australian or New Zealand wool contracts.

In practice, in almost all countries in which there are exchanges, they conduct the majority of regulations themselves, determining the day-to-day 'rules of the game' and setting down, in contract rules, the mechanisms for the settlement of disputes. There are many disputes between commodity traders, for example over the incorrect registration of trades, that are resolved through these procedures. Regulation in the more general sense of involvement by public authorities backed by law is, however, very common and extensive.

Regulators and economists argue that unregulated markets cause socially undesirable transfers of resources and thus bring themselves into disrepute; it is reasoned therefore that market regulation is cost-effective, at least in the long term. In financial markets, there are two kinds of market failure that justify intervention by elected or appointed authorities. Firstly, asymmetric information: trading companies and brokers know more about the workings of future markets and the evolution of commodity prices than members of the investing public and the public has a right to be protected from unscrupulous people posing as investment advisers. It is often felt that this danger is greater in the futures markets because the investment is highly leveraged — high profit opportunities are combined with equal opportunities for losses. Thus investors need to be protected, it is suggested by disinterested third parties, which in turn will encourage investors to participate in the markets, giving them much needed liquidity. To the extent that the economy as a whole has an interest in seeing that there are free and fair 'level playing fields' to determine prices, it is argued that regulation cannot be left to the market itself.

At the most basic level, regulators want to minimise malpractice in the market. A business of any complexity — such as a degree of internationalisation and with large sums of money involved — must necessarily be a target for various forms of crime. Futures accounts can be moved from one account to another in an attempt to avoid an audit or tax trail; clients can be cheated by being filled at worse prices than possible; and various methods such as imposing additional commission charges, 'churning' their accounts, or not passing on all the profits. Finally, the prices themselves could be manipulated for gain to create false markets that then become potentially very profitable for those in the know. Exchanges backed by legislation throughout the world, largely taking their lead from the US, have moved to eliminate abuses of this nature and have been largely successful in doing so.

Consider, for example, the movement of accounts. Clients' accounts — especially those of major companies whose actions, if known of in advance, can move the market — are kept secret by brokers. Brokers operate on a 'need-to-know' basis and branch offices often do not know the exact client involved. Traders could use such accounts to channel funds offshore to evade tax; they could illegitimately borrow money from clients' accounts to trade on their own account; or they could use accounts to launder money. The aim of regulatory agencies, through the regular inspection of accounts of broking firms, is to bring such abuses to light.

Brokers can use the market, in innumerable ways, to prevent best execution for their clients; ranging from the simple method of organising a crippling contract with high commission rates (uncommon now with consumer awareness rising, international tightness of the regulation of sales activity to private individuals increasing, and fiercer competition amongst brokers than in the 1980s) to more complicated patterns such as front-running (buying ahead of a large buy order from a client with the possible effect that the client only receives partial execution or execution at a higher price than he would otherwise have done). For the best analysis by regulators of such activity, orders are all timed producing an audit trail that a regulator can investigate. Brokers may try, however, to confuse the audit trail by trading through another broker (known as 'accommodation trading' in the US). Manipulating prices is an activity that exchanges and other regulators the world over seek to guard against. This can be achieved by triggering stop orders from clients by using house accounts, for example, or by agreements between market participants.

The real problem, which Cabinet Ministers and junior regulators alike refuse to face, is to decide where the bounds of illegality actually lie, and then to try to get international endorsement for the distinction and then to enforce it.

The second problem is that of maintaining the market (and, political critics of existing regulators would add, of developing it — for which regulators do not at present feel responsible). Financial markets lie at the centre of the economy, derivative markets are an increasingly important part of it, and chaos in these is obviously a very real economic issue. The 1987 crash is a good example. Objectives can prove to be conflicting though. For example, there is little doubt that brokers and traders swap contracts with one another under gentlemen's agreements to ensure that neither party loses money (called 'wash trading' in the US). Some may do this to cheat clients; or they may do it to get a market going in its first few months; or they may do it to ensure that on a particular day their company meets capital adequacy requirements. When should such activity, if at all, be illegal? And how should a regulatory agency go about establishing what happened? What criteria should the regulatory agencies be using in the first place?

Another excellent example of a type of trade that confuses the regulators is crossing, or self-trading. This type of trade involves the broker or trading house taking both sides of a transaction and passing it through the exchange in order to benefit from the clearing process. The broker takes the opposite side to a client's order. Some exchanges on introduction from their regulators specifically ban this type of trading; other are uncertain about it. (In the US it is called 'bucketing'). Arguably the client gets an excellent complete fill, so there is no regulatory issue to be faced, but it may be — when the client specifies a certain price rather than an at market order — that the broker can take advantage of a better position in the market to clear out his own position and take a risk free profit, using another market participant who by definition would have given his client a better fill.

Very importantly, financial regulation tends to be self-justifying, self-accelerating (for example in the alarming tendency of regulators to employ consultants) and stifling of the very initiatives that protect the system itself. Futures markets have been banned at various times — index contracts in particular were banned in the US until 1983, and in Japan (from 1868 until after World War II) and Germany (until 1986). Regulatory agencies have also taken steps to ban particular activities on markets, such as market-making, which runs the risk of stifling the market. In truth there is an equal danger if regulations are not enforced, or are too lax: this provides an environment where fraud can flourish and the public loses confidence in market institutions.

What really needs to be studied, and preferably at an international level, is the relative costs of the total amount of such activity and the costs of investigating it. It must be remembered that all compliance activity is unproductive and expensive, and the cost falls either on the entire derivatives industry (which resents the cost) or on the taxpayers (most of whom do not directly use the derivatives industry): it ought to be justified by performance.

Australia

The governing legislation was the Futures Industry Code, introduced in 1986. This was superseded by the Futures Law, which became effective in January 1991 and is consolidated in the Corporations Law under Chapter 8. With this Code the SFE's regulatory operations were strengthened and new futures industry legislation was introduced at a federal level. Regulation is overseen partly by the self-regulation of the exchange houses themselves and partly by the Australian Securities Commission (ASC). All foreign companies transacting business in Australia must register under the Corporations Law. Brokers and other advisers on exchange-traded derivatives must obtain licences from the ASC; segregation laws are in effect and these separate clients must be treated under the Corporations Law.

The SFE is a self-regulatory organisation within the Chapter 8 framework. The SFE says that, 'The activities of both regulatory bodies are closely related in a system of co-regulation which is achieved by:

(i) The licensing of futures brokers by the ASC. A pre-requisite of obtaining a licence from the ASC is obtaining the appropriate form of SFE Membership.

(ii) The registration of client advisers by way of completing the Registered Representatives course and exam, organised by SFE.

(iii) SFE Articles and By-Laws (Business Rules) to reinforce and add to the provisions of the Futures Law.

(iv) Exchange compliance and surveillance staff to monitor compliance with the Futures Law and SFE's Business Rules.

(v) The establishment and maintenance of a Fidelity Fund to compensate clients who suffer loss because of misappropriation or fraudulent misuse of money or property by an Exchange member.

(vi) The role of the Exchange's Committee for Inspection and Audit, the Arbitration Committee and the Fidelity Fund Committee to further reinforce its regulatory responsibilities.

(vii) Cooperation and coordination with the ASC in enforcing the Futures Law and Exchange's Business Rules.'

The SFE's rules have been recognised by the CFTC as consistent with the US regulatory framework, so SFE has been exempted from Part 30 of the CFTC's rules in respect of approved exchange members. However, agricultural contracts are excluded from this approval.

Canada

The complex system for regulating derivatives has at its apex the Provincial Securities Commissions under the relevant securities legislation. Audit supervision and enforcement have, however, mainly been shifted down to self-regulatory bodies along US lines, notably the Investment Dealers Association of Canada and the relevant exchanges. The Securities Commissions monitor the effectiveness of the self-regulatory bodies in their audit and compliance functions. Grain futures in Canada are largely self-governing but they come under the authority of the federal Grain Futures Act. A supervisor appointed by the Canadian Grain Commission ensures that Canadian futures markets 'operate in the best interests of Canada'.

France

To trade derivatives in France, traders must be authorised by the clearing house (Chambre de Compensation). Transactions in commodity derivatives by French residents but not in francs must be transacted through an agreed bank intermediary.

Hong Kong

Trading is regulated by the Commodities Trading Ordinance and the rules of the Futures Exchange. The Securities and Futures Commission enforces the rules and regulates brokers, who must comply with regulations concerning levels of capital and liquidity and segregation of client funds. Banks may trade OTC products amongst themselves.

Japan

In Japan, there is no one central organisation responsible for the regulation of all futures and options contracts. The choice of regulatory body depends rather on the particular instrument or commodity underlying the contract.

Commodity futures contracts, being agricultural commodities, are under the Commodities Exchange Act and are governed by the Ministry of Agriculture, Fisheries and Food (MAFF). Others such as precious metals contracts fall under the authority of the Ministry of International Trade and Industry (MITI). Protection for futures traders is achieved in a similar fashion: deposits of cash and securities are made with Commodity Commission Merchants (CCM) for margins. In order to protect clients against the potential bankruptcy of their CCM, the Commodity Exchange Law of 1950 was revised in 1967 and the 'guarantee money' system was established. The amount of the guarantee monies is determined by the Law. In July 1975, the 'Association of Compensation Fund' was established to supplement the guarantee money with which it is interdependent. Should a CCM conclude a compensation agreement with the Association, then the guarantee money requirements are halved: if the CCM becomes insolvent, and unable to discharge his liability to his clients, then the Fund will compensate the client up to the amount settled by the contract if the liability exceeds the guarantee money level. For the further security of clients' monies, there is also client segregation from house accounts and rules governing the use of clients' funds. In May 1988 cash-settled index futures and options became legal through amendments to the Securities and Exchange Law. In 1991, the Japanese Diet approved new legislation, the Commodity Investment Act, aimed at promoting and regulating the offering of domestic commodity funds in Japan, allocating supervisory responsibility amongst the various ministries. The guidelines for operation of this new law have now been completed and enacted. As a result of this legislation, a self-regulatory organisation, the Japanese Commodity Fund Association, has been established, aiming to promote the business development of such funds and to enforce existing consumer protection measures. There are already over 40 members. Further reform of the Securities and Exchange Law to expand the definition of security is envisaged, but no major reforms of the current system of regulation are planned.

Malaysia

The Commodities Trading Commission is an independent regulatory agency responsible for the regulation and supervision of the commodities futures industry. It was first established as the Commodities Trading Council under the

Commodities Trading Act of 1980. This was replaced in 1985 by another Commodities Trading Act that established the commission as a corporate body charged with the efficient functioning of the Exchange, the Clearing Corporation and the futures industry generally based on the principle of self-regulation.

The KLCE is a self-regulatory body whose rules and regulations broadly follow those of the US; the overall regulatory structure is administered by the Commodities Trading Commission, which also regulates brokers and traders. Any Exchange member dealing with customer commodity futures accounts must be registered as a corporate dealer under the Malaysian Commodities Trading Act 1985 by the Commissioner of Commodities Trading. Any dealer must also ensure that his representatives and dealing employees are also all similarly registered.

A particular feature of the KLCE is the reportable position limits. For the commodity contracts of the Exchange the reportable limits are 100 contracts net long or short, to be compared to maximum speculative positions of 500 (crude palm oil and RBD palm olein contracts), 200 contracts (tin) and 250 contracts (rubber) and 150 contracts in any one month and 300 total (cocoa). Hedgers are exempted from these position limits.

Netherlands

Securities legislation for derivatives was introduced for consumer protection reasons. The latest legislation dates from May 1986. Regulation is carried out by the exchanges and the implementation of the Securities Trading Act and the Securities Trading Decree. Brokers may only execute derivatives transactions with professional issuers, dealers and investors, unless the transaction is made with a licensed person. Licences are issued only after the finances and background of the applicant have been checked by the Finance Ministry. Members of certain bodies such as the US and Swiss Stock Exchanges are exempt from these rules.

New Zealand

In New Zealand, as in every country with an active derivatives market, the interests of investors have been protected through legislation. The safeguards in place include *Articles of Association and By-Laws*. These regulations form the basis of the day-to-day and long-term running of New Zealand exchanges. They include such issues as market protocol, membership requirements and trading practices. The *Securities Amendment Act 1988* makes it compulsory for all principals acting in the market who trade on behalf of others to be members of a recognised exchange. The NZFOE is the only so authorised exchange at present. All trading members of the Exchange must be clearing members of the

ICCH. Many of the Exchange's affiliate members are also clearing members of the ICCH. The Exchange operates a Fidelity Fund that aims to pay restitution in the event of the bankruptcy of a member. On 1 October 1990, Client Fund Regulations were introduced following Section 41 of the 1988 Act, outlining specific guidelines as to how client funds should be managed. In common with many other client fund rules, the object is that client funds become trusts in the event of liquidation, receivership or the appointment of a statutory manager for the broker concerned. Clients are therefore no longer just unsecured creditors of the company.

Singapore

The main regulatory body is the Monetary Authority of Singapore (MAS), which has statutory backing under the Futures Trading Act of 1986 to regulate the markets. The Singapore exchanges place limits on daily movements in contract prices. Brokers, dealers, and pool operators must be licensed as futures brokers or futures pool operators. Any person carrying on the business of advising others on derivatives contracts must be licensed as a futures trading adviser, which brokers do not need to be.

South Africa

The South African Futures Exchange (SAFEX) was established in 1990 as a move towards greater regulation of the South African derivatives market. SAFEX's rules are approved by the Registrar of Financial Markets and is controlled by the Financial Markets Control Act 1990.

UK

Regulation of derivative markets until the 1980s was a matter for exchanges themselves with overall supervision provided by the Bank of England. A politically pervasive but rather unclear belief in the UK that investor protection lacked either coherence or adequate legislative support, following revelations about price manipulation in a number of markets led to the commissioning of Professor Gower to write a complete review of the existing system. When acted on by government, this became the Financial Services Act of 1986 which came into force in April 1988 ('the FSA regime'). The FSA regime is widely held to have been introduced by the Conservative government in order to demonstrate a 'get tough with the City/protect the customers' attitude. After a series of expensive trials, however, such as Blue Arrow and Guinness, the FSA regime is widely recognised as an expensive mistake although the government has not yet realised this. The complex structure consists of the Department of Trade and Industry (DTI), staffed by professional civil servants with little or no market knowledge; self-regulation by the markets themselves; with an expensive intermediate bureaucracy, the Securities and Investments Board (SIB), executing strategic regulatory authority. The FSA covers all 'investment business' and certainly all derivatives except for short-term forward contracts. The derivative markets were allocated to the SIB, which directly authorises both exchanges as RIEs and clearing houses (LCH only) in the UK.

The SIB also authorises Self-Regulatory Organisations (SROs) that are in turn authorised to allow their members to enact particular types of investment business. The introduction of a self-regulatory body for futures and options was partly at the instigation of the futures industry itself which demanded a significant role in the regulation of the markets' members. This was consistent with the recommendations of Professor Gower. There were at one time more SROs than there are now. Sensibly, they are merging: for example the Association of Futures Brokers and Dealers (AFBD) has merged with the Securities Association to form the Securities and Futures Association (SFA) which is the SRO for commodity futures in the UK. The SFA has the primary responsibility for authorising and supervising member institutions and operates in the following areas:

- codes of conduct;
- standards of reporting and accounting;
- segregation of clients' funds from those of the broker;
- investigation of complaints;
- compensation for non-trading related losses.

All firms and individuals wishing to transact business in derivatives, as in other financial services, are closely examined to try to ensure the company and its officers are 'fit and proper'. That is to say, the company must be financially sound and must meet minimum capital requirements. Those who are engaged by the recognised companies have to be honest and competent to undertake business on behalf of customers. The intention, of course, is to avoid any possible malpractice and to safeguard the interests of clients at all costs.

Those under the auspices of the SFA who fail to observe any of the codes or rules are answerable to the SFA in the first instance. They are subject either: to fines, for minor offences; or, for grave offences, the company or individual may be prevented from continuing business by the Authority and may well be referred to the Department of Trade and Industry for criminal prosecution. For although the SFA has the power to punish and control companies and individuals for breaches in codes of conduct or rules, it is not empowered to institute legal proceedings.

The SFA can and does investigate member firms' adherence to rules on compliance procedures, capital adequacy (both base capital requirement, position and counterparty risk requirement), segregation of client funds, and record keeping and business conduct. The SFA can and does impose fines, discipline members and *in extremis* expel firms. The SIB, which authorises the exchanges, can recommend prosecutions through the DTI to the Director of Public Prosecutions. The SFA is, however, only concerned with the conduct of those it regulates and their relationship with their clients

Clearing members of London exchanges — for commodity purposes, IPE, LME or LCE members — will normally be authorised themselves under the FSA (either by being themselves directly regulated by SIB or by being members of the SFA). LCH says, 'Having obtained all necessary memberships, the clearing member is then bound to adhere to the various rules, regulations, procedures and reporting requirements of these bodies. Failure to do so may result in disciplinary action and/or the possible curtailment of his business activities.' Institutions such as the Bank of England, the exchanges and clearing houses and Lloyd's of London are exempt persons under the Act.

In addition, and complementary to the SIB/SFA rules, IPE, LME and LCE each has their own rules and regulations in respect of conduct on the Exchange between members themselves. The Exchanges have Compliance Officers and floor officials, who monitor conduct to ensure gentlemanly behaviour; they settle minor disputes and enforce market regulations. Serious breaches are reported to the relevant committees of the Exchange for investigation as well as to the SFA and SIB. If misconduct is proven, either the firm or the individual employee may be fined, suspended from trading or even expelled from the Exchange altogether.

For the time being the Bank of England continues to regulate banks and swap dealers in the money markets according to the 'Grey Paper' regime. These do not generally impinge on straight commodity market operations except for swaps.

The SIB in 1991 permitted the establishment of futures and options funds that are slowly developing in the UK. An increasing attempt is being made to simplify the complicated rules of the SROs, beginning with the 'New Settlement' following the departure of the first Chairman of the SIB, Sir Kenneth Berrill. He was replaced by Sir David Walker. Currently the 10 principles set down by the SIB are called the 'first tier' of regulation; the 40 core rules are the 'second tier'; also set by the SIB, and through the SFA (and other SROs) the 'third tier' for firms under their jurisdiction. The SIB wants consistency across SROs but also flexibility.

The summary picture of UK regulation in the 1990s is that it is stuck with an inappropriate and expensive structure of regulation that, despite its high cost to the industry (it is funded by the derivative industry itself) does not cover all the relevant markets or have a clear mission statement that is fully compatible with trying to develop the UK's status as a major centre for derivatives. A whole industry of Compliance Officers has grown up to service the FSA regime. By early 1992 moves were once again afoot to reform the FSA regime, which many commentators (especially those sympathetic to the Conservative Party and to commerce generally) said had erred, since its introduction, too far in the direction of investor protection at the expense of all the other objectives of financial services regulation. Recent recommendations by Large and Alexander suggest that a single all-embracing City regulator may eventually be required to prevent the unnecessary confusion — and expense —that exists currently between different sources of regulation, as well as to anticipate eventual privatisation of the Bank of England. However, it was clear that whatever was thought privately, the lack of legislative time for several years, and the desire not to be seen so obviously to have erred, would deter Ministers from introducing any reforms seen as unduly sympathetic to 'City interests'.

US

The rules set out in 1865 by the CBOT formalised the practice of futures trading in the US and served as a world model. In subsequent years, all US commodity exchanges developed and improved the basic rules for their members. The Commodity Exchange Act of 1936 dealt with market abuses by traders and futures commission merchants (brokerage firms). Price manipulation became a criminal offence. Federal governments began to play a role in regulating trading activity in 1922 when the Grain Futures Act was passed. The law required the exchanges to be licensed and to prevent price manipulation by their members.

The CFTC was created in 1974 by an act of Congress and in 1975 it replaced the older Commodity Exchange Authority. The former body was under the authority of the Department of Agriculture, since futures trading was primarily in agricultural goods. The growth in financial futures trading made a move from Department of Agriculture control logical. The CFTC has two main objectives, and has a wide range of legal powers to enforce its views. Firstly, the CFTC aims to ensure that futures trading meets its main purpose, so it has power to approve the operating rules of an exchange and to approve any new contract before it begins trading. It fulfils both functions very thoroughly. The CFTC also monitors positions held by traders and can impose limits on positions held, to prevent market manipulation. Secondly, the CFTC regulates the dealings of the futures industry with the US public as whole. This gives it the authority to create and maintain minimum standards of training of brokerage staff, capital adequacy standards for brokers and the segregation of clients from brokers' funds. Firms and individuals that violate rules of professional ethics and conduct or that fail to comply with strictly enforced financial and record-keeping requirements can, if circumstances warrant, be permanently barred from engaging in any futures-related business with the public. The enforcement powers of the CFTC are similar to those of other major federal regulatory agencies, including the power to seek criminal prosecution by the Department of Justice when thought necessary.

The self-regulatory organisation for futures and options within the US structure is the National Futures Association (NFA), established in 1981. It is subject to CFTC rules and supervision. Its purpose is to regulate the activities of its members (brokerage firms and their agents). Firms and individuals that conduct futures trading business with the public are subject to regulation by the CFTC and by the NFA. It exercises regulatory authority over Futures Commission Merchants, Introducing Brokers, Commodity Trading Advisors, Commodity Pool Operators, Leverage Transaction Merchants and Associated Persons (salespersons) of all of the foregoing. The NFA also has the responsibility for registering all the individuals and firms that are required to be registered with the CFTC. The NFA staff consists of more than 150 field auditors and investigators.

Futures Commission Merchants who are members of an exchange are subject to not only to CFTC and NFA regulations but to regulation by the exchanges of which they are members. Exchange regulatory staffs are responsible, subject to CFTC oversight, for the business conduct and financial responsibility of their member firms. Violations of exchange rules can result in substantial fines, suspension or revocation of trading privileges, and loss of exchange membership, and there are mandatory jail sentences for violation of even trading floor practices.

No individual or firm may offer futures contracts for purchase or sale unless those contracts are traded on one of the nation's regulated futures exchanges and unless the person or firm is registered with the CFTC. Moreover, persons and firms conducting futures-related business with the public must be members of NFA. In a number of cases, sellers of illegal off-exchange futures contracts have labelled their investments by different names — such as 'deferred delivery', 'forward' or 'partial payment' contracts — in an attempt to avoid the strict laws applied to regulated futures trading.

The CFTC is also responsible for monitoring the futures and options exchanges themselves, although not all the time, but it does frequently intervene in the markets. Although the exchanges are self-regulating, the CFTC approves their trading rules, terms and procedures, and the introduction of new futures and options contracts. Often its decisions are challenged by the exchanges in the courts and this has gone some way to establishing case law to support the legislation. Regulation for the US exchanges is still very much of a sensitive subject after the FBI investigation into the CBOT in 1989. Traders are still extremely suspicious of federal involvement.

There has been a long running dispute between the CFTC and the Securities and Exchanges Commission (SEC), the body responsible for the regulation of securities markets in the US. It has long been thought anomalous that trading in stocks should be regulated by one body whereas trading in stock index futures should be regulated by another. This feeling was reinforced by the events in the October 1987 stock market crash, when there was debate over the role played by futures markets in the market decline. It seems likely that some redefinition of responsibilities between the two bodies will be inevitable, although the Chicago exchanges, especially the CME and CBOT, whose lobbying power in Washington is formidable, have in the past expressed a strong preference to remain under the authority of the CFTC, which they regard as more sympathetic than the SEC.

In 1991 Congress continued to deliberate over CFTC re-authorisation, with the House and Senate eventually passing different versions of a re-authorisation bill. Differences between the two drafts continued into 1992, but both versions of the bill contain increased penalties for commodities law and regulation violations, tighter floor trading control, restrictions on dual trading by floor members and conflict of interest guidelines for board and committee members. Both these latter provisions are opposed by the industry as likely to restrict competition, reduce the effectiveness of markets for hedgers and reduce market participation by committee and board members. In 1992, however, the exchanges in the US switched positions and protested serious doubts about the re-appointment of the CFTC. The re-authorisation process this time around for the CFTC was not easy, given the frankly competitive relationship between the SEC and CFTC. In July 1992 the Chicago exchanges actually threatened to withdraw their support from the legislation, and eventually they succeeded in preventing substantial changes to the existing regime, with the result that the re-authorisation process was finally completed in October 1992.

As in most countries, swaps and hybrid instruments have posed almost insuperable obstacles for regulators. Regulations were issued from 1987 onwards governing these instruments but there is still far from comprehensive regulation. Administrative 'no-action' relief for products falling outside CFTC guidelines, and the threats of private litigation as well as enforcement action under state law remain. The latest legislation, now approved by Congress, is contained in the re-authorisation of the CFTC which allows the exemption of swaps that meet certain criteria but generally ensures that OTC transactions fall within the CFTC ambit. The Bankruptcy Code amendments enacted by

Congress in 1990 provide that bankruptcy itself has no more protection against creditors for swap transactions than for other forward or futures transactions. Definitions of futures and forward contracts for regulation by the CFTC are still not entirely clear and there are exemptions for some traded options and forward contracts. The rules for all commission merchants, on matters such as the segregation of customer funds, capital adequacy, client relationships and trade reporting are all regulated by the CFTC under the latest Commodity Exchange Act.

Chapter 10: International accounting rules

The timing of profit or loss results on commodity futures and option transactions is necessary to account for open positions. An active and liquid market enables positions to be closed out at any time so keeping a position open is the same in principle as closing out. Open positions should be revalued at market value ('mark-to-market'). The difference between this value and the value of the positions at their original prices is the profit or loss on open contracts at the time of valuation. This policy involves recognising unrealised profits. It therefore leans towards the accruals concept and not towards prudence. In practice, accounts must show a 'true and fair' view and analysts believe that mark-to-market prices do show this for the following reasons:

- Market liquidity should ensure that profits and losses could be taken at the time of valuation. So as transactions can be closed out, a profit or loss is made when the market rate moves, and it does not depend on a decision to close out the position. In practice, the larger the position and the less liquid the market, the less applicable is this argument.

- Mark-to-market is consistent with the practice of banks and others in the accounting of forward foreign exchange transactions and other types of securities.

- Profits or losses have already been paid over in the form of margins.

- The close connection between options and futures contracts makes it difficult to argue for different treatments for them.

- Mark-to-market protects against manipulations which might result from the flexibility either to leave open or to close out contracts on a selective basis.

- Performance is evaluated only by reference to the current market values of all open contracts.

The risk is that the accounts will be completely accurate when prepared, but inaccurate when published. The more important the derivative is for the company, and the more volatile it is, the bigger the problem. It emphasises the need for an electronic accounts system backed by full legislative approval. There is as yet no such system anywhere in the world.

The alternative is to state futures and options positions at cost value (with options written at the higher of proceeds or market value) if this is more financially attractive for the company. It is understandable however, that this is increasingly rejected as an accurate representation of the true financial position.

Such a possibility of manipulation and the evaluation of performance can be illustrated by the following example. Suppose a trader had only two contracts open at his year end, one showing a profit and the other a loss (whether these are option contracts or futures contracts is irrelevant). If the trader had an accounting policy other than to value the open contracts at market value then the results could be varied for the year simply by closing out, or leaving open, the profitable contract. Prudence requires provision for the loss making contract whether or not it has been closed out. A difference would arise depending on whether or not the contracts are closed out despite the fact that a particular accounting policy had been applied consistently. The results could be manipulated, and avoided only by valuing open contracts at the closing market price.

Results declared as a result of different accounting policies for open contracts

	Provide all losses $	Provide net losses $	Value at market $
Contract 1 - loss $500	(500)	(500)	(500)
Contract 2 - Gain $2,000	—	500	2,000
Accounting results			
If both contracts open	500	Nil	1,500
If contract 1 closed	500	500	1,500
If both contracts closed	1,500	1,500	1,500

Clearly, by the selective closing out of contracts, the accounting result can be varied unless a mark-to-market policy is adopted.

Recognition of profit and loss

The accounting period in which to place the profit or loss must be decided and this depends on the underlying reason for the transaction. Hedging and trading decisions should be considered separately. In practice, in a complex trading position it is oftcn impossiblc to dctcrminc which is which and the company treasurer may be able to allocate them as seems desirable from an accounting standpoint. In theory, the accounting for a trading transaction is relatively straightforward. Once the profit or loss is known on a mark-to-market basis, it is all immediately recognised. Each day a trader decides whether to close out or maintain all and each of his positions: taking profits and losses both on a daily basis recognises the effect of that decision in the period in which it was made. The consequence of this is that the profits and losses of even a very complex trading position can be easily assessed. The overall position is simply the total net profit or loss of all marked-to-market open positions, plus the profits and losses of closed out contracts.

Trading transactions

The accounting treatment for a trading transaction is relatively straightforward. Having determined the profit or loss on the trading transactions on a mark-to-market basis the whole profit or loss is recognised immediately, because each day a trader decides either to keep a position open or to close it out. Taking profits or losses on a daily basis recognises the effect of that decision in the period in which the decision was made.

Consider the following situation:

Day 1: A dealer buys a June 90.00 call option on a pearl future at a premium of 0.65.

Day 2: The price of the option rises to 0.70.

Day 3: The dealer closes out his position by writing a June 90.00 call option on a pearl future at 0.7.

The dealer makes a profit of five points (70–65). Assuming the approximate profit per point on the pearl futures contract equates to $10.00, a profit of 5 x $10.00/point = $50.00 has been made. Suppose also that the organisation's year end for accounting purposes is day two.

If the transactions described above were entered into as a trading transaction, all the $50.00 profit would be recognised on day two even though the position was not closed out until day three. This would have the effect of recognising the whole of $50.00 profit before the accounting year end.

However complex the trading position constructed, the calculation of the profit and loss is straightforward. The mark-to-market method of valuations is applied to each contract individually and the resultant net profit or loss is seen immediately together with any profits or losses on closed out contracts.

Hedging transactions

The rationale behind the accounting treatment of hedging transactions is completely different from that applied to trading transactions. The following three criteria are a guide to the identification of a hedge:

- *Intent*
  The transaction should be *intended* to be a hedge and this will involve evidence. At the time the futures or options transaction is entered into, its purpose should be specifically identified and documented, including the asset or liability being hedged and the period that the hedge is intended to cover.

- *Certainty*
  In the case of anticipatory hedges (ie, in respect of a transaction intended to occur at a future date) there should be a reasonable expectation that the cash transaction will be fulfilled. This will obviously also need to be demonstrated by experience.

- *Correlation*
  The price of the futures/options contract and the hedged asset or liability should show a high correlation so that they will move in the same direction and with similar magnitude. This will involve matching the contract as closely as possible to the hedged asset or liability in terms of the sensitivity to price changes, principal amount, effect of other economic changes, delivery date or exercise period.

Of the three criteria intent is crucial. If the intention is that the transaction is a hedge it should be possible to record that intention (and the reason) at the time the transaction is initiated. For internal control, the nature and the intent of the transaction should be recorded for subsequent monitoring and reported to management.

When the second criterion of certainty is relevant, that is with regard to anticipated cash transactions, plans for future cash transactions must be clear. The auditor expects to see a good track record of effective planning and subsequently actioning the plans by entering into the cash transactions projected. This criterion is particularly relevant to the hedging of uncertain future currency payments or intake of commodities and has a fundamental effect on the way such transactions are accounted for.

The third criterion of correlation is more factual. Reasonable correlation, or a reasonable expectation of correlation, is a factor that should be studied prior to entering a hedge transaction by reference to information to which others, including the auditors, should be able to refer.

Even with the criteria established for identification of hedges, some difficult assessments may still be required. As more complex hedging techniques are used it may become increasingly difficult to establish whether a transaction really is a hedge or not. Even if the transaction can be identified as a hedge, the determination of the period over which the hedge is running and/or the identification of the asset/liability being hedged may still prove difficult. The auditor will probably assume that a transaction is a trading transaction unless it can reasonably be proved otherwise. The onus will therefore be placed on the hedger to justify his actions. There will, for example, be situations where hedges are part of general asset/liability management and based on aggregates of assets and liabilities rather than individual items. This should not invalidate hedging treatment but it will undoubtedly complicate their identification.

Hedging contracts normally extend at least until the date of the anticipated cash market transaction to avoid exposure between the time the contracts are closed out and the time when the cash market transaction is made. Avoidance of this exposure can be achieved by the use of successive contracts, ie, by closing out a position for one delivery month and simultaneously opening an equivalent position for a subsequent delivery month. The hedge is therefore 'rolled' forward to a later date.

If the rolling forward of the hedge can be properly viewed as an integral part of the hedge operation (an especially relevant question where anticipated hedge transactions have been delayed) then it should be possible for the relevant transactions to be viewed as part of that hedge and to be accounted for accordingly.

Hedges may be discontinued, for example, because the anticipated cash market transaction is not to take place. In this case it would seem appropriate to treat the entire result of the hedge transaction as a trading transaction once it becomes apparent that the anticipated cash market transaction will not take place. Conversely, if a hedge transaction is left open after the point when the relevant cash transaction has taken place, or after the point when the hedge has been deemed to be discontinued, it would be appropriate for the results of the hedge that arose after that point to be treated as a trading profit or loss if material.

A hedge may also be discontinued because expectations of the trend in commodity prices have changed or that prices have peaked or troughed. It would seem appropriate to continue to view the results of the transactions as a hedge provided that intentions in this respect can be clearly established.

These criteria determine whether or not a futures/options transaction qualifies for treatment as a hedge. General rules are useful in giving guidance but each situation must be viewed on its merits. The auditor will tend to regard all transactions as trades unless there is positive evidence to the contrary, because in practice in a complex trading situation it is often virtually impossible to allocate them accurately between the two and auditors prefer to err on the side of caution in analysing derivative contracts. The distinction between trading and hedging is also often crucial for taxation purposes.

In July 1988 the UK Inland Revenue released a *Statement of Practice* in respect of hedging; an amended version was subsequently issues in November 1991. The Statement sets out the criteria by which the Inland Revenue proposed to judge whether profits and losses on futures transactions were from hedges or trades. As a result the grey area that previously existed, in respect of the taxation of profits and losses on futures contracts, was much reduced. The distinction is of considerable importance: if the transaction is regarded as hedging then the treatment of gains and losses in the futures will follow that of the underlying transaction. So if a fund manager is able to show that the futures contracts were entered into in order to hedge a portfolio, any gains on the futures contract will be regarded as capital. This is important for those financial institutions such as unauthorised unit trusts and investment trusts. In contrast, authorised until trusts and pension funds have enjoyed exemption from tax for all futures and options transactions since July 1990.

The principle is that the profit/loss on the futures or options hedging transaction should be recognised over the same time period as the income or expense generated by the underlying transaction being hedged.

The effects of this principle are best demonstrated by an example. Consider the same deal as described above except that instead of the transaction having been entered into as a trade, it has been executed to hedge: an OTC option written; or a six month rollover on a deposit with a bank.

In the first case, the $50.00 profit should be recognised in the same way as the profit or loss on the OTC option. Often the profit or loss on the OTC option will have been calculated using a variation of the mark-to-market method and this profit or loss will also be recognised immediately. The $50.00 profit on the traded options transactions will in these cases also be recognised immediately.

Thus the profit has been recognised in the same period as it was when the transaction was a trade. But the reasons for it being recognised in this period are quite different. In the case of the hedger of the OTC option, the profit is recognised on day two as this is when the profit or loss on the OTC option is also recognised.

For the second situation described above let us assume that the bank deposit rolls over on day three. The profit on the option contract should be carried forward in the balance sheet and taken to the profit or loss account at a sixth rate a month for the six months beginning on day three.

The rise in the price of the options contract on day two reflects a rise in the price of underlying futures contracts which in turn is a result of higher physical pearl prices. Thus the pearl price at which the deposit rolls over is higher on day three than it would have been on day one and the reduced return resulting from this higher price is recognised over the six month period commencing on day three. The purpose of buying the traded option was to afford protection against such increases in pearl prices and it is therefore appropriate for the profit on the options transactions to be recognised over the same period as the higher prices demanded for the pearls.

Matching profits and losses on a hedge with the corresponding income and expenditure on the underlying transactions may involve carrying forward profits and losses in the balance sheet for recognition at a later date. In order to prevent profit manipulation, particularly where losses are being carried forward, trades and hedges must be differentiated. Thus in designating a futures or options transaction as a hedge, it is important that the three criteria for determining a hedge are satisfied.

Accounting issues

General accounting principles

In the UK the main guideline for the accounting treatment of derivative products is the *Statement of Recommended Accounting Practice on Contingencies and Commitments (SORP),* issued by the British Bankers' Association in conjunction with the Irish Bankers' Federation. These represent a codification of best accounting practice set out in the *Statement of Standard Accounting Practice (SSAP) No. 2* and have been incorporated into successive Companies Acts. Central to the accounting of futures and options in the UK is the accruals concept, which permits the matching of costs and revenues, subject to prudential concerns. The UK principles are similar to those adopted in other countries with active derivatives markets.

In the US the Financial Accounting Standards Board's FASB80 does address the methods of accounting for futures. There are currently no authoritative guidelines on accounting for either options or financial futures in New Zealand. The method of accounting for options and futures derived from the fundamental accounting concepts set out in the *Statement of Standard Accounting Practice (SSAP) No. 1* of the New Zealand Society of Accountants is typical of international derivative accounting treatment. It can be summarised as follows:

1 The going concern concept (the entity is assumed to continue in business for the foreseeable future).

2 The accruals concept (revenue and costs are accrued, matched and dealt with in the accounting period to which they relate).

3 The consistency concept (like items in the accounts and from period to period are treated consistently).

4 The prudence concept (revenue and profits are not anticipated but are recognised only when realised and provision is made for all known liabilities as soon as they can reasonably be determined).

The application of the going concern and consistency concepts is straightforward in relation to commodity futures and options transactions and warrants little attention. The most important concept in determining how to account for options and futures is the accruals concept, which permits costs and revenues to be matched. This concept must, however, be tempered by the prudence concept where the outcome of a position is uncertain. It is these generally accepted fundamental accounting concepts which provide the justification for the policies which follow.

There are four main accounting issues that need to be addressed in accounting for financial futures and options transactions. These are:

- The valuation of open positions.
- The recognition of profit and loss.
- The consideration of the underlying asset/liability.
- The treatment of margins.

Figure 1: Accounting overview

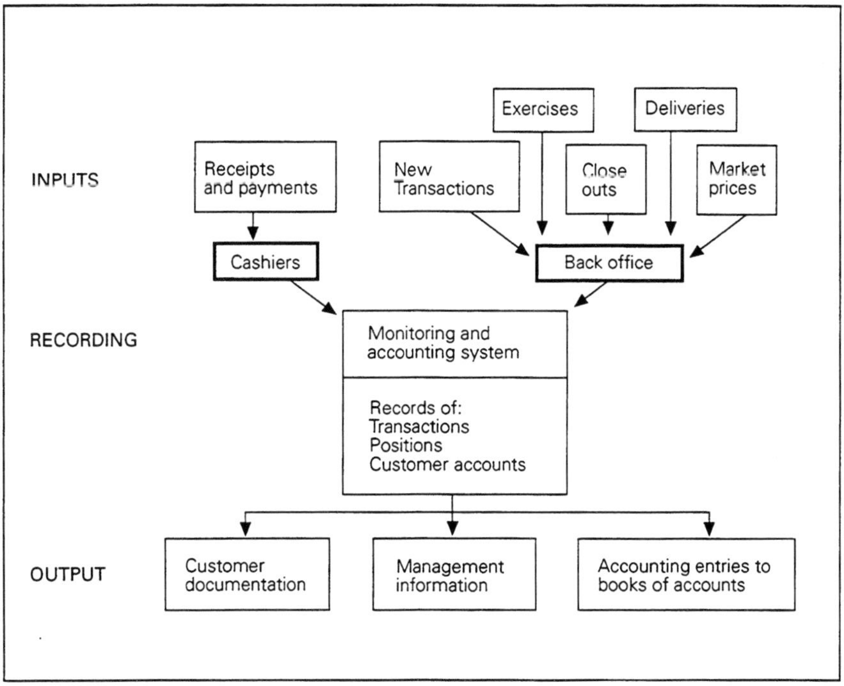

The determination of the time period over which the results of a hedge should be recognised may not be straightforward, especially where the transaction is a general hedge. It is important, therefore, that where there is any doubt as to the period, this should be specified when the hedge is undertaken, together with the rationale for such a treatment.

Underlying assets/liabilities

Consideration of the balance sheet treatment of the assets or liabilities underlying a futures or option contract depends on the legal nature of such contracts. Title does not pass until delivery or exercise respectively. Actual delivery or receipt of underlying assets is not essential as contracts may be closed out prior to delivery/exercise, and some contracts are cash-settled anyway. It is therefore appropriate that the underlying assets and liabilities should not be shown on the balance sheet. This reflects the economic reality of the transaction, and is consistent with that adopted for forward foreign exchange transactions.

More important is the valuation of hedged assets and liabilities. Where the hedge protects an asset value then the valuation of the asset either at cost, at lower of cost and market value or at market value may affect the recognition of the hedge result. Where the hedge protects the value of an underlying asset, the resulting net book amount (the cost of carrying value of the asset plus its hedge result) should be reviewed. It may be appropriate to compare this combined amount with the market value, or realisable value of the underlying asset being hedged.

The original book amount for the hedged asset should *not* be compared with its market value in isolation since this could indicate the need for an amount to be written off to the profit and loss account when a hedging profit has been received partly or wholly offsetting such a write-off.

Treatment of margins

Deposit margins are collateral, remaining on the balance sheet of the depositor as an asset; they are unlikely to be other than current in nature. They are payable in respect of all futures contracts taken out, but margining systems allow increasingly for a reduction in deposit margins where offsetting positions are held in related contracts.

Variation margins, reflecting profits and losses on open contracts, have to be met daily by both members and non-members. Mark-to-market requires the immediate recognition of these profits and losses in the case of trading transactions. For hedging transactions mark-to-market will still be applied but the resultant profits and losses may be carried in the balance sheet. These profits and losses will again reflect the variation margins paid or received.

Margins paid or received each day represent the net movement in deposit and variation margins for the previous day. The variation margin itself may well be the net effect of profits and losses for the day on all open trading and hedging positions. If there are many parts to the margins paid or received, each requiring a different accounting treatment, it is often better for this margin to be posted to a clearing account pending analysis into its elements.

Disclosure in financial statements

The main purpose of disclosure is to enable a set of accounts to assess the impact on the business (including risk) of the transactions undertaken. Materiality is obviously fundamental. There is a wide range of possible disclosures but no specific requirements or overpowering case for any particular one and, unfortunately, there is a wide variation in current standards of disclosure internationally and between various users of the market. In the absence of authoritative guidance and until an accepted market practice evolves, this must be a matter of judgement by management and auditors. A comprehensive accounting policy is an essential starting point and this should be disclosed whenever involvement in commodity futures and/or options can be regarded as material. An appropriate company accounting policy would be as follows:

'The company is using commodity futures contracts and options contracts as part of its overall risk management strategy. Gains and losses on contracts used in trading operations are recognised currently using the mark-to-market method of accounting and are included in trading results. Gains and losses on contracts used in asset/liability management are deferred and amortised over the lives of the hedged assets or liabilities.'

Financial statements do not generally provide a comprehensive summary of the various risks to which an enterprise is exposed. A more common disclosure under the contingent liability note is a statement to the effect that open financial futures and options contracts exist.

In some countries, disclosure in financial statements is required of the nature of all outstanding futures and options contracts. In the UK the disclosure requirements are contained within the SORP mentioned above, which contains the applicable provisions of the EC Bank Accounts Directive. This recommends that an off-balance sheet table exposure is included within the financial statements. This should include contracts analysed as between their types — whether futures, options, swaps or other forms of OTC derivative — and between commodities and parts of the business. The SORP also suggests, although this is not mandatory, that additional information be disclosed on off-balance sheet instruments such as OTCs. The SORP suggests that information could be provided from the risk based capital framework established by the Basle Committee on Banking Regulations and Supervisory Practices' recommendations in the International Convergence of Capital Standards; this would show the gross amount of the contract or the underlying principal amount, the credit equivalent amount — the value at risk plus an additional amount as determined by regulators relating to potential future credit exposure, a risk weighting also determined by regulators and a risk weighted balance. Such a disclosure, the SORP recognises, is not ideal and for that reason it is optional.

Aside from such disclosures, it is rare to disclose any other information in the financial statements in respect of commodity futures and options. Concepts of truth, fairness and materiality however, must clearly remain paramount. If commodity futures and options dealing constitute a material part of an organisation's business, then further disclosure may well be necessary.

The role of the accounting function

The principal functions of any accounting system are:

- to produce documentation for third parties;
- to produce the management information needed to monitor operations and manage the business effectively, and to generate the necessary accounting entries as a basis for providing documentation, management reports and figures for incorporation in periodic financial accounts;
- as a requirement of any regulatory bodies involved.

For commodity futures and options the role of the accounting department will need to be viewed in the context of the organisation as a whole, and this can best be illustrated as follows:

Figure 2: Organisation of functions

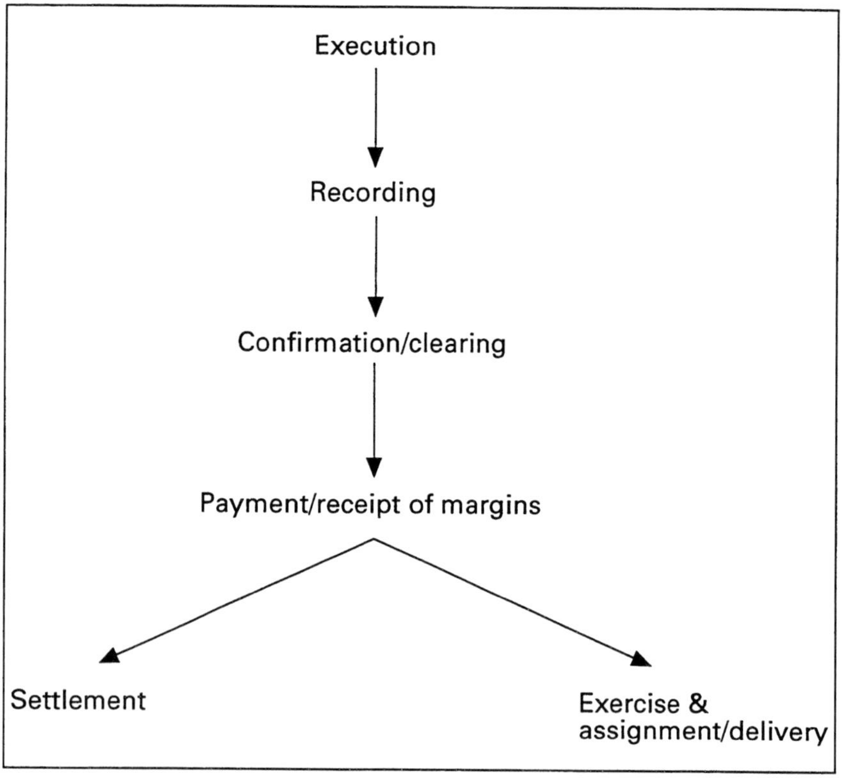

It is normally appropriate to segregate the accounting function from the dealing, back office and cashiers functions in order to ensure that there are proper internal checking procedures as part of good internal control.

Although the principal functions set out above are common to all types of organisations engaged in futures and options activities, the scope of the systems and of the accounting records required will vary considerably, depending on the role of the user in the market. The structure of accounting records, and hence the appropriate accounting entries, will likewise be affected by: the scope of activities; whether or not customer account ledgers will be required; the need to identify hedging profits and losses; and so on.

The figure below illustrates the key elements of a monitoring and accounting system to handle financial futures and options transactions.

Figure 3: Elements of monitoring and accounting system

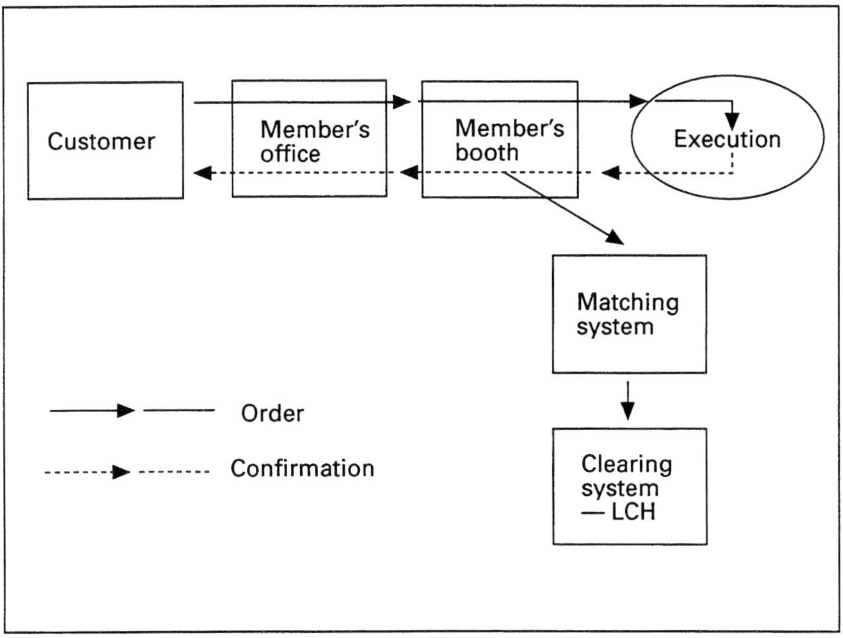

The elements illustrated in this figure should be present in any monitoring and accounting system, whether computerised or not. It is probable that computerised data processing facilities will be needed by most users of the commodity futures markets, and will almost certainly be required where there is any significant amount of options transactions. However, it is feasible to have an entirely manual system provided that the volumes involved are sufficiently low.

The origin of 'new transactions' input will vary depending on the user. For members, the execution of a transaction on the exchange floor will trigger the input into the accounting system. For non-members, transactions will originate in the dealing room. Whatever the origin of the transaction, it is the responsibility of the back office to ensure that details of all transactions are received from the department responsible for ordering or executing the transaction and then to check each transaction against an independent deal confirmation.

Transaction details should be input into the monitoring and accounting system immediately, with allocation to particular customers if appropriate; this input should be subject to the general control measures over system entry described later in this chapter.

Like new transactions, exercises of purchased options will tend to be dealer originated, particularly if the options have been purchased as part of a dealing strategy rather than as a hedge against a non-dealing asset/liability. Again, it is the responsibility of the back office to ensure that they receive details of all options exercised and that these are checked against an independent confirmation. The fact that an option has been exercised should be entered immediately into the monitoring and accounting system.

In this respect it is useful for the options accounting and monitoring system to interface with those for other types of trading. For example, the exercise of an option on a futures contract will clearly generate a futures position. It is both inefficient and time consuming for the exercise of the option to be recorded on one system and the generation of a futures position to be recorded on a completely separate system with a separate input. A much better solution would be for the recording of the option exercise automatically to feed the necessary input into the futures system.

The valuation of unrealised gains or losses on open positions within a system clearly depends upon the regular input of the market price data. Daily input of the official settlement prices is necessary to ensure:

- accurate margining of customers;
- reconciliation of internal records with margin statements received.

It is also desirable to be able to input market prices at any time during the day to check margin requirements arising from positions being taken by dealers or customers.

The back office must ensure that details of the contracts closed-out are entered into the organisation's own internal monitoring and accounting system, including accurate entries for individual customers, where appropriate. For the customers, internal systems input may be raised from the settlement statement sent by the member (once this has been checked against the settlement request). It is evident, for both new transactions and settlements, that part of the system output of a member (customer documentation) then serves an input role as far as the customer's system is concerned.

In a similar way to close-outs, the back office must ensure that all details of deliveries on futures contracts are entered into the monitoring and accounting system. Such input will include the cancellation of the futures position and the generation of the accounting entries necessary in order to create the corresponding cash positions. The exact entries required will depend on the precise details of delivery and hence will vary from futures contract to futures contract. It may be desirable for the accounting and monitoring system to store the delivery details for each type of futures contract and to generate the necessary entries upon the completion of a standard input routine for deliveries.

The processing and input of cash receipts and payments will be essential if customer account balances are to be maintained within the system.

In addition to these categories of input, which correspond to the elements shown in Figure 1, there are various other items to be considered which can be broadly classified into two further sub-categories as follows:

- *System information*
  information relating to contract specifications, customers, levels of charges and interest rates, currencies, margin scales and so on will need to be maintained on file.

- *Invoices and debit/credit notes*
  although not part of the system overview in Figure 1, the processing of any documentation creating a charge or credit to a customer's account is a vital part of any accounting system. Whether entries are raised within a suite of input screens or on an integrated back office/accounting system or posted separately by the accounting records section, strict control must be exercised over inputs, as described below.

Whether a system is manual, batch entry or on-line entry, proper control and validation of input are essential. In particular:

- Responsibilities for particular input tasks should be clearly allocated, with password control on screen operators.

- Input routines should require a standard format containing all relevant details, eg, for a new transaction details of the date of transaction, customer, full transaction data, commission rate indicator and any specific instructions from an approved list.

- Source documents should be stamped or otherwise marked to indicate that they have been actioned by the back offices.

- All input should be subject to validation routines, eg, computer proof listings of new transactions entered requiring confirmation, and any necessary correction to take place before updating transaction files. It may be possible to build in many of the validation checks automatically.

- A unique reference number should be assigned within the system to each item of validated input.

The system must create and maintain complete records of all transactions segregated by customer where appropriate. Specific user output would be a 'daily dealing' statement which should be reconcilable to the trading statement from the clearing house or member.

Open positions
It is essential that each input transaction or settlement is accurately reflected in statements of position and that the transactions comprising an open position, either for a particular customer, or in total, may be readily identified.

Margins and equity
From the open position, margin reports may be generated, by customer or in total, showing the net variation and deposit margin requirements in each case. This information may then be summarised and compared with the current ledger balance (again by the customer, or in total) to update the open equity position. Commission due must be properly calculated and posted to the relevant customer account.

Exception reports
These assist effective monitoring by highlighting potential risk situations, for example:

- Position limit excesses
  - A customer's equity falling below a certain level.
  - Contracts nearing delivery date or expiry.

Appropriate customer documentation will be required for:

- *Confirmation of contract*
  Customer confirmations should normally be produced on at least a daily basis for new business.

- *Settlement (or difference) account*
  This will advise the customer of details of contracts closed out and the profit or loss posted to his account. Settlement accounts should also be produced at the end of each day as required.

- *Statements of positions, margins, account balances and equity*
  These are the equivalent customer documents to the internal position/customer records discussed above, and will indicate to the customer any amounts immediately due in respect of margin payments.

- *Customer account documentation*
  It will, in addition, be necessary to invoice customers for charges and to provide periodic (eg, monthly) statements of account.

Much of what has been described as 'position records' can be regarded as part of the overall information required to manage the business. In addition to this 'immediate monitoring' data, however, information is required to evaluate past performance to forecast futures results and to adjust the strategy as necessary to achieve planned results. Such information may include:

- Profitability reports presented in various ways:
  - By department/individual dealer.
  - By market/contract.
  - By customer/group of customers.
  - By period – showing performance trends.

- Cost analyses.

- Commission analyses.

- Market reports.

- Cash flow projections.

Detailed ledgers for financial futures and options should be designed to meet the circumstances of the user. The system must be able to cope with the special problems associated with accounting for futures and options transactions, particularly the volume and date, the speed of processing and the likelihood of more than one currency being involved.

The structure of the financial futures and options accounting records, and particularly the level of integration into the overall accounting system, will depend on a number of factors. In particular:

- whether these activities form a major part of the overall activities;
- whether the system is computerised;
- whether the organisation is principally concerned with hedging or trading;
- the nature of participation (ie, customer, non-clearing or clearing member). This will determine whether individual customer ledgers are required.

The accounting systems for financial futures and options may be an integrated part of the overall accounting system or may be completely separate. If separate it will, however, need to generate suitable total accounting entries for recording the results and balances relating to futures and options in the general ledger. A multi-currency system may also be required if contracts in more than one currency are dealt in.

The ledger accounts required might include the following:

- Profits and losses on trading, to record the performance on trading as distinct from hedging transactions. This account in turn could be sub-analysed by type of contract, trader, sales office or customer.
- Deferred profits and losses on hedge transactions, to record the profit or loss which has not yet been written off.
- Profits and losses on hedging, to record the amounts of the deferred profits and losses now written off to the profit and loss account, having been released in symmetry with the profit and loss effect on the hedged item.
- Brokerage paid, to record brokerage costs where an organisation deals through a broker.

- Brokerage received, where members are acting as brokers.

- Deposit margins paid, to record deposit margins paid to the clearing house or to the member.

- Deposit margins received, to record the deposit margins placed by customer. A separate account or sub-account for each customer will probably be required.

Each of the above accounts will be required in respect of both financial futures and options.

In summary, the importance of internal control to both members and non-members, in minimising the risks associated with futures and options activity, cannot be overstated. Exchanges have paid great attention to the need for effective controls in establishing the rules and other arrangements for the operation of the market itself.

There is necessarily a business risk associated with any investment that members and others make in order to participate in the market. For example, costs will be incurred to acquire seats on the exchange (for members), for staffing the operations, training, accommodation, administration and systems, etc.

Benefits gained from participation in the form of trading profits, or the protection provided from hedging activities and the income from acting on behalf of customers, need to cover and justify this expenditure. There is clearly an important need for careful evaluation of the likely viability of participation, together with subsequent close monitoring of costs and benefits.

Users of the market holding open positions in either futures or options contracts are always subject to the risk that prices will change unfavourably and they will incur losses. The volatility of market prices means that this risk is particularly acute.

In any business there is always a risk that losses may be incurred as a result of human error, skimping on procedures, poor communication, lack of understanding, unauthorised activity (including fraud), boredom or tiredness, inadequate monitoring or other systems breakdowns. Operations in the financial futures and options market are not exceptions in this respect.

Acknowledgement is made to the extensive use of material in this chapter taken from the Accounting and Administration Booklet published by The New Zealand Futures & Options Exchange in conjunction with Price Waterhouse.

Chapter 11: Conclusion

Some exchanges have seen tremendous volume growth during the 1990s; LIFFE is a good example as are the NYCE and the IPE. Futures contracts are, to some extent, beneficiaries of recession; market participants scrabble to ensure some protection against prices that they often fear are falling. Energy prices have been highly volatile, and the energy futures exchanges have been seen as effective price mechanisms within the energy market. IPE officials believe that with the oil industry facing higher costs due to environmental pressure, and with continued Middle East crises threatening price stability, the future for oil prices is always uncertain and there will therefore be an increased demand for effective price management mechanisms; if not exchange-traded — and it is in conflict with OTC products such as the oil paper forward markets that the IPE and other such exchanges see the real challenge — then OTC. From this evidence, the message for exchanges appears very clear: meet the need, make the money. There is, according to this theory, nothing 'old hat' or essentially limiting about commodity derivatives. One argument that the derivatives industry seems clearly to have won is regarding the input of derivative market trading on the volatility of the underlying commodity's price. The latest research from the University of Warwick, for example, notes that empirical studies find little or no relationship between margin requirements (or the introduction of derivatives) and price volatility.

Research suggests that volatility increases significantly only in the extreme case when investors are ignorant of any forced margin selling, and instead believe they may be motivated by superior information. This leads to low market liquidity and the possibility of crashes. The research findings concluded that the introduction of low margins (or derivatives with low margins) should be accompanied by the best possible data on the potential amount of forced margin sales that could occur. If such information can be made widely available to investors, the liquidity benefits of low margins can be realised with minimal impact on market volatility. This conclusion is widely accepted and is under current research on option margining under the SPAN system, for instance.

Problems do however still exist for the derivatives industry in the 1990s. A combination of factors combine to suggest that the great days of expansion are coming to an end. A warning sign from the financial sector came in the 1991 Touche Ross and Moody's Investor Services reports; it was suggested that one implication of derivatives is that credit risk management becomes more difficult because creditworthiness itself becomes more volatile. As companies cut back, risky transactions and new ventures become the first to go, and with them the need to hedge. Global trade growth has slowed to negligible amounts and industrial production has actually fallen back. The slowness with which the swaps market has filtered through to soft commodities, the paucity of successful new exchange-traded contracts, and the downward trend in soft commodity exchange volumes, all clearly indicate that the halcyon days are over. The most impressive thing about many contracts now are the glossy and expensive brochures that the exchanges produce about them. Recessions do end however, and exchanges and derivatives experts can be assured that after the recovery there will be a further expansion.

In the 1980s many authors were exceptionally optimistic about the future for derivative markets. Writing as late as 1990, James Gray said, 'Plans are already afoot for a whole variety of European interest-rate contracts, for electricity, property, high-protein soyabean meal, tanker freights, tea, rice, reinsurance, apples, eggs, a European Stock Index, Arabica Coffee, diamonds, gold and sheep-meat, no doubt among other, even more abstruse commodities.' LIFFE interest-rate contracts have succeeded to some varying extent, but no successful commodity futures have been launched in the UK since white sugar in 1987 with the exception of the IPE's sour crude contract. Few successful commodity contracts are likely to be launched in the 1990s anywhere in the world — the NYCE world cotton contract, backed by the international cotton trade is an honourable exception to the general trend of plenty of willing sellers and a critical lack of buyers, and therefore a lack of liquidity.

This, and the slow growth of electronic trading has wide implications for the numbers and independence of exchanges worldwide. Mergers are indeed already happening throughout the world. In Japan, which will eventually have a futures volume the size of the US, a merger is already underway between the Kobe Rubber Exchange, Osaka Grain Exchange and Osaka Sugar Exchange. In the UK, in 1991, London Fox merged with the Baltic Freight Exchange. The LME and IPE continue to stand alone, but this does, one suspects, have much to do with continued reservations about electronic trading and the lease on Commodity Quay (home of Fox and the IPE) than other more fundamental factors. Moreover, once electronic trading does become widespread, then the importance of separate exchanges becomes more academic. Separate exchanges then become relevant only in the disposition of the revenue from trades for the production of marketing literature, the presentation of seminars and any other investment, for example, in compliance or market information systems. It is clear, however, that this is an issue not for the next decade but for the twenty-first century. In the 1990s it is likely that there will be a further international diffusion of the industry, with most of the growth coming from new exchanges in the developing countries and the former Soviet bloc.

The main reason cited for the likely future survival and development of the markets is that ever since there has been a trade in commodities, markets have proven to be highly efficient conduits of activity. Over time, central market-places have been shown to be indispensable to trade. They have grown or developed to ensure the survival and progress of trade. Apart from the Dark Ages, progress has been steady and continuous; markets have grown in complexity, volume and numbers of users. Markets, their practices and their users have responded to economic and political changes. They have served to distribute goods, and have thereby reduced regional inequalities and even price volatility below that which only local markets would have been able to achieve.

Fresh developments in commodity markets are extremely likely, not just quantitative improvements — such as the gradual rise of electronic trading, offset arrangements, mutual international recognition of exchanges and trading regimes, and new increasingly different derivative contracts — but also new types of instruments that cannot be predicted.

There may, however, be another threat to the futures markets that has not yet received adequate study: the combination of the New World Order, rising global environmental concerns and improved commodity technology. New World Order means world peace, international collaboration and opportunities for developing countries to be maximised. The UN will act to supply more food when famine threatens, for instance. Humanity is setting itself an agenda of self-control. Part of that objective — to stop threats to the effective international trade of commodities, especially of oil and oil products — will be met by massive force from the US. In 1973 the Organisation of Petroleum Exporting Countries (OPEC) was able to double the oil price within weeks and Kissinger's intervention threats were considered in the light of possible Soviet retaliation. Now it is oil producers who depend on the US for their security. When the Gulf crisis broke, IPE oil volumes were indeed tremendous, but there was no huge price rise and the next time Saddam, or another dictator, acts there may not even be such a tremendous surge in volumes. In other words, US military power, or the threat of it, will restrain commodity price volatility. Rising global environmental concern will also mean greater attention to conserving resources rather than producing, trading and consuming them. It may be possible that derivatives contracts will be developed on renewable energy resources such as wind and water, although it will be difficult. Better commodity technology will mean more effective production management, quicker production response to shortages and surpluses, cheaper, improved quality and more efficient, if not more extensive storage. This will happen more effectively and in a market framework, rather than the artificial environment of post-war international commodity agreements. Prices need not fluctuate so substantially. The sad truth is that if real success is achieved in a human agenda of self-control, of dominating nature and acting in a planned and rational way, then there is no place for commodity futures markets.

This doomsday scenario is, however, unlikely to materialise within the next hundred years and if it does, financial futures markets may find themselves equally pressured. The flexibility and sophistication of derivative markets, however, together with the considerable capital that exchanges and major firms in particular are prepared to invest in exploring new areas for expansion, make it very likely that the explosive growth in volumes for individual contracts seen since 1945 is now at an end. What is likely to replace it is a widening of the interests in derivative markets to cover an increasing number of different types of risks. Once the property and insurance markets have been cracked, then the way is open for the eventual construction of company and even personal hedging strategies that will enable virtually all risks to be removed.

Notes:

James Gray, *Shipping Futures*, LLP, 1990 London, 2nd edition

Glossary of futures and options terminology

A

Account executive

The agent/employee of a Futures Commission Merchant (FCM) who serves the customer/traders by entering their commodity futures and options orders, reporting trade executions, advising on trading strategies etc.

Actuals

The physical or cash commodity, as distinguished from futures contracts.

Adjustments

Physical shares are subject to many adjustments, such as capital distribution payments, dividend payments, rights and bonus issues, stock splits or consolidations and others.

Against actuals

See **Exchange of futures for physicals**

American style option

An option that may be exercised into its underlying instrument at any time up until expiry. *See* **European style**

Automated Pit Trading (APT)

Developed by LIFFE, the APT system is a high performance trading system (capable of handling 100 transactions per second), which emulates the principles and characteristics of trading by open outcry.

Arbitrage

The purchase (or sale) of an instrument and the simultaneous taking of an equal and opposite position in a related instrument when the pricing relationship is out of line. This takes advantage of profitable opportunities arising from mispricing anomalies. This is normally a relatively risk free strategy ('closed' arbitrage) although higher risk arbitrage is also undertaken.

Articles of Association and By-laws

These regulations are the basis of the day-to-day and long-term running of the exchange. The by-laws contain specifications for each contract traded on the exchange.

Assignment

Notice to an option writer that an option has been exercised by an option holder. An assignment notice is generally issued by the clearing house for exchange-traded options.

Associate member

A member having the right to trade in options on the exchange.

At-the-money

The strike/exercise price closest to the current price of the underlying instrument. A call or put option that is 'at-the-money' has not intrinsic value and it will not be worthwhile to exercise it.

Automated Trading System (ATS)

The computerised trading facility provided by the exchange. All offering and bidding is conducted through the ATS. The same computer system is used to generate the trading documentation for brokers, and provides continuously updated information on trading.

Automatic exercise

A procedure for exchange-listed options whereby the clearing house automatically exercises in-the-money options at expiration.

B

Backwardation

(Inverted Market): When the nearby month is trading at a premium to later months.

Basis

The difference between the price of a futures contract and the futures equivalent price of the underlying instrument. Normally quoted as cash price minus futures price, ie, a positive number indicates a futures discount and a negative number indicates a futures premium. *See* **Crude basis and fair value**

Basis point
The standardised minimum price movement of a futures or options contract. Also known as a 'tick'.

Bearish
A market view that anticipates lower prices — whether in futures, options or physicals.

Bear market
A falling market.

Bear spread
Being short the nearby month and long the later month, whether in futures, options or cash. The bull spreader will profit if the spread strengthens (ie, if the nearby gains on the deferred month).

Bid price
The price at which a trader or market maker is willing to buy an instrument.

Black & Scholes
Commonly used formula for pricing options.

Blue month
In order to facilitate price quotation in the pit, the Blue month is used in some exchanges to identify the most actively traded contract month. As positions are rolled over from the front month to the next, and trading activity switches accordingly, a decision is taken by the Floor Committee and exchange officials to make the most actively traded month the Blue month.

Bonus issue
A free issue of shares to existing shareholders, usually in a predetermined ratio.

Box
(Trade type: X): Buy call and sell put, buy put and sell call at higher strike.

Break-even point
The futures price at which a given option strategy is neither profitable nor unprofitable. For call options, it is the strike price plus the premium. For put options, it is the strike price minus the premium.

Broker
A person or organisation acting on behalf of another in the market-place.

Brokerage
Brokers charge commission either at a fixed rate or on a percentage basis.

Bucketing
Directly or indirectly taking the opposite side of a customer's order into the handling broker's own account or into an account in which he has an interest, without execution on an exchange.

Bullish
A market view that anticipates a rise in prices, whether in futures, options or physicals.

Bull market
A rising market.

Bull spread
Option trading strategy combining two exercise prices. Being long the nearby and short the later month, whether in futures, options or cash. The bull spreader will profit if the spread strengthens (ie, if the nearby gains on the deferred month).

Butterfly
(Trade type: B): Buy put (call), sell two puts (calls) at higher strike, buy put (call) at equally higher strike.
To achieve delta neutrality, buy or sell the appropriate number of futures.

Buyer
The purchaser of either a call option or a put option. The buyer also may be referred to as the option holder. Option buyers receive the right, but not the obligation, to enter a futures market position.

Buy in
If an option writer does not hold enough assets to deliver to the option buyer at exercise, he will 'buy in' the assets in the market.

Buy on close
To buy at the end of a trading session at a price within the closing range.

Buy on open

To buy at the beginning of a trading session at a price within the opening range.

C

Calendar spread

(Trade type: E): An option strategy involving the purchase and sale of two option contracts of the same type that have the same strike prices but different expiration dates. Also known as a horizontal spread.

Call

An option contract which gives the buyer of the option the right (but not the obligation) to buy a specific quantity of shares at a fixed price on or before a specific future date. The seller of the option has the obligation to sell the specific quantity of shares at a fixed price on or before a specific future date should he be exercised against.

Call

(Put) Spread (Trade type: D): Buy call, sell call at higher strike. (Buy put, sell put at lower strike). To achieve delta neutrality, buy or sell the appropriate number of futures.

Call option

An option that gives the buyer the right (but not the obligation) to buy a specified quantity of the underlying instrument at a fixed price, on or before a specified date. The writer (seller) of the option has the obligation to deliver the underlying instrument if the option is exercised by the buyer.

Call writing

The writer of an option is an option seller.

Cash commodity

The actually physical commodity as distinguished from a futures contract.

Cash market

The market is the underlying financial instrument on which a future or options contract is based. The cash market is for immediate delivery and payment for the actual physical commodity. *See* **Underlying instrument**

Cash price

The price of a physical commodity at a particular cash market. Also referred to as spot price.

Cash settlement

In the case of those futures and options contracts where it is impossible or impractical to effect 'physical' delivery, open positions are closed out on the last day of trading at a price (EDSP) determined by the spot 'cash' market price of the underlying instrument (eg, FT-SE 100, Short Sterling futures).

Ceiling price

The maximum purchase or sales price that a strategy provides. Note: Not all strategies have a ceiling price.

Cancel Former Order (CFO)

Cancel former order.

Commodity Futures Trading Commission (CFTC)

The Commodity Futures Trading Commission is the independent federal agency created by Congress to regulate commodity futures trading.

Class of option

All calls and puts on the same underlying financial instrument. For example all options on Brierley shares would be in the same option class.

Clearing

The process of registration, position maintenance, settlement and provision of the 'guarantee' of an exchange-traded transaction. *See* **Guarantee**

Clearing house

The organisation which guarantees performance and settlement of exchange-traded contracts for those exchanges which do not clear contracts themselves.

Clearing member

A member firm of the clearing house or association. Each clearing member must also be a member of the exchange. Not all members of the exchange, however, are members of the clearing association. All trades of a non-clearing member must be reported to and eventually settled through a clearing member.

Client agreement

The legal document between the broker and the client, setting out the conditions of the broking relationship. It is governed by Self Regulatory Organisation (SRO) and exchange requirements (as set out in its Rules).

Client Fund Regulations

See **Futures Industry (Client Fund) Regulations 1990**

Close, The

The period at the end of the trading session. Sometimes used to refer to the closing price. *See* **Opening, The**

Closing purchase transaction/close out

A transaction which leaves a zero net position in the market. This is effected by a purchase if the initial transaction was a sale and vice versa.

Closing range/range

The closing price (or price range) recorded during the period designated as the official close. (Settling Price).

Combination

(Trade type: J) The term 'combination' shall mean two or more commodity contracts acquired simultaneously and comprised of:

(i) a long futures and a long put option (synthetic long call);
(ii) a short futures and a short put option (synthetic short call);
(iii) a short futures and a long call option (synthetic long put);
(iv) a long futures and a short call option (synthetic short put);
(v) a long futures, a long put option and a short call option;
(vi) a short futures, a short put option and a long call option.

The delivery month must be the same for all commodity contracts in the combination and, if applicable, the striking prices for any two option positions in the combination must be identical.

Commission

A fee charged by a broker to a customer for executing a futures or options transaction. Usually, it is a round-turn fee that covers both the initiation and liquidation of the contract.

Commission house
An organisation which trades commodities and/or futures and options contracts for customer accounts in return for a fee. Often used synonymously with brokerage house.

Commitment
A trader is said to have a 'commitment' when he assumes the obligation to accept of make delivery on a futures contract.

Commodity
Any and all goods, articles, services, rights and interests in which contracts for future delivery are presently or in the future dealt in, on or subject to the Rules.

Commodity contract
Contracts for the future delivery of commodities, options on commodities or on contracts for the future delivery of commodities, and any other interests or instruments traded on the exchange.

Commodity Pool Operator (CPO)
Individuals or firms in businesses similar to investment trusts or syndicates that solicit or accept funds, securities or property for trading in commodity futures contracts.

Commodity Trading Advisor (CTA) (US)
Individuals or firms that, for pay, issue analyses or reports concerning the advisability of trading in commodity futures or options.

Condor
(Trade type: W) Buy put (call). sell put (call) at two equally higher strikes, buy put (call) at yet higher strike. To achieve delta neutrality, buy or sell the appropriate number of futures.

Contango (carry market)
When the nearby month is trading at a premium to the deferred months.

Contract
A contract is an agreement to buy or sell a specified amount of a specified commodity at a specified price of a specified grade within a specified time period in the future. Purchase of futures contract(s) binds the buyer to accept delivery of the commodity and binds the seller to sell and provide the

commodity according to contract specification, if the position is not liquidated prior to first notice/last trading day.

Contract grade

The grade of a commodity that has been officially approved by an exchange as deliverable in settlement of a futures contract.

Contract month

The month in which futures contracts may be satisfied by making or accepting delivery.

Convergence

The process by which the futures price moves towards the equivalent price of the underlying instrument as delivery or cash settlement approaches.

Conversion

A riskless arbitrage transaction involving a long futures, a long put option, and short call option. The put and call options have the same strike price and same expiration date.

Cost of carry

See **Fair value**

Cover

The purchase of futures to offset a previously established short position.

Covered option

A written option is covered if it is matched by an opposing cash of futures position in the underlying asset, or by an opposing option position of specific characteristics.

Covered writing

The sale of an option covered by a position in the underlying futures contract. For example, short call and long futures.

Clearing Processing System (CPS)

Developed by LIFFE, the CPS is fully integrated with TRS and further extends the post trade support available to LIFFE members. CPS facilities include real time position keeping, including delivery and exercise instructions, end of day processing of deliveries, exercises and settlements, margin calculation.

Crude basis
The simple difference between the price of a security or currency in the primary (ie, 'cash') market quoted in futures equivalent terms, and the prevailing futures market price.

Cum-dividend
Shares that are being sold with the right to the current dividend.

D

Day order
An order that is placed for execution, if possible, during only one trading session. If the order cannot be executed that day, it is automatically cancelled.

Day trade
The purchase and sale of a futures of an option contract on the same day.

Day trading
Refers to establishing and liquidating the same position or positions within one day's trading.

Deck
The orders a floor broker holds in his hand.

Declaration date
The last day on which the option taker must state his intention to exercise. (Also known as exercise or expiry date.) Note. If an option is not declared by this date it is automatically abandoned.

Default
Failure to perform on a futures contract or option as required by exchange rules, such as failure to meet a margin call or to make or to take delivery.

Delivery
Settlement of a futures contract during delivery month or at expiry, by receipt or tender of a commodity (physical delivery) or by cash settlement.

Delivery day
The day on which delivery takes place. In some cases (eg, Long Gilt futures) delivery can take place on any day during the delivery month.

Delivery equivalent

The cash price at which it becomes economical to take or stop delivery during futures expiration. For example, suppose factories are bidding $20/kg over the July futures for pearls. If one owned receipts in a delivery location acceptable to the contract, the receipts would be valued at $11/kg over the July (comprised of $5 for load out plus $6 for interest and storage in this example). It would be said that the cash bid for pearls is $9 over delivery equivalent, for delivery intentions are usually difficult to predict.

Delivery/expiry month

See **Contract month** and **Delivery**

Delivery notice

A notice presented through an exchange's clearing house by a clearing member advising of the intention to deliver the actual commodity in satisfaction of a contract obligation.

Delivery points

Those locations designated by an exchange at which delivery may be made in fulfilment of contract terms.

Delta

The amount by which an option premium changes relative to a change in the price of the underlying futures contract. Deltas are positive for bullish option positions and negative for bearish option positions. Deltas of deep in-the-money options are equal to one; deltas at-the-money options are around 0.5; and deltas of deep out-of-the-money are zero. Delta is an instantaneous rate of change and varies by a factor 'gamma' with respect to the underlying futures price.

Designated broker scheme

A scheme initiated by LIFFE to sustain liquidity in some new contracts. In return for publicity and support in the form of literature, speakers and information from LIFFE. Designated Brokers undertake to market actively the new contract prior to and after its launch, and to provide a full time broker in the pit for a specified period following the launch of the contract. This scheme was first introduced when the Bund contract was launched.

Designated market maker

To ensure liquidity in new (ECU futures) and existing (options) contracts, LIFFE has introduced a Designated Market Maker scheme. In return for fee concessions and publicity by LIFFE, the Designated Market Makers undertake to provide two-way and updated prices in the pit, within a pre-determined bid-offer spread, and to have a physical presence in the pit throughout the trading day.

Diagonal calendar spread

(Trade type: F) Sell near put (call), buy far put (call) at a different strike. To achieve delta neutrality, buy or sell the appropriate number of futures.

Diagonal straddle calendar spread

(Trade type: P) Sell Straddle in near month, buy straddle in far month at different strike. To achieve delta neutrality, buy or sell the appropriate number of futures.

Discount

The amount by which a future or option is priced below its theoretical of 'fair' value or below the price of the underlying instrument. This term is applied to both fair value and crude basis.

Discretionary account

An account over which any individual or organisation, other than the person in whose name the account is carried, exercises trading authority or control.

Dividend

The distribution of net profit to shareholders. Expressed as a percentage of the par value or as cents per share.

E

Early exercise

The option buyer has the right to exercise an option before the expiration date.

Exchange Delivery Settlement Price (EDSP)

When a contract reaches maturity/expiry, the EDSP determines the price for physical delivery of the underlying instrument, or for cash settlement.

European style options

Options that are only exercisable at expiration.

Exchange of futures for physicals (EFP)

(EFP, Against Actuals, AAs) In the Exchange of Futures for Physicals one party buys the physical commodity and simultaneously sells (or gives up a long) futures contract while the other party sells the physical commodity and simultaneously buys (or receives a long) futures contract. The price of the exchanged futures position, the quantity of the futures and cash commodity to be exchanged, the price of the cash commodity, and other terms are privately negotiated by the parties rather than being competitively executed in the pit.

Ex-dividend

Share traded after a dividend has been paid.

Exercise

The action taken by the holder of a call if he wishes to purchase the underlying futures contract, or by the holder of a put if he wishes to sell the underlying futures contract.

Exercise day

A day on which the holder (buyer) or an option may exercise the right to buy or sell the underlying instrument. In the case of LIFFE this can be any day in the life of the option. *See* **American style**

Exercise price

(Strike Price) The fixed price at the level at which the option may be exercised and the underlying share bought (call options) or sold (put options). Exercise price is determined by the exchange with reference to the contract By-Laws.

Exercise/strike price

The price at which an option holder has the right to buy (with call options) or sell (with put options) the underlying instrument, if the option is exercised.

Expiration date

The last date on which the option may be exercised. Although options expire on a specified date during the month prior to the named month, an option on a November futures contract is referred to as a November option, since its exercise would lead to the creation of a November futures position.

Ex-pit transaction

Transfers of positions made for certain technical purposes, in a location other than the regular exchange trading ring.

Extrinsic time
Same as **Time value**

F

Fair value
The level at which a futures contract should trade to be at a level economically equivalent to the underlying instrument, taking into account the net financing costs related to that contract. For options, the fair value premium is calculated using a mathematical option pricing model, eg, Black & Scholes, Cox Ross Rubinstein.

Fast market
Term used to describe hectic market conditions (ie, large volume of business with frequent price fluctuations).

Fees
Variable amounts charged by the exchange and clearing house for each option contract entered into.

First notice day
The first date, varying by commodities and exchanges, on which notices of intentions to deliver actual commodities against futures are made.

Flat market
A market in which the bid and offer are the same price.

Floor broker
A member who executes orders for the account of one or more Clearing Members. A floor broker executing customer orders must be licensed by CFTC.

Floor price
The minimum purchase or sales price that a strategy provides. Note: not all strategies have a floor price.

Floor trader
A member who trades only for his own account or for an account controlled by him, or who has such a trade made for him. Also referred to as a 'local'.

Forward contract
A cash market agreement in which a seller agrees to deliver a specific cash commodity to a buyer sometime in the future for a predetermined price.

Full carry
Formula is the price of the commodity X interest rate over a year giving the cost per month. The local storage rates must be added in, per month, for full carry. Full carry is rarely recognised at terminals regular for delivery, most hedgers look to lock in between 60–80% of full carry.

Full member
A member having the right to trade all exchange futures contracts and exchange options.

Fundamental analysis
Analysis concerned with economic factors rather than price data, as are studied in **Technical analysis**.

Futures contract
A legally binding agreement on a nationally recognised exchange to make or take delivery of a specified instrument, at a fixed date in the future, at a price agreed upon at the time of dealing.

Futures equivalent price
Refers to the pricing of the 'cash' market instrument being put on the same basis as the futures contracts pricing so that direct comparisons can be made.

Futures Industry (Client Fund) Regulations 1990
Regulations that reinforce the exchange's requirement for the separation of client funds from a broker's house funds, and require all client funds to be immediately paid into client bank accounts with registered banks.

Futures prices
The price of a particular futures contract is determined by open competition between buyers and sellers on the trading floor of a commodity exchange.

G

Gamma

The rate of change of the delta relative to the asset price is called the gamma of the option. It measures how much the delta will change if the market price of the underlying instrument changes; it corresponds to the acceleration of the option premium.

Give up

(1) At the request of the customer, a brokerage house that has not performed the service is credited with the execution of an order;

(2) In the trading ring, a broker 'gives up' the name of the firm for which he was acting to another member with whom a transaction had just been completed.

Granter

The seller (writer) of an option.

Good Till Cancelled (GTC)

This is an order to a broker to buy or sell at a fixed price. The order holds until executed or cancelled.

Guarantee

The primary role of the clearing house is to guarantee contract performance. It becomes the actual counterparty to all contracts registered in the name of its clearing members. This removes bilateral obligations and counterparty risk between the original counterparties, as the clearing house becomes the buyer to every seller and vice versa, and permits netting of positions.

Guts

(Trade type: G) Buy call, buy put at higher strike. To achieve delta neutrality, buy or sell the appropriate number of futures.

H

Halos

The option strategy newsletter produced by the exchange.

Hedge
The buying and selling of offsetting positions in order to provide protection against an adverse change in price. A hedge may involve having positions in the cash, futures, or options markets.

Hedge ration
The ratio of a position's exposure to that of an individual long futures contract. The term is usually applied to aggregate positions and individual options contracts (where it is identical to delta).

Hedger
An individual or company that owns or plans to purchase a cash commodity and is concerned that the price of the commodity may change before buying or selling it in the cash market. A hedger achieves protection against changing cash prices by initiating a futures and/or options position opposite his cash market position. When the cash market transaction occurs, the futures and/or options position is offset.

Holder
The buyer of an option.

I

Implied volatility
The volatility of the underlying instrument implied by current option prices.

Initial margin
The returnable collateral deposited when initiating an open position. This is required by the clearing house from clearing members as protection against default of a futures or options contract. The exchange requires the level of initial margin set by the clearing house to be the minimum required by (clearing) members from their clients. The level is subject to changes in line with market conditions.

Interest rate
The prevailing risk free interest rate that affects the option price.

Intermarket spreads
The relationship between different futures contracts.

In-the-money

For call options where the exercise price is below the price of the underlying instrument, and for put options, where the exercise price is higher than the price of the underlying instrument. Exercise of an in-the-money option results in the realisation of its intrinsic value; it is the amount that would be realised if the option were immediately exercised (ie, the amount by which the option is in-the-money).

Intramarket spreads

The relationship between different expiration months in the same contract.

Intrinsic value

The intrinsic value (in-the-money) for a call option is the amount by which the market price for the share exceeds the exercise price, and for a put option the amount the exercise price exceeds the market price.

Iota

The rate of change of an option premium with respect to interest rates.

Iron butterfly

(Trade type: I) Buy Straddle, sell Strangle. (eg, Sell put, buy put and call at higher strike, sell call at equally higher strike). To achieve delta neutrality, buy or sell the appropriate number of futures.

L

Ladder

(Trade type: L) Buy call, sell call at higher strike, sell call at equally higher strike. (Sell put, sell put at higher strike, buy put at equally higher strike). To achieve delta neutrality, buy or sell the appropriate number of futures).

Last trading day

The final day for dealing in a futures or options contract for a particular delivery or expiry month.

Leverage

The potential to increase financial gains as a percentage of an investment. Futures are seen to be highly leveraged — the initial commitment required is usually less than five per cent of the market value of the contract, whereas the trader gets the benefit of full price movement of the contract.

Limit
The maximum permissible price move up or down from the previous session's settlement price for a given commodity for any one day's trading; the maximum amount a futures price may advance or decline in any one day's trading session.

Limit order
An order given to a broker by a customer specifying a certain maximum (or minimum) price, beyond which the order is not to be executed.

Liquidation
A transaction that closes an open futures or options position. There are two ways to liquidate an open futures position;

(1) offsetting the initial sale or purchase;
(2) taking or making delivery.

Open options positions can be liquidated by

(1) offsetting the initial sale or purchase;
(2) exercising the option;
(3) letting the option expire.

Long
The position that is established by the purchase of a futures contract or an option (either a call or a put) if there is no offsetting position.

Lot
Any definite quantity of a futures commodity of uniform grade; the standard unit of trading.

M

Mark to market
The process by which contracts are revalued daily for the calculation of variation margin.

Margin
In commodities, an amount of money deposited to ensure performance of an obligation at a future date. Buyers of options do not post margin, since their risk is limited to the option premium, which is paid in cash when the option is purchased.

Margin calls
Additional funds that a person with a futures position or the writer of an option may be called upon to deposit if his margin account falls below requirements or if margin requirements are increased. Buyers of options are not subject to margin calls.

Matching
The process by which bought and sold details of transactions in the pit are verified (matched) by TRS before being passed to CPS and the clearing house.

Maturity
See **Last trading day**

Maximum price fluctuation
The maximum amount the contract price can change up or down during one trading session, as fixed by exchange rules.

Member
Most futures exchanges have an international membership that is widely representative of the financial service industry. To become a member of the exchange one must usually purchase a share in the exchange, although frequently it is possible to lease-in a trading permit from a shareholder. Only exchange members are allowed to trade on the exchange floor.

Minimum price fluctuation
Smallest allowable increments of price movement in a given contract.

Marked If Touched (MIT)
A price order that automatically becomes a market order if the price is reached.

N

Naked option
An options position with uncovered risk and no offsetting option or share position.

Naked
Writing a call or a put on a futures contract in which the writer has no opposite cash or futures market position. This is also known as uncovered writing.

Nearby basis
The difference between the current cash price and the nearby futures contract price.

Nearby/front month
The closest (in terms of expiry date) available month for trading.

Notice day
A day on which notices of intent to deliver pertaining to a specified delivery month may be issued.

Novation
The process by which the clearing house effectively substitutes one contracting party to a future contract for another party. Novation permits holders of futures positions to close out with the market generally, irrespective of the party with whom the original trade occurred.

Number of possible contracts (Total number of possible contracts) (Japan)
This term refers to the total number of possible contracts at the subject price and refers to the following totals for buy and sell contract orders.

(1) Total number or market orders.
(2) Number of contract orders for prices better than the subject price.
(3) Number of contract orders at the subject price.

O

Offer/ask price
The price at which a trader or market marker is willing to sell a contract.

Offset
Liquidate a futures or options position by taking a second market position opposite to the initial position, ie, buy if you first sold a futures or options contract or sell if you first bought a futures or options contract. Options can be offset at any time up to the expiration date.

Omnibus account

An account carried by a futures commission merchant in which the transactions of two or more persons are combined and carried in the name of the clearing member rather than designated separately.

Opening, The

The period at the beginning of the trading session officially designated by the exchange during which all transactions are considered made 'at the opening'. (*See* **Close, The**)

Opening call

The process of opening up each contract (futures and options) on a month-by-month basis for each commodity month, the process is usually about five to 10 minutes long. In this process, all contract months of a specific commodity trade in sequence within the first half hour of the opening bell.

Opening price

The price for a given futures commodity that is generated by trading through open outcry at the opening of daily trading; the first sale in the opening range.

Opening range

The range of prices that are traded through open outcry during the process of the Opening Call.

Opening transaction

A purchase or sale that establishes a new position.

Open interest

The sum of futures contracts in one delivery month or one market that has been entered into and not yet liquidated by an offsetting transaction or fulfilled by delivery.

Open outcry

A method of public auction for making verbal bids and offers for contracts in the trading pits or rings of commodity exchanges.

Open position

A long or short position that has not bee offset by an equal and opposite position eg, at the end of the day, a position held with the clearing house.

Option

See **Call Option** and **Put Option**. The right to buy or sell a given commodity, stock, bond or currency in the future at a mutually agreed price (ie, the strike price). Options can be for physical or cash exercise. Options exercise can take one of three forms

(1) Physical exercise (eg, currency options);
(2) Cash exercise (eg, LTOM FT-SE 100 options)
(3) Futures exercise (eg, LIFFE Bond futures).

Order shortage (Japan)

This term refers to a situation during fixing in which contracts cannot be established even though there is an equal number of orders because fixing conditions are not met. In this type of situation, the Japanese katakana character 'fu' is displayed in front of the sell indication. In this type of situation, orders received after the start of fixing are added. Once the conditions for fixing are filled, fixing is performed. In closing price fixing, fixing can be performed even when there is an order shortage.

Out-of-the-money

The relationship between the share price and the exercise price determines whether a share is out-of-the-money. The call option can be classified as out-of-the-money if the share price is less than the exercise price. A put option is out-of-the-money if the share price is greater than the exercise price.

Over-the-counter option (OTC)

An option traded over-the-counter as opposed to on a listed exchange. There is a direct link between buyer and seller, and no standardisation of exercise prices and expiration dates.

P

Purchase and Sale (P & S) Statement (US)

A statement sent by a FCM to a customer when any part of a futures position is offset, showing the number of contracts involved, the prices at which the contracts were bought and sold, the gross profit or loss, the commission charges, the net profit or loss on the transactions, and the balance.

Pay-off diagram

Options can be illustrated by the use of pay-off diagrams that are derived from the profit and loss profile of the position.

Physical delivery

Settlement of a futures contract by receipt or tender of a financial instrument eg, gilts, US Treasury bonds. *See* **Delivery**

Pit

A designated area on the trading floor of the exchange where all trading in a particular future or option must take place during prescribed floor trading hours.

Possible contract price range (Japan)

To guarantee the selection of a fair price and maintain price continuity, a range of possible contract prices is established based on the standard price. This price range moves with changes in the standard price, and is established separately for each commodity in accordance with the rules for conducting systems trading.

Position limit

The maximum position, either net long or net short, in one commodity future or in all future of one commodity combined which may be held open or controlled by one person or firm, in its own name, as prescribed by an exchange or the CFTC. Does not apply to bona-fide hedgers.

Premium

The price of a particular option contract that is determined by open outcry between buyers and sellers on the trading floor of a commodity exchange. Premium does not include related brokerage commission fees. The premium is the maximum amount of potential loss to which the option buyer may be subject. The premium will depend upon the option's exercise price, the underlying physical price, the market's volatility, the length of time before expiration and prevailing interest rates.

Prompt date

The day on which delivery against a declared option contract must be made. (Also known as Value Date)

Protected Payment System (PPS)

Method by which a clearing member authorises its bank to credit/debit its account with unspecified amounts from time to time on the instruction of the clearing house. It is used to facilitate daily initial and variation margin flows.

Put option
An option that gives the buyer the right (but not the obligation) to sell a specified quantity of the underlying instrument at a fixed price, on or before a specified date. The writer (seller) of the option has the obligation to take delivery of the underlying instrument if the option is exercised by the buyer.

Put-call party
The value of a call at a certain exercise price and expiration date can be deduced from the value of a put with the same exercise price and expiration date.

Put writing
The writer of an option is an option seller.

R

Range
The difference between the highest and lowest prices recorded during a given trading year.

Red month
The 5th, 6th, 7th and 8th contract months that are most actively traded eg, if Blue month is June 1990, the Red months will be June 1991, September 1991, December 1991 and March 1991.

Required number of contracts for allotment (Japan)
It is the minimum number of contract orders to establish contracts at a certain price during fixing, one of the main conditions for fixing. Refers to the following totals for sell and buy contract orders. In closing price fixing, however, contracts can be established even if the required number of contracts for allotment condition is not satisfied.

(1) Total number of market orders;
(2) For the sell order side, the total number of limit orders below the subject price. For the buy order side, the total number of limit orders exceeding the subject price.
(3) Number of members that placed orders at the subject price.

Resting order
An order away from the market, waiting to be executed.

Reversal
A position in which the investor sells the underlying short, sells a put and buys a call with the same terms.

Recognised Investment Exchange (RIE)
A Recognised Investment Exchange in the UK authorised by the Securities & Investment Board (SIB), conforming to Section 4 of the Financial Services Act (1984). LIFFE is an RIE.

Ring
A circular area on the trading floor of an exchange where traders and brokers stand while executing futures and options trades.

Risk-management strategy
A trading strategy using futures and/or options contracts to reduce or eliminate the price risk associated with a cash market position. Also referred to as a hedging strategy.

Roll over
The transfer of a futures or options position from one delivery/expiry month to another — always involving the purchase (sale) of the nearby month and simultaneous corresponding sale (purchase) of a further out delivery month.

Round trip
The opening purchase (or sale) of a future or option and the subsequent opposite and closing transaction in the same contract. Transaction costs are usually quoted on a round trip basis.

Round turn
The sale and purchase of an option in the same options series.

S

Segregated accounts
An account holding segregated client funds (to which the SIB Client Money Regulations apply). Such accounts are maintained on behalf of clients by brokers and the clearing houses. Segregated funds are protected should the broker go into liquidation.

Seller
Also known as the option writer or grantor. The seller of an option is subject to a potential obligation if the buyer chooses to exercise the option.

Series (of options)
Options of the same type (ie, either puts or calls, but not both), covering the same underlying futures contract or physical commodity, having the same strike price and expiration date.

Settle/settlement
See **Closing purchase transaction/close out**

Settle-to-market
The process whereby the profits or losses determined under the mark-to market basis are received/paid in cash by way of variation margin as the contracts are deemed to be closed out at closing market price at the same price.

Short
The position created by the sale of a futures contract or option (either a call or a put) if there is no offsetting position.

Special indication (Japan)
This term refers to a situation during continuous trading when a contract price cannot be determined for an incoming order because all of the prices for opposing orders are outside of the possible contract price range. In this type of situation, the Japanese katakana character 'to' is displayed in front of the sell indication. In this type of situation, the market can be returned to a regular continuous trading state by determining a price.

Speculating strategy
A trading strategy using a futures and/or option contract to profit from changing prices.

Speculator
A market participant who tries to profit from buying and selling futures and/or option contracts by anticipating future price movements. Speculators assume price risk and add liquidity and capital to the marketplace.

Spot price
See **Cash price**

Spread

A strategy whereby a trader buys one future and/or options contract and simultaneously sells a different but related futures and/or options contract. A trader would put on a spread to profit from a change in the price relationship between two or more contracts. In futures this may be the common calendar spread (intermonth or straddle) eg, Long March cocoa — Short June cocoa or across commodities in an intercommodity spread eg, Long Fox cocoa Short New York cocoa. In options, such strategies as ratio'd, horizontal and vertical spreads are used across strike prices and expiry months. Spreads can also be generated by combinations of options and futures. A trader would initiate a spread to profit from a change in the price relationship between two or more contracts.

Spread margin

A reduced rate of margin to holders of limited risk spread positions in futures and/or options position.

Standardisation

The exchange sets the quantity of shares, the fixed buying and selling price of those shares and the specific future date at which the option expires. These factors are standardised so that the only variable traded us the price of the options contract (*see* **Premium**).

Standard price (Japan)

The standard price is the market's target price and fluctuates according to the following rules from the start of accepting orders until the close of the final session.

(1) When orders are first accepted in the morning, the closing price from the previous day is used as the standard price. From this point until the start of the morning session (09.00), the standard price is automatically revised to the price with the largest number of possible contracts every 10 minutes.

(2) After the opening price is determines, it becomes the standard price. During continuous trading, the standard price automatically fluctuates in accordance with nearby prices.

(3) When orders are accepted for the afternoon session at 12.30 the closing price of the morning session is used as the standard price. Thereafter, the same pattern as the morning session is followed.

Straddle

(Trade type: S) Buy put, buy call at same strike. To achieve delta neutrality, buy or sell the appropriate number of futures.

Straddle calendar spread

(Trade type: N) Sell Straddle in near month, buy Straddle in far month at same strike. To achieve delta neutrality, buy or sell the appropriate number of futures.

Strangle

(Trade type: K) Buy put, buy call at higher strike. To achieve delta neutrality, buy or sell the appropriate number of futures.

Strike price

The price at which the holder of a call (put) may choose to exercise his right to purchase (sell) the underlying futures contract.

Synthetic futures and options

Futures and options positions combined in such a way that forms risk/reward characteristics resembling another futures or options position.

Systematic risk

The risk inherent in a market as a whole, eg, the UK equity market, rather than the risk in an individual stock.

T

Taker

The buyer of an option.

Technical analysis

Analysis concerned with price data rather than economic factors, as are studies in **Fundamental analysis**.

Theoretical value

The fair value of a futures or options contract. *See* **Fair Value**

Theta

The rate of change of an option premium with respect to time. A portfolio of options with a positive theta will gain in value as time elapses (and nothing else changes); whereas a portfolio with a negative theta will lose as time elapses.

Tick

The standardised minimum price movement of a futures or options contract.

Time decay

The time premium is a wasting asset in the hands of the option buyer or holder.

Time value

Is equal to the price of the option minus the intrinsic value (also called extrinsic value). It is a combination of volatility and time to maturity. The longer the life of the option, the higher the time value element of the premium. The closer an option is to maturity, the more sharply its time value declines.

Traded options

Usually refers to options that are traded on an exchange, eg, LIFFE, and cleared through a clearing house, eg, LCH to distinguish them from options that are bought and sold 'over the counter' (OTC options).

Trade Registration System (TRS)

Developed by LIFFE, the TRS is a real time trade matching system. Within TRS trades are matched, allocated and assigned to accounts. TRS makes it possible for LIFFe trades to be matched within 30 minutes of the trade taking place, and confirmed within 60 minutes. *See* **CPS and APT**

Two by one ratio call (put) spread

(Trade type: H) Sell call, buy two calls at higher strike. (Sell put, buy two puts at lower strike). To achieve delta neutrality, buy or sell the appropriate number of futures.

U

Uncovered/naked position

An option where the writer (seller) has no cover against a market move in the buyer's favour. The writer of a naked call does not have the underlying commodity to deliver and the writer of a naked put has not sold the commodity short.

Underlying instrument
The financial instrument upon which a futures or options contract is based (often referred to as 'cash'). These tend to be homogeneous, or a basket of like instruments, eg, three month sterling interest rates, German government bonds with 8–10 years to maturity. (In the case of options on futures, the underlying instrument is the futures contract).

Unsystematic risk
The risk associated with individual components of a stock index, for example. This will include such factors as an individual company's profitability, earnings, etc.

V

Variation margin
Actual debits (losses) and credits (profits) arising from the mark-to-market process on existing futures and options positions are posted as variation margin. In the event of a shortfall, as a result of an adverse price move, a call will be made on clearing members for additional funds to cover the realised loss. Conversely, realised profits may be called from the clearing house, which settles contrasts to market daily.

Vega
The rate of change of an options premium with respect to volatility. A portfolio with a positive vega implies that it will gain in value if volatility falls.

Volatility
A measure of the amount by which an asset price is expected to fluctuate over a given period of time. Normally measured by the annual standard deviation of daily price changes. Called implied volatility when estimated from the market price of options.

Volatility trade
(Trade type: V) Buy put, buy future to give zero net delta. Buy call, sell future to give zero net delta.

Volatility trades

'Delta neutral' trades whereby options and their related futures contract are transacted simultaneously in the options pit. Designed primarily for professional users who wish to take a specific trading view on the level of (implied) volatility of the underlying contract rather than the direction of price movement.

Volume of trading

The number of contracts traded during a specified period of time. It may be quoted as the number of contracts traded or in the total of physical units, such as bales, bushels, pounds or dozens.

W

Warning point

This is a price set ahead of time to monitor price movements in the market and provide a warning when the standard price approaches the price limit. This warning price is established separately for each product in accordance with the rules for conducting systems trading.

Weaken

Refers to basis movement where the price of a cash commodity at a local market declines relative to the price of a specific futures contract. A long hedger benefits from a weakening basis.

Writer

The seller of an options contract who is obliged to deliver ('short' call) or take delivery ('short' put) upon notification of exercise by the buyer (holder).
The seller (granter) of an option.

Index

A

B

C

D

E

F

G

H

I

J

O

P

Q

R

S

T

V

W

U

W

Z